Surfing the Zeitgeist

Surfing the Zeitgeist

Gilbert Adair

faber and faber
LONDON · BOSTON

First published in 1997
by Faber and Faber Limited
3 Queen Square London WC1N 3AU

Typeset by Faber and Faber Ltd
Printed in England by Clays Ltd, St Ives plc

A CIP record for this book
is available from the British Library

ISBN 0–571–17991–6

10 9 8 7 6 5 4 3 2 1

Contents

Acknowledgements vii
Preface ix

On names 1
On film history 4
On aboriginality 7
On postmodernism 10
On beginnings and endings 13
On melody 16
On the circus 19
On snow 22
On *The Triumph of the Will* 25
On outtakes 28
On American presidents 31
On actemes 34
On emotion 37
On special effects 40
On the theatre 43
On fame 46
On nostalgia 49
On sweets 52
On silence 55
On boredom 58
On decadence 61
On *film noir* 64
On craftsmanship 67
On Freud 70
On transtextuality 73
On journalism 76
On word-of-mouth 79

On a theory of television 82
On Aids 85
On titles 88
On event freaks 92
On style 95
On conceptual art 98
On art movies 101
On critics 104
On pop music 107
On Mae West 110
On ordinariness 113
On set-pieces 116
On stereotypes 119
On actors 122
On avant-gardism 125
On Tintin 129
On clichés 132
On video 135
On portraiture 138
On running times 141
On the Imp of the Integral 144
On poetry 147
On rape 150
On the future 153
On the critical faculty 156
On 'liveness' 159
On naked children 163
On domestic art 166
On opera 169
On controversy 172

On soup 175
On Ellis Island 178
On intervals 181
On personality 184
On Wallace and Gromit 187
On Generation W 190
On newspaper cartoons 193
On pedantry 196
On posterity 199
On genius 202
On Hollywood 205
On cultural nationalism 208
On light music 211
On Americana 214
On a cultural revolution 217
On technology 220
On the *Titanic* 223
On the Death of the Author 226
On interpretation 229
On updating 232
On 'quotation marks' 235
On the Queen 238
On the death of a poet 241

Index 244

Acknowledgements

Grateful acknowledgement is made to the *Sunday Times* for permission to reprint, in a revised form, the essays collected in this book.

Preface

In an issue of the *New Yorker* dating from the late spring of 1996, the magazine's film critic, Anthony Lane, English-born but now, apparently, the toast of the American cinema establishment, reviewed, in tandem, Jan de Bont's *Twister* and David Hogan's *Barb Wire* (with Pamela Lee Anderson). Lane 'led', as we say in the trade, with *Twister*, of which he basically approved ('rich in astonishment, punishing to the senses'), even if he found it wanting by comparison with the previous title in the de Bontian canon, *Speed*. He certainly liked it well enough to use its unrelenting theme-park viscerality to pummel poor *Barb Wire* with. 'The true sadness of this picture,' he wrote of the latter, 'is that it remains unutterably funless' (meaning: unlike *Twister*). And, as though afraid he still had not sufficiently established his demotic credentials, he began his next sentence with the magnanimous-sounding 'I don't mind that it's rubbish . . .'

I don't mind that it's rubbish. In the context of a review which was not a review at all but a string of witty putdowns – Lane *is* witty and *Barb Wire* (which, like most people, I never saw) surely deserved no better – those six words were unlikely to have impressed an average *New Yorker* reader as any sort of emblematic statement on the crisis in which cultural criticism finds itself at present. Yet that is exactly what they were. For I would say (rather, I would once have said) that one of the definitions of a critic, whatever his or her chosen medium, is: *someone who minds that it's rubbish*.

Lane himself is no more than a symptom of the terminal disarray, the defection of intellectual duty, endemic to contemporary criticism in a world in which too much is changing too fast, a world in which, so long as it can seek shelter under the capacious, candy-striped golf umbrella of postmodernism, most anything goes. Faced with such a world, disoriented critics have tended to assume one or other of two main attitudes. The first, typical of film journalism in particular and, more generally, of those magazines (*Esquire*, *GQ*, *Loaded*, *Vanity Fair* and the like) which have become the repository of postmodern populism, consists of decreeing that any art form which elects not to communicate to its potential audience in what Mallarmé called *les mots de la tribu* ('the idiom of the tribe') is thereby boring, smug, pseudy and, in a word, 'funless'; of rejecting any cultural phenomenon not in thrall to the facile, whorish seductions of spectacle;[1] and, ultimately, logically, of *not minding that it's rubbish*. The second attitude, favoured by critics of a more traditionalist stamp, is simply to ignore the fact that today's culture is in a state of constant ebullience and to continue to turn out, or churn out, week after week, month after month, the kind of article, a complacent conflation of artistic intentions and critical impressions, which could have been written, virtually verbatim, thirty, fifty or a hundred years ago – even when, as seldom but sometimes occurs, the work of art so written about could itself *not* have been produced thirty, fifty or a hundred years ago.

I may seem to be inflating the importance of workaday reviewers, who have never loomed very prominently in the history of either art or ideas. Yet they are, after all, the guardians of the living culture; it is to them, at the very least, that the task of keeping that culture greased and awhir has historically been assigned. If books were read by as many as read book reviews, then practically every book would be a bestseller. If every newspaper purchaser took at its face value his pet critic's ritual admonition to 'beg, buy, borrow or steal a ticket' for some 'unmissable' production of Ibsen, Chekhov or Alan Ayckbourn, if he actually did beg, buy, borrow or steal a ticket, theatres would be sold out. Let's put it bluntly. The health, and hence the future, of our culture is in the hands of hacks – hacks of whom it may be said that, when they die, it will be as though, professionally, they never lived, as though their opinions were never expressed (who now remembers, or gives a tinker's curse, what W. A. Darlington wrote about the theatre, or C. A. Lejeune about the cinema, or even Desmond MacCarthy about literature?[2]), as though the millions of words, the literally *millions* of words, which they committed to print during their lifetimes failed to make the slightest impact on either their own posterity or on that of the medium to which their careers were dedicated. Given the stratification of our society, we have no choice but to entrust the management of its culture industry to these hacks, as we have no choice but to entrust the management of our social and economic welfare to politicians. That, however, is no reason why we should regard the former as any more intelligent, any less obtuse,[3] than most of us do the latter.

A preface's function is, by definition, to be prefatory, and space permits me to cite only a few of the anomalies and aberrations of the culture (or critical) industry as it now operates in Britain, anomalies and aberrations which derive either from a chronic absence of distance (from the present) or perspective (on the future). The idea of film criticism, for example, as word-of-mouth personified, of the critic as the more or less servile minion of the Hollywood majors, pointing his readers in the direction of films which they do not need him to tell them to see and paying damningly faint lip service to those mostly non-American productions for which a public requires, precisely, to be cultivated, a climate to be created. The rampant little-Englandism of our current cultural fads, tastes and appreciations (or little-Anglo-Americanism, since, whatever route the country's foreign policy takes in the next few years, its culture long ago lost its heart to the vast and bountiful continent across the water). The ubiquitous critical tic, common even among those academics who regularly moonlight as literary reviewers, of alluding to 'the greatest' (as in 'Auden, the greatest poet of the century'), when what is meant, so one hopes, is only 'the greatest British'. The demotion of television criticism to nothing more than a daily or weekly sounding-board for some so-called critic's 'wit'. The wild disproportion of space, in the books pages of newspapers and magazines, between the coverage of an artist's biography and the far more niggardly coverage reserved for the achievements which presumably gave rise to the biography in the first place. (Although, on the surface, a fairly trifling journalistic malpractice, this is in fact one of the surest signs of a debased culture.) Above all, the persistent and concerted stroking of our national ego, as though it went without saying that ours was one of the Golden Ages of artistic endeavour.

Briefly, about that Golden Age. The louder the hyperbole, the more vociferous the self-trumpeting, the harder it becomes to credit that anyone is truly taken in (even among the trumpeters themselves – Salman Rushdie, for one). I offer no counterargument here, as it would be a waste of both time and space, the naming of names being all that is really needed. So, to cast the net no further back than to the last of the genuine cultural Golden Ages, the first fifty years of this century, I name: Picasso, Mondrian, Matisse, Kandinsky, Stravinsky, Debussy, Bartók, Schoenberg, Proust, Joyce, Kafka, Mann, Rilke, Yeats, Brecht, Pirandello, Genet, Chaplin, Ozu, Dreyer, Vigo. I could go on, as I am sure the reader could (for there are innumerable more where these came from), but it would be as pointless an exercise as would be pitiful any attempt to match such names from the past with those of supposedly comparable creators from the present. Only an idiot or an opportunist or a congenital optimist would dare to suggest that ours is anything but a period of profound cultural mediocrity and stagnation. That is neither an insight nor an idea but an inescapable fact.

Yet, for whoever is prepared to admit the multiple diversifications of contemporary culture (culture, that is, in the least restricted sense of the word), whoever is prepared to engage with them, embrace them, if not unconditionally, then at least without encumbering himself with too many festering twinges of nostalgia for the past's redundant credos and repertories, there is no especial cause for despair, since we are also living through a hugely stimulating period of what might be termed *perpetual transition*. As everyone knows, we now find ourselves at the centre, in the *eye*, as is said of hurricanes, of an electronic explosion, a cybernetic 'twister'. In a previous collection of essays, *Myths & Memories*, published in 1986, I wrote of the strange concordance – in the collective paranoia of that particular zeitgeist – of cancer and the atomic bomb, a malignant tumour and a nuclear cloud, and concluded that 'the mushroom thus becomes the great cryptic motif of the eighties'. If these rather less apocalyptically minded nineties have their own great, albeit not so cryptic, motif, it is the *screen*.

I composed this very text on a screen. It was edited and corrected on a screen. It may one day, possibly sooner than I imagine, be made available for consultation on a screen. Films are watched on screens, as are TV programmes and, increasingly, operas and ballets. Children study on screens and do their homework on screens. Cosmologists no longer peer at the firmament through telescopes but generate models of its space and structure on screens. We can riffle, if we wish, through atlases on screens, and dictionaries, and encyclopaedias, and we will no doubt one day read novels on screens, and poems, and diaries, and letters, and the biographies of those who wrote them, not to mention the biographies of their biographers. It may take five years, or ten, or twenty, but it will happen: newspapers will eventually be rendered obsolete by screens, just as will magazines and, so I believe, books. If that, too, is not yet an inescapable fact, it is as close to one as dammit.

In the screen, then, and for better or worse, has been invested the future (and already, to a degree, the present) of our culture. To be sure – just as there existed in the fifteenth century, when Johann Gutenberg invented the first movable-type printing press, numerous monkish mandarins who had devoted their lives to the cult and exquisitely hand-crafted fabrication of the illuminated manuscript and who viewed the advent of the mass-produced book as not only a threat to their own livelihoods but as the first nail in the coffin of Western culture – there will always be critics, commentators and indeed artists temperamentally incapable of abandoning the security of certain ancient cultural harmonies which they alone will continue to deny have been forfeited for ever. They are, though, alas for them, destined to go the way of their now forgotten predecessors.

The screen is to our culture what the mass-produced book was to that of half a millennium ago – a truth it has become the proper and primary vocation of the contemporary critic to confront. If he does not, he will find himself deleted from the history of that culture as swiftly, nonchalantly and definitively as waste material is deleted from a computer. He will be consigned, if I may borrow a dated but still operative cliché, to the dustbin of history – or, should I say, to the minuscule dustbin whose icon can be found in the lower right-hand corner of every modern computer screen.

The eighty essays which comprise this collection were written over a period of three years, roughly from 1993 to 1995, and (with a single exception) published in the *Sunday Times*, a newspaper to which I would like to express my gratitude for its having taken me under its roomy wing. What Roland Barthes wrote in the preface to *Mythologies*, a book which, after forty years, remains the prototype of all enduring analyses of contemporary culture, be it of the populist variety or not, I could equally write in the preface to mine: 'These essays do not pretend to show any organic development: the link between them is one, rather, of insistence and repetition.'[4] In short, this collection purports to give its readers, not the satisfaction of an evolving and infinitely extensible argument taking off from the first page and alighting with a heavy, recapitulative tread on the last, but a series of extrapolations and digressions (chronologically ordered extrapolations and digressions, nevertheless) from that very absence of a thematic core. I do not claim to be the 'critic of the future' whose contours I have outlined above. My book aspires to be no more than a *transitional* object, offering less a discourse on culture as such than a whimsical *meta-discourse* on the prevailing discourse – one to which, short of taking monastic vows, none of us can ever contrive to close our ears. Like the glinting surfaces of a Calder mobile, the essays which its covers enclose have been fashioned to reflect random but, I hope, significant fragments of our more conspicuous cultural agendas.

Since there is something Zen-like (as well as quintessentially postmodern) about the idea of extrapolating and digressing from nothing, my original title for this collection was the fittingly but staidly gnomic 'Variations Without a Theme'. Then, deciding that I would prefer the book to sound (why not?) as flippant and sassy, as feisty and 'zeitgeisty', as the events, artefacts and phenomena with which its pages are crammed, I opted for *Surfing the Zeitgeist*. As a title, and vulgarly catchy as it must appear, it does at least have the merit of saying just what it means to say and also just what I mean to do in the pages that follow.

Notes

1 No word – as the journalist Nicholas Lezard once acerbically wrote of the theatre – exists for actors (and, one might add, for directors, dramatists and critics, too) until it has been transformed into a *spectacle*, until it has been *declaimed*.

2 And these are among the very, very few whose names still ring a faint bell.

3 There are exceptions, there are always exceptions.

4 From the English translation, ever so slightly amended, of Annette Lavers.

On names

Whatever the name 'Marguerite Duras' may now convey to a British reader, it was long a potently conjurable one in France. There Duras was a *grande vedette*.[1] With her courage and stamina, her plaintive, faintly garrulous lyricism and, not least, her diminutive, neckless frame, she was what might be described as the Edith Piaf of the intellect.

Towards the end of her life, however, she was the victim of a very public practical joke. A mischievous young journalist, Guillaume Jacquot, whose esteem for Duras had clearly remained well this side of idolatry, appropriated one of her early novels, *L'Après-midi de Monsieur Andesmas*, gave its characters a new set of names, retitled it *Margot et l'Important*, retyped it on manuscript paper and submitted it, unsolicited, under his own name, to Duras's three regular publishers, Gallimard, P.O.L and Editions de Minuit. It was of course rejected by all three. I say 'of course' because, had it not been rejected, the story would not be worth telling.

And it is a story, precisely, about names. On the primary level, by appearing to prove that her work, or at least one example of it, was incapable of making its own unlabelled way in the world (Doris Lessing pulled a similar stunt some years ago), what it exposed was the drawing power of Duras's own name. On a more subtle level, though, the joke was also on the prankster himself. Jacquot, as I say, altered the names of the novel's characters – a natural enough precaution if such a hoax is to be successfully perpetrated. But what he forgot was that much of the bewitchment of Duras's novels derives from those very names, which are neither arbitrarily chosen nor interchangeable. Duras is, in fact, one of the great namers among contemporary novelists. They may not mean much to the British, but names like 'Monsieur Andesmas', 'Lol V. Stein', 'Anne-Marie Stretter', 'Aurélia Steiner', 'Nathalie Granger' and 'Véra Baxter', names that recur with extraordinary frequency throughout her oeuvre and are reiterated with mantralike insistence in any one novel (or, for that matter, film), function as instant signifiers, *protonyms*, of her imaginative world, and it would be a trifle unreasonable to expect anyone to want to publish her without them. (Only think of Dickens without *his* names, or Joyce, or Shakespeare.)

What an alluring entity is the printed name! Consider the following: Steffi Graf, Bill Clinton, Woody Allen, Vanessa Redgrave, Salman Rushdie, Yves Saint Laurent, Umberto Eco, Elizabeth Hurley, Martin Scorsese, Gary Lineker, Anita Brookner. Practically the only thing they have in common is that this essay happens not to be about any of them. Yet how their capital letters glitter on the page – so much so, it is not inconceivable that more than one reader, scanning the essay to see whether it contains anything worth reading, will have been arrested not by its opening paragraph, which is how these things are supposed to work, but by this fourth paragraph, merely on the strength of the names above. It scarcely matters that nothing at all has been made of them, that nothing new, interesting or juicy has been said about them, that the cumulative effect is akin to that produced by some *trompe l'oeil* portrait by Gainsborough in which what seems from a distance to be an intricately, even finickily, rendered satin gown turns out, on closer inspection, to be nothing but a fuzzy, meaningless blur of brushstrokes – it is, nevertheless, just such a bundle of names that is calculated to attract the lazy, unprimed eye. And it has now reached the point where a newspaper or magazine page without its statutory quota of proper, and preferably household, names is as dispiriting to behold as a bridge hand with nothing in it but threes and fives and eights. Household names are, in short, the face-cards of journalism.

If that in itself is news from nowhere, a more disturbing development is that the mania for names has started to infiltrate other, traditionally more elevated forms of printed information. Books, for example. In these recessionary times 'literary' fiction has become all but unsaleable, and the average British book buyer has come to remind one of that fabled American cinema owner of the thirties who begged the Hollywood studios not to send him any more historical dramas, any more of those pictures in which, as he put it, 'people write with feathers'. Readers, it appears, no longer want books *by* people who write with feathers, they want books *about* people who write with feathers. Life is the thing, as witness, of late, a whole slew of biographies: biographies of (and here comes another whoosh of upper-case adrenaline, another 'fix' of gorgeous proper names) Max Beaverbrook, Henry Kissinger, Maggie Smith, Stephen Spender, Ottoline Morrell, Rupert Murdoch, Edmund Burke, Benjamin Britten, Eugène Delacroix and Jesus. Nor, you will note, is it essential that the names in question be of living luminaries: obituaries, too, have enjoyed a conspicuous popularity in the last few years.

The growing public estrangement from fiction, then, is most likely related to the form's absence, not of facts, but of names. Yet, even in fiction, the proper name is contriving to map out a new space for itself. One of the codified properties of the postmodern novel is the threading of real names through the textures of an otherwise nonfactual narrative; which means that, if they feel like dropping names, novelists are no longer obliged, as Proust was, to invent them. On a less eminent plane, the 'shopping-list' prose of a Jackie Collins or a Julie Burchill tends to be characterised by the systematic way in which it attaches brand names to everything its creator's protagonists eat, drink, wear and sit on. In the cinema this is called 'product placement' and it has to be paid for. So it may well be that in the future (unless it has already happened) companies like Benetton and Laura Ashley and TWA will routinely make the same kind of deal with bestselling novelists.

Just as Alice sighed, 'What is the use of a book without pictures and conversations?', so a current grown-up sigh might be 'What is the use of a book without names?' For there it is, the course (and perhaps also the curse) of the writer in the postmodern age – from *The Name of the Rose* to the irresistible Rise of the Name.

Notes

1 Until her death in March 1996.

On film history

As every informed cinephile knows, there exists, 'out there', elusive, invisible and (save possibly to statisticians) more or less inaccessible, a nebulous set of opinions on the cinema that are collectively known as 'the orthodoxy' or what Barthes, in a more general context, termed 'the Doxa'. Whenever a film is regarded by such a cinephile as 'overrated' or 'underrated', whenever a director is considered by him to be 'too famous' or 'unfairly neglected', it is at the received wisdom peddled by just that spectral orthodoxy that an accusatory finger is being pointed. For the serious buff the Doxa is an insidious and ubiquitous creature, a many-headed dragon whose powers of self-preservation and self-regeneration are so phenomenal it can only be defeated by the Saint George of posterity arriving, belatedly, to the rescue of artists, like damsels, in distress.

On occasion, fortunately, Doxa the Dragon will consent to emerge from her lair (and here endeth the first Metaphor), granting one a rare opportunity to contemplate her in all her sublime banality. Such an occasion is the publication of Barry Norman's *100 Best Films of the Century*. (I must have missed an earlier companion volume, *100 Best Films of the 19th Century*.)

Where to start? With the fact that, out of the hundred films listed in the book, no fewer than eighty are English-speaking productions? For Norman, where 'the best' is at issue, the international cinema is evidently of scant relevance beside the good old US of A (and what might be called, given the realities of film funding, the good old UK of A). Or with the fact that he appears not even to have *heard of* Rossellini, Ozu, Mizoguchi, Vigo, Ophüls, Dovzhenko, Feuillade, Tati, Tarkovsky and Paradzhanov, and relegates such living masters as Resnais, Rivette, Rohmer (whom he Teutonises as 'Erich'), Antonioni, Wenders, Pialat, Oliveira, Bertolucci and Bresson (Bresson!) to the status of also-rans? (To be sure, the blacklisting of these marginal figures from his Pantheon leaves him ample room for such imperishable masterpieces as *Butch Cassidy and the Sundance Kid*, *Cabaret*, *Genevieve*, *Gregory's Girl* and *Sleeper*.) Or else with the fact that, when he does choose a film-maker of genius, he invariably plumps for the one film of which the public is likeliest to share his opinion before seeing it expressed? Chaplin? *The Gold Rush*, naturally. Welles? What else but *Citizen Kane*? Hitchcock? Why bother looking further than *Psycho*? British Hitchcock? *The Thirty-Nine Steps* – stands to reason. Eisenstein? Everyone knows his best film was *Battleship Potemkin*, so why upset the apple cart by proposing a title of which some reader 'out there' might never have heard?

In effect, the crux of the matter is the phrase 'everyone knows' rather than the choice itself. In his preface Norman pleads the anthologist's customary defence against carpers. 'There are films included,' he writes, 'that would undoubtedly appear on every-body's list but equally there are several, maybe many, which would not appear on any but mine.' What on earth, one wonders, can these latter films be, since his list so uncannily reflects a prevailing, off-the-top-of-anyone's-head notion of great cinema it could just as well have been compiled by polling its potential readers in advance of publication and printing the results. If Norman were one day to publish an anthology of his *100 Best Musical Compositions of All Time*, there can be no doubt that Beethoven would be represented by the Fifth Symphony. For what is Beethoven's Fifth (besides a masterpiece) but the *Battleship Potemkin* of classical music, a warhorse, a cliché, a philistine's-eye-view of the medium's history and accomplishments?

This is a tactic I call, precisely, *taking the Fifth* – meaning, in cultural matters, *don't stray too far from the beaten track or you will run the risk of incriminating yourself*. After all, if I were to assert that *The Magnificent Ambersons* or even *Touch of Evil* was a greater film than *Kane*, that *Monsieur Verdoux* was an infinitely more subtle comedy than *The Gold Rush*, or that some little B-movie western by Samuel Fuller had more vitality in it than all the rootin', tootin', high-falutin' pretensions of *High Noon*, I would have to defend my choice. I would have to fight my corner. I would not be able to fall back, as Norman repeatedly does, on such waffling critical shorthand as 'superbly crafted', 'enduringly popular' and 'splendidly orchestrated'. (What literary critic would ever call Joyce's *Ulysses* 'superbly crafted' or Proust's *Recherche* 'splendidly orchestrated'?) But then, I would also have a chance to extend, instead of remaining warily within, my readers' own pre-existent frame of reference.

Am I coming down too heavily on a pointless, harmless book, one written not by a real specialist but by a television personality whose basic function is to amuse the audience between film clips, like those luckless stand-up comics who alternated with the strippers at the old Windmill Theatre? Is there no room for the common man's approach? Certainly there is: the snag is that, these days, less and less room has been left for anything else. What troubles me is that, just as its centenary is being celebrated, the cinema is still taken far less seriously in Britain than in almost any other European country I know; that entire swathes of film history (and geography) are ignored by those critics whose role it is, or should be, to form and foster public taste; and that, even if Barry Norman is perhaps no longer all that representative of the current film-critical climate, his influence must still be commensurate with his popularity.

Paradoxically, this book of his, a book which one presumes was written to provoke and promote an ever higher regard for the medium of film, risks having exactly the opposite effect. Yes, I myself have enjoyed many, if far from all, of the films on his list; and, yes, it is one of the glories of the cinema that it has never lost touch with its populist roots. But if these mostly middlebrow entertainments are enshrined as its *very best*, then it can only reinforce the still dominant British opinion that film is a minor art form, unworthy of comparison with literature, painting, poetry and music. And that, you see, *just isn't so*.

On aboriginality

Jean-Jacques Annaud's film version of *The Lover*, Marguerite Duras's bestselling autobiographical novel, was an abject failure on absolutely every level; watching it, I needed no more than five or six minutes to realise that I would be incapable of staying the course. But how, and when, to walk out? I could hardly take my leave *before* the first of its notorious sex scenes, which would have been grotesquely high-minded of me, not to mention professionally remiss, since it was that very scene which had caused all the fuss and pother. I could not plausibly leave *during* the scene, which would have given my colleagues (I saw the film at a press screening) the mortifying impression that I had been so outraged by it I had been unable to stay put in my seat an instant longer. And I certainly could not leave immediately *after* the scene, since that would have given the equally mortifying impression that it was all I had come to see. (For the record, I hung on for about half-an-hour before sashaying, as negligently as I knew how, to the exit.)

I mention that little predicament of mine not as a prelude to exploring the politics of leaving a film halfway but in order to highlight the tension still generated by representations of the naked body, to illustrate the degree to which, in nearly all imagery of human nudity (painterly, photographic or filmic), two rival points of convergence compete for the spectator's attention – the public and the private parts, the face and the sexual organs. Our eyes (deny it if you will) tend to flit from one to the other and back again, as though carrying out a series of subliminal spot checks.

This no longer applies, though, to just any nudity. What made Annaud's film so sleazily scandalous was, first, that its actress, Jane March, was sixteen years old when she appeared in it; and, second, that she was rumoured to have been personally deflowered during the shoot. Without that fact and that rumour *The Lover* would have attracted exactly the attention it merited – which is to say, none.

Similarly, in the case of a film almost as awful, Polanski's *Bitter Moon*, it was the self-conscious kinkiness of its sexual shenanigans which provided the talking point – most notably, Peter Coyote's verbal description of a 'golden shower' so comically ecstatic it must have provoked a wave of golden showers among the public, with audiences collectively pissing their pants – not the mere fact of simulated sex in itself, a fact we have all learned to take pretty much for granted.

We have come a long way since the fifties, when Otto Preminger's *The Moon Is Blue* was condemned by the American Catholic League of Decency because of a line of dialogue that included the apparently incendiary phrase 'a professional virgin'; when any manifestation of outright nudity on a cinema screen was simply unheard-of; and when, for an adolescent like myself, the only hope of a glimpse of it elsewhere was in the glossy pages of *National Geographic Magazine* or in some exotic television documentary. Such nudity as was available, moreover, was exclusively that of the Other, of the Non-White, of the 'Native'. Like, I fancy, many youths of my generation, I knew what a woman of Papua New Guinea looked like without her clothes on before I ever knew what one from my own environment did. Nor were these women ever photographed in interiors. Feminine nudes could be sanctioned as 'natural', and hence erotically unarousing, only if they were presented in such a way as to blend in (fat chance!) with an environment that was itself unambiguously natural, even 'savage'. And for the potential voyeur they were further de-eroticised by the tacit understanding that, if they were naked (more accurately, half-naked), it was not because they had taken their clothes off but because, very much less enticingly, they had never worn any in the first place. Although such a term was not yet in currency, theirs was an *ecological* nudity – green, so to speak, rather than blue.

We have, I say, come a long way since then. And for most of the way those individuals or institutions whose (frequently self-appointed) vocation it has been to stem the tide have been fighting a rearguard action against public sentiment on the matter. But there is one pertinent question that no one seems to have thought of posing. If, from the fifties to the nineties, we have progressed from the 'professional virgin' of Preminger's *Moon* to the 'golden shower' of

Polanski's *Moon*, what on earth will filmgoers be confronted with in the teens and twenties of the new century?

In that question is the implication that the process will continue to evolve in the future just as it has in the past and present, that representations of sex will become ever more explicit and 'raunchy'. Yet, interestingly, and even if it would be premature to regard it as a trend, there has arisen in the cinema of late, in *Dances With Wolves*, *At Play in the Fields of the Lord*, the two rival Christopher Columbus films and *The Last of the Mohicans*, a curious and unexpected phenomenon: the Return of the Native.

'Return' is perhaps not quite the word. Now that it is no longer tainted by the post-colonial condescension of the fifties, aboriginality, *nativeness*, has been transformed into a wholly positive concept, one defined by spiritual candour, societal harmony and a pantheist empathy with all things natural. And, in a strictly cinematic context, what this New Native represents is nudity without transgression and without guilt; nudity as an end, not a means; nudity as a point of departure, not a point of arrival; nudity flowering in surroundings in which nakedness is the norm, the nakedness of an animal or a plant as much as that of a human body; nudity, finally, as *the* elemental sign of moral superiority. In Ridley Scott's *1492* the baddie wears black, the goodies wear nothing. (Rather, they wear loincloths, that infallible signifier of the Native.)

By demonstrating that filmic nudity need not always be erotically sensitised, such a phenomenon may prove lastingly useful. Or it may instead turn out to be the same old hypocrisy in a new liberal guise.[1] Or it may be so ephemeral as to mean nothing at all. For the present, at least, it offers an agreeable alternative to the rancid vulgarities of Annaud and Polanski and a timely correlate to the erotic vegetarianism of safe sex.

Notes

1 In the contemporary cinema, however, there does appear to be a gradual weaning away from that immemorial double standard for male and female nudity, upheld nevertheless in both *The Lover* and *Bitter Moon*, whereby a woman is required to disrobe completely while a man is permitted to remain erogenously discreet.

On postmodernism

Postmodernism – there's a word to send a chill shiver rippling down the spinal cord! Postmodernism – that bulbous, green, reptilian, H. R. Giger-designed alien erupting out of the pudgy soft belly of the British intelligentsia! Of all the current cultural anxieties by which our intelligentsia is beset, none, it is safe to say, is more acute. Not only did an issue of the *Modern Review* flourish the unequivocal headline 'The Plague of Postmodernism' but the *Independent on Sunday*, almost simultaneously, conducted an enquiry into whether it was indeed a plague, culling quotes from experts real and imagined, including Jean Baudrillard, who claimed, quite understandably, to be 'exhausted' by the term and its by now Pavlovian application to his writing, and Toby Young, the *Modern Review*'s editor, who dismissed it all as 'a wank'.

Baudrillard, one of postmodernism's venerable old troopers, has certainly earned the right to shrug off identification with the phenomenon. But has Young? There is one fact, after all, that tends to be forgotten by its more fashionable fetishists – which is that postmodernism, far from being new, long predates the self-styled stylologists who now damn it as nonexistent. (At its most extreme, postmodernism might claim that it is they, rather, who do not exist.) Usage of the word can probably be traced back to architectural criticism of the early sixties; most commentators would date the rise of the thing itself, even if not yet named or theoretically articulated, from the demise of high modernism in the fifties; its inherently anti-tragic resonances (a postmodern work of art can be anything any other work of art can be except tragic) were first postulated by Walter Benjamin in his seminal essay, written in 1936, 'The Work of Art in the Age of Mechanical Reproduction'; and one prominent French theorist, Jean-François Lyotard, has argued that its true origins are locatable in the Age of Enlightenment. In Britain, as usual, we have leapt on to the bandwagon just as it is approaching its terminus.

But I referred above to postmodernism as, supremely, a source of *anxiety*. What is so alarming to the British is that a crucial super-structure of hierarchy would appear to have been cavalierly disman-tled from the cultural debate, with the result that the crudest of pop culture is now being analysed in the sort of unapologetically earnest idiom formerly reserved for classic texts. (On this superficial level postmodernism means *never having to say you're sorry*.) There is also the uneasy feeling abroad that postmodernism seeks to elevate comment above creation as the supreme aesthetic achievement and that its practitioners need art and literature only in the sense that a video recorder needs a television screen to be fully operational. And what is possibly most disturbing is that postmodern critics seem to have rendered the concept of originality so obsolete, so irrelevant and so confusing as to defy all attempts at elucidation. Consider comic strips. They existed for decades without Roy Lichtenstein's paintings, and Lichtenstein's paintings could never have existed without the prior example of comic strips. So which of the two is more deserving of study? It cannot be comic strips . . . and yet.

What is therefore required is a master-text that would map the mindset of postmodernism, that would enable even those unversed in the arcana of modern cultural theory to understand a little of what it all implies. Such a text exists, I believe, although to my knowledge it has never been cited in this specific context. I refer to Jorge Luis Borges's magnificent *jeu d'esprit* 'Pierre Menard, Author of Don Quixote', from the Argentine fabulist's collection of short stories *Ficciones* (*Fictions*), published in 1939 and one of the great books of the century.

Borges's Pierre Menard is a turn-of-the-century man-of-letters, one of whose uncompleted and unpublished projects is the writing of *Don Quixote* – literally. Menard, Borges insists, 'did not want to compose another *Don Quixote* – which would be so easy – but *the Don Quixote*'. And he continues: 'It is unnecessary to add that his aim was never to produce a mechanical transcription of the origi-nal; he did not propose to copy it. His admirable ambition was to produce pages which would coincide – word for word and line for line – with those of Miguel de Cervantes.' Menard's self-imposed destiny, in short, is to have 'contracted the mysterious duty of reconstructing literally [Cervantes's] spontaneous work'.

As Borges makes clear, however, this second *Don Quixote*, although a verbatim reproduction of the first, is 'more subtle than that of Cervantes'. If Cervantes superimposed on the realities of seventeenth-century Spain those myths of medieval knighthood that were still popular when he wrote his novel, Menard totally eschews the conventionalised, turn-of-the-century Spain of *Carmen* and castanets: 'his disdain for local colour,' remarks Borges, 'indicates a new approach to the historical novel.' When, via the character of Quixote, Cervantes is seen to pass judgment 'against letters and in favour of arms', the likeliest explanation is that he himself was a former soldier: in Menard's *Don Quixote* the selfsame passage patently betrays the influence of Nietzsche. As for the question of their respective styles, there the divergence could not be more radical. Cervantes wrote easily and gracefully in the Spanish of his period, whereas Menard's *exactly identical* prose was, for the early twentieth century, of a quite extraordinary archaism (traces of which, I might add *à la* Borges, can be found in the historical pastiches of Peter Ackroyd and the seafaring trilogy of William Golding).

There, surely, it is – the *Ur*-postmodern text. For what 'Pierre Menard, Author of Don Quixote' cunningly demonstrates is that, when decontextualised – and what is postmodernism about if not the emancipation of cultural artefacts from their immemorial contexts and the reprogramming of them very much as one pleases? – a literary work may serve to generate not just a new and different literary work but also one in which a critique of the original is embedded. And if Menard chose *Don Quixote* (a novel which, not by coincidence, stands in a precociously 'postmodern' relationship to the romances of Cervantes's own period), the principal points of reference for most contemporary postmodernists have been the key works of high modernism. To those, then, to whom nothing means anything unless it can be encapsulated in a snappy definition one might say that the postmodern is the postmortem of the modern.

On beginnings and endings

It is difficult for human beings to live on a spinning globe, to keep their balance, like acrobats, on a revolving planet.

That rather infantile reflection was prompted by the frequent use made, in the several scene changes of John Cox's production of Richard Strauss's *Die Frau ohne Schatten* at Covent Garden, of a tilted revolve stage. Revolves, to be sure, are nothing more than elaborate pieces of theatrical machinery, deployed to shift sets and shunt performers on and off the stage; they are not designed to emit any meaningful signals to the spectator. Nevertheless, as the Covent Garden revolve tilted and turned, and Strauss's Empress and Nurse slowly walked along it into the depths of the stage, I found, as I have often done, that it had somehow become invested with a vaguely metaphorical, allegorical quality. Perhaps because the operation of 'spinning', even if only of a coin on a tabletop, cannot help carrying with it just the faintest intimation of the cosmic, it felt almost as though the characters were ascending into the realm of myth, into eternity itself.

The more general point to be made is that, if one loves an art form in and of itself – if, to take the particular case in point, one responds to the abstract concept of 'opera' over and above the assemblage of individual works of which the international operatic repertoire is composed – then even something as utilitarian as a revolve is eventually transformed into an autonomous source of meaning and enjoyment. As is also, in its own way, the ritual warming-up of the orchestra before the conductor takes his place on the podium. Here, again, a purely functional activity is turned into a pleasure; for an opera buff, the discordances produced are poignantly evocative ones. At the very least, we reassure ourselves that, if the strings are a tad screechy and the brass a bit too brass-bandy, these problems will be ironed out once the opera gets under way, just as, in a restaurant, we trust that some slightly vinegary house wine will become more palatable once we start to eat. Beyond that practical consideration, however, an orchestra's collective throat-clearing is affecting because it sounds as though the musical instruments are animatedly chattering to each other prior to the dimming of the lights, just as we ourselves are doing in the auditorium. It is an onomatopoeic accompaniment to our own discordant buzz of anticipation.

One reason I never tire of opera is that it remains unashamed of even its corniest traditions and conventions. In this it differs from the theatre, a by now debased and hybrid medium, neither unrepentantly visceral nor unrepentantly intellectual, and more and more terrified of, precisely, theatricality. Whatever happened, for example, to the drop curtain (which *is* retained in most opera houses)? What was the argument for dropping it? When entering a theatre these days, we know that we must not expect that close-your-eyes-and-open-them-when-I-count-to-ten kind of surprise that we used to have when the curtain rose. We know that we shall be confronted with a bare, unpeopled, unlit set which we shall almost certainly have to like or lump throughout the entire evening. When staging whodunits, theatrical managements expect critics not to 'give away the ending'; by having dispensed with the drop curtain, what they themselves give away is the beginning.

As for the cinema, I do not suppose it makes much sense at this late stage to lament the passing of the luminous cone which formerly issued from the projectionist's cabin, even if (along with the sprocket holes on a roll of film and the earliest types of cameras with their enormous Mickey Mouse ears) it continues to be the medium's principal decorative emblem, omnipresent to this very day on albums and reference books.[1] On the other hand, I confess to a real nostalgia for two monosyllabic words which have all but disappeared from contemporary films: 'The End'.

If I say 'all but disappeared', it is because they seem to be staging something of a comeback. Terence Davies's *The Long Day Closes* managed to reinstate them by the simple expedient of moving all its credits forward to the start of the film – as was long the case. For that is of course why 'The End' has been made redundant: the fact that, in the majority of big new American films, the closing credit rolls may run for up to six or seven minutes. (Are all these credits absolutely necessary, by the way? No published book would seek to cram into its endpapers the name of every editor, typesetter and printer involved in its fabrication, and so far as I know none of these indispensable collaborators has been battling for individual recognition.)

The main consequence of 'The End''s disappearance is that one no longer quite knows when a film has finished. Is it when the last image has faded from the screen or is it instead when the last title has rolled? It may appear a matter of exquisite inconsequentiality that, while some members of a cinema audience, the purists, are still craning to catch every last and least credit, others, the impurists, are already shuffling towards the exit. Yet such non-uniformity of response, with some of us standing, some of us sitting, some of us moving, some of us staying, does have the frustrating effect of denying us, as a public, as an ensemble, that satisfying sense of resolution, that sense of a sudden, irreversible finality and closure – 'Ouf, it's over!' – that used to be one of the trivial but irreplaceable satisfactions of a cinema performance.

Not so much a question of *All's Well That Ends Well*, then, as of *All's Well That Ends*, period.

Notes

1 As an adolescent, I claimed to be able to deduce what genre a film belonged to merely by studying the shafts of dust caught in the headlights, as it were, of that cone.

On melody

Consider *Porgy and Bess*, recently staged at the Royal Opera House in a production by Trevor Nunn. Nearly everyone of a certain age must be familiar with at least some of Gershwin's score. 'Summertime', for example, the opera's first big number – nearly everyone, I repeat, must know its opening ten notes. Well, listening to those ten notes at Covent Garden, 'Sum-mer-time-an'-the-livin'-is-ea-sy', I asked myself a question I have frequently felt like asking when listening to some great but also ostensibly simple and, so one imagines, easily improvisable tune: *Why did it take so long to be unearthed?*

Reduce 'Summertime' to its substructure, to its unembellished, ten-note skeleton, and hum it to yourself: 'Dum-de-dum. Dum-de-dum-de-dum-*dum*-dum'. It is a memorable, even indelible, tune, which, once registered, is never likely to be forgotten. Yet there does not seem to be all that much to it. As the opera's defining aria, it is the theme instantly conjured up in our inner ears when we hear the words 'Porgy and Bess'; and, as a solo subjected to numerous diverse vocal treatments over the years, it must have made a small fortune for the Gershwin estate. So why did one of those hundreds, maybe thousands, of composers who had been improvising at pianos since the turn of the century – whether classical, popular or, like Gershwin himself, what is called 'crossover' – not hit upon its melody long before 1934, when the opera was staged, and earn the réclame, money and above all personal satisfaction that were to be his?

The question may well strike a musician as meaningless. But, speaking for myself, as a layman utterly without musicological expertise, I have always thought that melodic motifs were like spermatozoa, with only a privileged few ever breaking through to generate a real live tune. I have the sense, too, that they are already 'out there' before actually being composed – out there in the ether, waiting for a composer to appropriate them, begging to be chosen like the unborn children of Maeterlinck's *The Blue Bird*.

Actually, there are many such themes which impress me as having taken too long to be discovered. Think of the song 'Tonight' from *West Side Story*, again as it might be broken down into an elementary note-progression: 'To-night, to-night . . .' and so on. Surely, before Bernstein came up with it in 1957, someone could have chanced across that artless sequence of ascending and descending notes and immediately realised its melodic potential? Or think of Gershwin's own 'I Got Rhythm', which is virtually a parody of what I am talking about. Or the pounding central theme of Sibelius's *Finlandia*. Or the five crashing chords which announce, as though throwing down a challenge to the listener, the opening movement of Tchaikovsky's First Piano Concerto.

On the other hand, I cannot help feeling that the smoky, snaky complexity of the melody which makes up the entirety of Ravel's *Boléro*, or the wittily syncopated patterning, both vocal and verbal, of Cole Porter's 'Anything Goes' ('In-old-en-days-a-glimpse-of-stock-ing-was-looked-on-as-something-shock-ing . . .'), could never have been so nonchalantly plucked out of the air. Unlike those of Gershwin and company (to whose labours I am probably doing an injustice), the melodies of Ravel and Porter leave me with the distinct impression that, in their gestation, the element of chance must have been minimal.

Melody is really a most mysterious thing. Why are there tunes that one is *born* knowing? (In my own case, I might cite, out of hundreds, 'In the Hall of the Mountain King' from Grieg's incidental music to *Peer Gynt*, a tune I cannot remember ever hearing without already having heard it at least once before.) Given how few there are about today, how many memorable tunes, if any, remain to be composed? More specifically, does there still exist, in that same hypothetical ether that I invoke above, a configuration of notes and chords capable of producing, on our ears but equally on our souls, the kind of irresistibly uplifting effect which 'Land of Hope and Glory' produces? If Elgar had failed to compose 'Land of Hope and Glory' the first time around, would the tune have remained spectrally 'available' to some subsequent composer or would it have been lost to us for ever? Are there in fact lots of potential tunes still to be unearthed, tunes to which our ears are not as yet, precisely, *attuned* – just as those compositions by Stravinsky and Debussy and Bartók which were dismissed as tuneless by the first audiences to be exposed to them have long since ceased to strike our ears as melodically problematical? And will our descendants thus find themselves humming Berio and Birtwistle and Xenakis as they stand on the platform waiting for the 8.25 to Waterloo?

So many questions and so few answers. But the problem with music in general, and melody in particular, is that the gap between creator and consumer is an unbridgeable abyss. Everyone is able to write a little, paint a little, act a little, rhyme a little, but no one composes music 'a little'. And, to my knowledge, there exists no book for the layman which explains what exactly makes a melody a melody; which analyses the whole concept of melodic memorability, of 'catchiness'; which elucidates what it is about the best-known of Mendelssohn's *Songs Without Words* (the one commonly exploited by the cinema to denote a caricatural idea of prissy gentility) that causes it to stand out from the others like a radiantly healthy rather than a sore thumb, that makes me wonder whether it was genetically programmed into my being, that convinces me I could have whistled it in the womb. No one has ever shown me why that piece and not another should have imprinted itself on my consciousness.

Left to my own, metaphorical devices, and feeling the urge to end with a statement instead of a question, I would propose this definition: a melody is a piece of music which, like certain books, *one cannot put down*. It is feeble, I know, but it is a start.

On the circus

A paradox.

On the one hand, I have, and have had for as long as I can remember, a real predilection for the mytho-iconography of the circus ring. By that I mean, I like the circus's gaudy treadmill when it has been distilled and purified in the Barnum-and-ballet spectacle of Fellini's *8½*, Chaplin's *The Circus*, Bergman's *Sawdust and Tinsel*, DeMille's *The Greatest Show on Earth*, Tod Browning's *Freaks*, Victor Sjöström's *He Who Gets Slapped*, Max Ophüls's *Lola Montès* and, if now more metaphorically, the same director's *La Ronde*, with its famous merry-go-round (or perhaps I should say melancholy-go-round) construction. I like the wistful, tristful funambulists in the paintings of Picasso's Blue and Rose Periods, as also his unblushingly sentimental drop curtain for Satie's once scandalous ballet *Parade*.[1] I like the circus paintings of Degas, Toulouse-Lautrec, Seurat, Dufy, Léger and Chagall.[2] I like the circus writings of Cocteau, who compared the silvery aerialists drifting high above his head in the canvassy cosmos of the Nouveau-Cirque to wisps of 'phosphorescent snot'. I like Rouault's dolorous Christ-clowns, whose arched eyebrows resemble a matching pair of poised and praying angels from a child's transfer album. I like, finally, the circus ring settings of Wedekind's *Pandora's Box* and (if, again, only metaphorically) Brecht's *Mother Courage*, and the circus band music of Milhaud's *Le Boeuf sur le Toit*, Sauguet's *Les Forains* and Shostakovich's *Hypothetically Murdered*.

On the other hand, not to put too fine a point on it, *I hate, detest, abhor and abominate the circus itself*. Not even six wild white horses from the Camargue, glitzily caparisoned, could drag me to a performance under the loathsome Big Top.

How can such an abyss between representation and reality be explained? Naturally, much of it has to do with the world's currently acute sensitivity to the mortification and possibly maltreatment of the animals involved: even as an infant, I was more distressed than diverted by the spectacle of snarling caged lions, elephants perched with repulsive daintiness on their hind legs and seals playing 'Pop Goes the Weasel' on the xylophone. Nor do I warm to the now presumably irreversible mediatisation of the medium. Yet my hostility is more deeply rooted than that.

For me, what the circus primarily represents is, to the nth degree, the intensification of the *live*. In the theatre, as we know, each individual performance is subtly different from all those which precede and follow it; we know equally, though, that this difference tends to be of fairly minimal import, virtual rather than truly perceptible. By contrast, a great deal of the circus's (supposed) appeal is founded upon just that differential, upon just those variables which are inherent in every live performance. One can actually establish a hierarchy of sorts. Thus: when we watch a film, we know (and are obscurely reassured by the fact) that we are watching *exactly* the same film as everyone else; when we watch a play, we know that we are watching *almost exactly* the same play as everyone else; but, when we are at the circus, we cannot help wondering whether (and hoping that?) *tonight*, for our benefit alone, the trapeze artist will plummet to his death or the lion tamer will be savaged by one of his own lions or, more modestly, the equestrienne's horse will deposit a mound of steaming manure right in front of us. Just as farms are clearly 'closer to' nature than are factories, so circuses are closer to the historical 'one-off' essence of spectacle than are either films or plays.

This exacerbated sensation of 'liveness' is inseparable from the circus experience at every level: for once, all our senses are called into play. There is, to start with, a heightened, even hyperbolic, quality to the *acoustics* of a circus tent, acoustics comparable only to those of a public swimming pool or skating rink, acoustics whose effect is reminiscent of nothing so much as that produced when one claps one's hands over one's ears then abruptly withdraws them. In like manner, when part of a circus audience, we become sensitive to odours to a degree that would be inconceivable (fortunately) inside a cinema or theatre. The very air seems visible, a pixilated powder which smarts the eyes and has to be dusted from the shoulders like spangly dandruff.

The problem is that intimately linked with the circus's 'liveness' is a debilitating deadness, the deadness of an art form which has survived through tradition alone and seeks to command our respect and support in the sole name of that tradition. In this it can be equated with such other moribund but 'worthy', 'seasonal', 'quintessentially British' entertainments as pantomimes, Punch-and-Judy shows, Highland Games, Royal Tattoos and related Eistedfodder, all of which blackmail us (there is no other word) into attending them as though we were enjoined by a moral imperative, as though it were somehow our duty, to do so.

Gorgeous though its iconography may be, the circus itself is dying. The circus is dying because, in this postmodern *fin de siècle* of ours, and whether we regret it or not, the ubiquity of technological reproduction in general, and of television, video and compact discs in particular, means that 'liveness' is no longer perceived as a necessary condition for any of the performing arts, no longer perceived as a cultural value at all. (For most children the wild animals of the circus ring have been quite satisfactorily replaced by the tame animatronics of the theme park.) The circus is dying, ultimately, because the *live* is dying.

Notes

1 I have often thought it would be an amusingly apposite experiment for *Parade* to be revived *complete with its scandal* – which is to say, complete with dancers costumed as outraged bourgeois spectators who, strategically positioned in the auditorium, would leap up on to the stage during the performance.

2 If I include Chagall here, it is because he painted barnyards the way his fellow artists on the list painted circus rings; because, after all, the circus may be regarded as the aesthetic sublimation and glamorisation of the farm.

On snow

Notwithstanding its perennity in December's television schedules, *White Christmas* is actually a pretty undistinguished film. But there is one scene in it which, trite and manipulative as it unquestionably is, has never failed to move – well, let us say, touch – me. Dean Jagger has invited two former army buddies, Bing Crosby and Danny Kaye, to top the bill in a revue at the ski lodge he has purchased in Vermont; unfortunately, because of an embarrassing absence of snow, its opening night threatens also to be its closing night. All appears lost until, on Christmas Eve, just minutes before the curtain is timed to rise, Jagger, tipped off by a member of his staff, draws apart a pair of folding panel doors to reveal, impeccably on cue, the long-awaited snowfall. The lodge, thank heaven, has been saved, and Crosby and Kaye, accompanied by Rosemary Clooney and Vera-Ellen, all of them in Santa Claus drag, bring the film to its conclusion with a chorus of what is still, apparently, the single most popular song in the history of American music, 'I'm dreaming of a White Christmas . . .'.

Curious, I recall thinking the first time I heard that song, that its lyrics should refer to 'dreaming of', rather than 'hoping for', a white Christmas. Or maybe it is not so curious after all. In Britain, more especially in its southern regions, the idea of a white Christmas, considering the extreme rarity of the actual phenomenon, may well belong to the realm of fantasy rather than that of any credible expectation. And it is doubtless for that reason, for all but hopelessly irreclaimable curmudgeons, that there has arisen, around the theme of snow in general, and of Christmas snow in particular, what can only be called a *mystique*.

A book could be written on the poetics of snow as one of the obligatory if all too infrequently satisfied conditions of a perfect Christmas. It is a poetics which dates from the Victorian era[1] and more specifically, of course, from Dickens. The latter has always been the crucial reference. As Borges writes somewhere, the uniqueness of Dickens's novels is that, however lavishly he piles on the agony, the agony of poverty, neglect, violence, solitude and death, the ineradicable conviviality of his style guarantees that the fictional world which his characters inhabit, and for which the word 'Dickensian' was coined, remains unfailingly lovable and livable-in. Well, I would argue that, in the context of our own experience of Christmas, *snow serves exactly the same function as Dickens's style*. Its effect is above all to remind us of its contrary – snow is, paradoxically, a signifier less of cold than of *warmth*, less of cheerlessness than of *snugness*. In spite of certain negative associations (which range from Andersen's Little Matchgirl and Captain Scott perishing gallantly in the Antarctic wastes to the tribulations of the Cardboard City homeless of the nineties), a frosting of snow on a bedroom window-pane has the same magical appeal for us as the sound of rain pelting down on a bedroom roof. It reinforces that sense of security, of comfort, of cosy 'indoorness', that is essential to the spirit and success of a contemporary British Christmas.

Not only does the whiteness of snow match that of several other traditional motifs of the season (the whiteness of Santa Claus's beard, of the lining of his costume, of the icing on a Christmas cake), but its potentially alienating chill is offset by the fact that, in each of these instances, it automatically generates an adjacent, compensatingly warmer hue of redness (the overall redness of Santa Claus's costume, of an open fire glowing in a fireplace, of a sprig of holly on a Christmas pudding, of a robin's breast, even of Rudolph the Reindeer's nose). One colour, in short, is never in evidence without the other. And they become inextricable in the quintessentially Christmassy (and Dickensian) image of the rosy cheek, an image that contrives to convey a sensation of, simultaneously, coldness *and* warmth.

Easy as it is to forget the fact, however, Christmas is a festival as well as merely a holiday, a celebration of Christ's birth, a birthday we all celebrate together. Such a festival necessitates special conditions if it is to retain its ritualised authenticity, and at Christmas the special condition is snow. In the iconography of Christmas-as-festival, as represented in the older-fashioned type of card, it is not at all unusual, for example, to find the Magi depicted traversing a starlit tract of snow-mantled desert on their no doubt baffled camels.

In its more humdrum application to the jollities of Christmas-as-holiday, meanwhile, what a coating of snow provides is the winter's equivalent of a *beach*. Children build snowmen instead of sandcastles out of it. Grown-ups ski instead of jog on it. It softens the feel of the ground under our feet, just as the sand on a beach does. It smooths and planes the world's angles and edges. It Disneyfies cities and blankets the countryside in a quasi-abstract purity and simplicity. In our hands it turns into a playful putty, a pristine plasticine. It looks gorgeous and, when we step on it, it sounds delicious. It is, in short, the season's primary agent of mindless, instinctive hedonism.

And yet, there you are, it practically never happens. It is a fantasy of Christmas, familiar to us from countless films (notably, Frank Capra's *It's a Wonderful Life*, which is the exact filmic counterpart to *A Christmas Carol*), but, in life, destined to be more dreamt of than experienced. Dreamt of – but also remembered. For, unless I am now fantasising backwards, there *have* occurred a handful of white Christmases within my own lifetime. Which is all perhaps as it should be. Perhaps, for a white Christmas to conserve its potency and allure as an *ideal*, it should always remain the stuff, the raw, powdery material, of nostalgia, existing either in the past as a memory or in the future as a dream but never, never, in the present as a lived reality. Perhaps, when all is said and done, there are no snows *but* the snows of yesteryear.

Notes

1 The most vivid symbol for me of a true Victorian Christmas is an item of nineteenth-century clothing whose disappearance I have always regretted: the muff.

On *The Triumph of the Will*

Not long ago I watched a rare television screening of *The Triumph of the Will*, Leni Riefenstahl's famous, infamous documentary on the sixth National Socialist congress held in Nuremberg in 1934. The screening itself was preceded, as by a health warning on a packet of cigarettes, by a *causerie* in the studio with, among others, Professor George Steiner, the contemporary German filmmaker Hans-Jürgen Syberberg and the American cinema historian Annette Insdorf. And, for a viewer like myself, with only the vaguest memory of a film I had last seen twenty-odd years before, the experience was a revelation.

By now everyone must be aware of the unique nature of Riefenstahl's reputation, that of an indisputably major artist who made the catastrophic error of aligning herself, whether through ideological conviction or professional opportunism, with the rise of the Nazi Party. It is a reputation which, with minimal shadings of opinion, the studio debaters were all content to endorse and which I, too, had always lazily assumed was an accurate measure of her status and stature. Then the film – produced, according to its credits, 'by order of the Führer' – started to unfold and the scales fell, one by one, from my eyes. *The Triumph of the Will* is not a great film *in spite of* its subject matter but a bad film of enduring interest exclusively *because of* that subject matter. By any scrupulously cinematic criteria, it is as tedious and risible as the congress itself must have been to all but the most fanatical Nazi. Far from having destroyed a career of the highest promise by making the regrettable decision to lend her 'genius' to a disreputable cause (a decision, it should be noted, which she made twice: the second film for which she is celebrated is the rather more accomplished *Olympiad*, a documentary record of the 1936 Olympic Games in Berlin), Riefenstahl can count herself extremely lucky to have filmed these, shall we say, Olympian games, for without her association with Hitler she would now have been completely forgotten. (A comparison with another work of propaganda for one of the twentieth century's defining isms, Eisenstein's *October*, a hymn to Soviet communism, is crushing for the German director.)

It is not just the gallery of obscene Nazoid faces, those of Goebbels, Hess, Streicher, Frank, etc., that one finds so disheartening; not just the drivelling speeches by all present, speeches of an unrelieved and well-nigh indistinguishable banality (each of them succeeded, as night succeeds day, by carefully calibrated spasms of canned applause); not just the endless goosestepping parades (as though Riefenstahl were endeavouring to do for uniforms what she was later to do for glistening nude bodies in *Olympiad*); and not just the gruesome military marches on the soundtrack (oh, for a little Wagner!). Worse by far are those passages of the film in which Riefenstahl aspires to the *sublime*. There is, supremely, the opening sequence of Hitler's airborne arrival in Nuremberg. Apart from the fact that the exaltant imagery of clouds parting to allow the Führer's plane to pass constitutes visual kitsch of the purest water, and would have been judged laughable by Steiner and Syberberg if they had been confronted with it in a painting instead of in a film, its premise recalls nothing so much as that of the crassest Hollywood adventure movies, with the Great White God descending from the skies upon awestruck 'natives'. That such imagery had an immense impact on German audiences of the period is, of course, of interest to social historians. That it should also continue to be held as evidence of Riefenstahl's brilliance as a filmmaker beggars belief.

Virtually any unpretentious newsreel footage of the Nazi era is more haunting than Riefenstahl's pseudopoetic ravings. In terms of the cinema's own documentary tradition, such less prestigious practitioners as Chris Marker, Georges Franju and Frederick Wiseman have achieved results incomparably more subtle and disturbing. And, simply on the level of mass choreography, there can be absolutely no comparison between Riefenstahl and, yes, Busby Berkeley, whose garish spectacles, like hers, were conceived primarily with film in mind, Berkeley's with women, Riefenstahl's with men.[1]

'Fascinating Fascism', Susan Sontag called it; while the English journalist Philip Norman has argued, persuasively if perhaps a trifle

prematurely, that certain decorative configurations of thirties total-
itarianism have started to make a worrying comeback in contemporary logos – those, specifically, of the Conservative Party and British
Telecom. Yet it is difficult to see how this repetitious, long-winded
bore of a film, a film almost entirely deficient in the macabre glamour which is promised us by its reputation, could present any real
danger to the fast-forward generation of the nineties, to all those
neanderthal neo-Nazi thugs whom one has seen parading through
the streets of the new unified Germany and who could scarcely be
more unlike the virginal and supernaturally clean-cut Hitler Youth
apotheosised by Riefenstahl. They would simply be incapable of sitting through it.

Neo-Nazism is one of the most ominous developments of our
ebbing century, but little purpose is served by obsessively relating its
rise to the emblems and artefacts of its historical upper-case prece-
dent. For if *The Triumph of the Will* remains a problematic film, the
problem that it poses is not whether such a 'brilliant' work is capable of seducing neo-Nazi skinheads and pinheads but why such a
trashy one continues to impress liberal intellectuals.

Notes

1 Berkeley, whose organisation of filmic space makes Riefenstahl look like an
  amateur, sometimes tempers the more sinisterly regimented aspects of his production numbers with conceits reminiscent of the gala traditions of Chinese
  rather than Soviet communism. I am thinking of those moments in his films
  when a bevy of chorines, as they say, brandish above their heads a grid of inter-
  locking squares which turn out to form a giant composite portrait of Ruby
  Keeler.

On outtakes

Here is a gag, a magisterially timed and executed one, that I chanced to see on television. In medium shot, in the centre of the screen, in the main aisle of a crowded provincial shopping mall, a newscaster reports on an item of local current affairs. Passersby pass by, mostly unfazed by the camera, although there is the odd surreptitious glance in its direction. Then, suddenly, in the upper left-hand corner of the image, just behind the newscaster, the tip of a white cane appears, tap-tap-tapping away, left, right, left, right, left, right. In his turn, the cane's blind owner enters the picture, making an involuntary beeline, slow, unerring and inexorable, for the unsuspecting reporter. They collide, naturally – but what prompts our laughter is less the collision itself than its foreplay, the exquisitely paced suspense that prepares us for it.

It is a gag, though, that did not feature in any regular comedy show. It was an outtake, screened in one of the several editions of Denis Norden's *It'll Be Alright* [sic] *on the Night*. And the odd thing is that, if the same gag had featured in some other show, it would not have been so funny.

Why not? What is the appeal of these ragbag anthologies of film stars 'corpsing' (to err is human), newsreaders stumbling over their presumably autocued lines (to 'er . . .' is also human), animals misbehaving and ordinary people simply falling over? What makes us laugh at their various misadventures not just in a quantitatively but qualitatively different fashion? This, first of all: that the unwittingly funny will always be funnier than the wittingly funny, because humour, almost by definition, is never more effective than when founded on an absence of premeditation.[1] An obvious remark, perhaps, but it does enable us to isolate the peculiar charm of *It'll Be Alright on the Night*: which is that, in the tightly regulated and standardised framework of television comedy, outtakes alone contrive to introduce the otherwise alien concept of the unpremeditated and the accidental.

If those screened by Norden are infallibly funny, it is because they offer a series of textbook demonstrations of Bergson's once famous theory of humour – that it derives essentially from the abrupt collapse of a chronically rigid being. A professional comedian can never be that funny because he only pretends to 'collapse'. And, in fact, the least funny of the outtakes screened on the show are those which involve actors, in particular actors who have specialised in comedy (most glaringly – and in spite of the fact that Norden routinely refers to it as a 'classic' and constantly reruns it 'by public demand', or so he alleges – the one of Peter Sellers convulsed in giggles during a *Pink Panther* shoot). For it is in the nature of actors to remain in control of such a situation, however sticky, and attempt *in extremis* to milk it for all it might be worth (for the benefit of the studio crew if no one else). It may even be the case, given the current popularity of outtakes, that some actors are now prepared to fluff their lines deliberately in the hope of turning up on *It'll Be Alright on the Night*.

The huge success of Norden's show, however, can also be linked to what is, on the part of the British, a veritable cult of *failure*. How enchanted we are when things go wrong! Think of all those ludicrous little books – token books which we give to other people at Christmas like book tokens – chronicling disasters in the theatre and opera house. Think of Stephen Pile's bestselling collections of grandiose flops. Think of the perverse pleasure viewers took in watching a whole evening of so-called *TV Hell* – an evening of programmes, in short, which they had turned off in disgust the first time around. Why, even many of our national success stories appear to have had their origin in failure. On the one hand, there is the egregious 'Gazza', who became a household name for having wept after being cautioned during a World Cup soccer match; on the other, Nigel Short, the finest chess player Britain has produced in a century yet whose perceived nerdishness means that he finds himself regularly, and with relish, compared to Adrian Mole.

One might attribute this extreme indulgence towards failure to a longstanding British weakness for the heroic flop, to our tradition of revelling in disaster (Dunkirk) instead of, as is proverbially claimed of Americans, obstinately refusing to acknowledge its existence

(Vietnam). Equally, it might be interpreted as a reflection, albeit in a minor, frivolous key, of the wider sense of political and social inadequacy which has pervaded the culture of this country (the country that lost an empire and failed to find a role) in the latter half of the twentieth century. Or one might view it, as I myself do, as a specifically post-eighties, postmodern phenomenon. In a period in which almost everything can be recuperated as a marketable commodity, failure, too, has been transformed into a value, a realisable asset.

For this is just one of the many mottoes of the postmodern: If at first you don't succeed, who cares? There will always be a market for your failure.

Notes

1 Rather surprisingly, the same rule can be applied to wit, or verbal humour. All else being equal, an impromptu *mot* invariably strikes us as funnier than one we suspect has been prepared in advance.

On American presidents

I never saw Stephen Sondheim's *Assassins*. In view of the fact, though, that it clearly represented a new and courageous departure for the composer, I was intrigued to note that, for some of his admirers, it foundered on the sheer *monotony* of its subject matter, on the fact that the psychopathology of political assassins turned out to be less rich, complex and various than one had generally supposed. And I wonder whether it would not have made better sense for him to have focused instead on their victims.

At least from what one has read of them, American presidents are more interesting creatures than their assassins – more 'theatrical', too, particularly in the context of the modern American theatre. For consider: what is that theatre if not, above all, the theatre of revelation, the theatre of 'You mean . . .?' You mean . . . you were such a cheapskate that when I had tuberculosis you refused to pay for the services of a proper doctor (son to father in O'Neill's *Long Day's Journey into Night*)? You mean . . . you sold spare parts to the army in wartime knowing them to be defective (son to father in Miller's *All My Sons*)? You mean . . . your best friend committed suicide because you rejected his advances (Maggie to Brick in Williams's *Cat on a Hot Tin Roof*)? Now consider: by what has the contemporary American presidency been marked if not by a similar series of second-act revelations concerning the true, albeit sometimes long submerged, natures of one national father-figure after another: Kennedy's promiscuity, Nixon's mendacity, Reagan's Irangate and Bush's Iraqgate.

When in full oratorical flight, American statesmen even sound like characters in search of an author – from Kennedy's second-hand speechifying about the fear of fear itself[1] to Lloyd Bentsen's famous putdown of Dan Quayle: 'Senator, you're no John Kennedy!' (One can almost see the second-act curtain slowly descending on Bentsen, ideally played by someone like Burgess Meredith, as he delivers the line to a woebegone Quayle.) And it might be amusing, with Bill Clinton's inauguration imminent,[2] to look back over the various presidencies since Kennedy's and imagine, in the style of a college revue or indeed of a Sondheim musical, how they would have been portrayed by some of the more prestigious American dramatists.

The Kennedy story itself – his assassination, his brother Robert's assassination, the pursuit of the whole Kennedy clan by those same Furies who once set the house of Atreus aflutter, and the still suspect succession of Lyndon Johnson (already libellously lampooned in a squib of the period, *MacBird*) – would naturally demand nothing less than the florid cloth-ear eloquence of an O'Neill. *Mourning Becomes Jackie*, perhaps. With the accession of Nixon (who was also debunked in a cod-Shakespearean satire called, if memory serves, *Dick Deterred*), we at once switch gear to the squalid, five o'clock shadow world of Mamet's *Glengarry Glen Ross*, the only difference being that the expletives that we associate with Mamet's dialogue would have to be deleted. Next in line was Ford, the spitting image of Paddy Chayefsky's lonely, lovelorn, chronically cack-handed butcher Marty ('Whadda you wanna do tonight, Marty?' 'Gee, I dunno, whadda *you* wanna do?'). Carter, for his part, I see in a play entitled *A Streetcar Named Retire*, as an ageing, wilting Southern beau reminiscing about the big white house in which he used to live and on whose estate the calla lilies were ever in bloom. Reagan and Bush were dead ringers for Lennie and George in Steinbeck's *Of Mice and Men*, with moronic Ronnie trotting contentedly beside his smarter Vice-President: 'Duh, George . . . we gonna live off duh fat of duh land, right, George?'[3] Then there was Bush himself, having finally paid off his mortgage on the White House, like Willy Loman in Miller's *Death of a Salesman*, and haplessly peddling his wares from door to door on that tricky Tokyo route.

And Bill Clinton? It is with him that we return to Sondheim, one of whose lesser-known musicals is *Merrily We Roll Along*, an updated adaptation of the play of the same title by George S. Kaufman and Moss Hart. Although that play, too, is structured on a series of revelations, the particular conceit that distinguishes it from the others cited above (a conceit it shares with Pinter's *Betrayed* and

Martin Amis's *Time's Arrow*) is that its narrative unfolds in reverse chronology. When the curtain rises, its by now middle-aged playwright protagonist is already shown to have sold out, to have sacrificed his artistic integrity in pursuit of easy commercial success. Whereupon Kaufman and Hart invert the arrow of time and lead us backward through their hero's life to the play's climax at which (oh, the subtle irony of it!) we find him still at college brimming with optimism and vowing to be forever true to his youthful ideals.

It is doubtless a prematurely harsh claim to make at this point,[4] and it would be grotesque to be a total fatalist about such matters; yet, as we look at the two young (or youngish) faces of Clinton and Gore, those faces of the future, so fresh, so full of promise (more precisely, full of promises), it cannot help striking us that, just as in the closing scene of *Merrily We Roll Along*, all that youth and freshness and promise have *already* been contaminated by the failures and errors and compromises which we know, we *know*, are in store for us during the next four years.

In the beginning is the end, and the fact that we shall be living these years forward instead of backward is neither there nor here.

Notes

1 Borrowed from FDR.

2 This piece was originally published in 1993.

3 Reagan could not be given his own role in any such adaptation: he was not good enough an actor to play so bad a president.

4 I was premature but right.

On actemes

Robinson Crusoe discovering a footprint in the sand. Oliver Twist asking for more. Heathcliff and Cathy on the moors. Gavroche on the barricades. Joseph K's arrest one fine morning. Marcel's *petite madeleine*.

What exactly are these? Being completely unfigurative, what they are not, in the literary sense, is 'images'. Nor would it be fair to reduce them to the status of 'famous passages from famous novels', since the spell they have cast over the collective imagination has tended to obscure their original novelistic context. (You do not have to have read *The Trial* to identify the reference above.) They have in a sense transcended language. They have detached themselves from the prose to which they were once canonically anchored and now float, free and untrammelled, in an aquarium of folk myth and memory. Such as they have been bequeathed to us, bereft of any genuinely measurable duration, any definitive verbal formulation, any real textual exactitude, they resemble nothing so much as dreams.

In fact, there is, or used to be, a word for them: actemes. (I say 'used to be' because, although the word gained a certain currency among linguistic theorists in the sixties and seventies, it has since, mysteriously, disappeared from circulation.) To simplify, an acteme is a single fragment of discourse from a not necessarily fictional text, a fragment which was initially generated by language but has subsequently come to drift through the reader's (and, of course, the non-reader's) mind as an extra-linguistic cloud of narrative. And if I revive the concept here, it is because it occurs to me that what is wrong with contemporary British fiction is its chronic shortage of memorable actemes.

The problem, to be fair, is not confined to the domestic output: there is, I venture to suggest, an international crisis of fiction. Yet from recent American literature one could at least cite the scene in which Sherman McCoy and his mistress take a horrendously wrong turning and find themselves astray in the Bronx; or, in the same novel, that of the inopportune death of a Jewish entrepreneur in a fashionable Manhattan restaurant: say what you like about the often questionable racial ideology of *The Bonfire of the Vanities*, Tom Wolfe's bestseller was a cornucopia of marvellous actemes. There exist, too, vivid examples in at least a handful of non-English-language novels from the last quarter-century: among others, Márquez's *One Hundred Years of Solitude*, Calvino's *Invisible Cities*, Süsskind's *Perfume*, Eco's *The Name of the Rose* and Pavic's *The Dictionary of the Khazars*. My own reading of current British fiction is likely to be as partial and incomplete as anyone else's, but from those novels I have read the sole instance I have come across of a haunting acteme (haunting in a minor key, which is precisely its charm) is in *The Remains of the Day*, in the scene in which, stranded in a West Country village, Stevens, Kazuo Ishiguro's butler protagonist, is befriended by its obsequiously amiable inhabitants. It is a strangely beautiful moment by virtue of the fact that it seems not to have been programmed into the novel's genes, being, in the best and least pejorative sense of the word, *gratuitous*.

Are actemes indispensable to a novel's power to survive? The fiction of the nineteenth century bulged with them (Dickens, Dostoevsky, Balzac, Stevenson, etc.); interestingly, though, the advent of high modernism proved to be by no means incompatible with their invention. I have already referred to Proust and Kafka (whose unfinished *Amerika* – as it is usually known – strikes me, from this angle if no other, as the greatest novel ever written, by anyone, anywhere), but I could just as well have listed Joyce, Hemingway, Beckett, Céline, Genet, Mann (what is *Death in Venice* if not one long acteme of seventy pages or so?), and many, many more. And whatever the theories to which contemporary novelists feel obliged to pay lip service, however they attempt to justify the pallor and anaemia of their work in terms of what might be called the Naturalistic Imperative, most readers still instinctively dislike books without conspicuous actemes.

Which surely explains why the century's most potent and popular story-telling medium is not the novel at all but the cinema, the dream factory, the acteme factory. Since its origins in the waning years of the nineteenth century (origins from which it has never quite managed, perhaps fortunately, to distance itself) the cinema has been an inexhaustible generator of actemes – from the slaying of King Kong, that Quasimodo of the Empire State Building, to the shot of Cary Grant mounting a staircase in Hitchcock's *Suspicion*, his path lit by a spookily glowing glass of milk like a candle in the hand of a dozy child. (Actually, Hitchcock has a claim to be considered the twentieth century's most fecund creator of actemes in any medium.) Even now, when the cinema itself, certainly the American cinema, is no longer what it was, its actemic hold over the public has if anything been reinforced rather than weakened. Just as a rash contributor to *Cahiers du Cinéma* once, in the fifties, defined Charlton Heston as an 'axiom', so I am now tempted to propose Arnold Schwarzenegger as a living, breathing acteme.

Naturally, film has an enormous advantage over fiction in this regard, not merely because it is itself primarily a visual medium but also because of the publicity machine which it has at its disposal – a machine designed to crank out stills, posters, advertisements, trailers and the like – and which is crucial to the propagation of filmic actemes.[1] It was, nevertheless, not just the supremely great but countless lesser novelists of the nineteenth and early twentieth centuries who possessed the secret of the novelistic acteme, and it would be disastrous to write it off as a lost cause. For what an unforgettable acteme does is what Walter Benjamin demanded of all art: that it 'transform the inaccessible into an event'.

Notes

1 How many readers familiar with the photographic acteme of Marilyn Monroe standing astride a Manhattan sidewalk grating, her skirt billowing about her thighs like a giant white orchid, would be able to name the film from which it was extracted? The answer, for the record, is Billy Wilder's *The Seven Year Itch*.

On emotion

I happened to speak to a couple of acquaintances who had been to see, independently of each other, Nicholas Hytner's production of *Carousel* at the National Theatre and who had both been enchanted by it. Nothing peculiar in that: the show was almost universally admired. But what surprised, what even startled, me about their enthusiasm was the word which, in involuntary unison, both of them used to describe it. The evening had been, they said, a tremendously *moving* experience.

Moving. It was only after hearing that word twice in as many days that I realised how extremely uncommon it has become as a response to a work of art in practically any medium. *Brilliant, sensitive, dazzling, disturbing, original, audacious, stimulating, exquisite*, what you will – there are adjectives aplenty in the codified lexicon of cultural approval, but *moving* has been all but expunged from it. It is as though a legitimate distaste for sentimentality has finally prevailed over an immemorial craving for emotion. In the case of *Carousel*, for example, the reservations of the one national theatre critic to have remained grouchily unconvinced, Michael Billington of the *Guardian*, were directly related to the unashamed emotionalism of 'You'll Never Walk Alone'. And the debate around Chaplin's art, revived by the release of Richard Attenborough's ghastly biopic, has refocused attention on the 'pathos' that is supposed to have undermined his pantomimic genius, in stark contrast to the aristocratic purity of Keaton, the rival idol.[1] Pathos and bathos, those two Musketeers so frequently confused by schoolchildren, are now one and the same, and the arbiters of cultural fashion have decreed that hearts are no longer to be worn on sleeves.

Or, rather, that is what I used to believe – that it was entirely a matter of the public mood, of the zeitgeist. On reflection, I have come to realise that if audiences are no longer moved it is probably because artists no longer feel impelled to move them. Certainly, in an era of the cinema when the great 'bel canto' melodramas of the past, the melodramas of Douglas Sirk and Max Ophüls and Michael Curtiz, are an extinct species, and 'love at first sight' has been ignominiously reduced to 'meeting cute', it is hard to remember the last time that, as the cinema curtains closed over the screen, a curtain of tears had also, mortifyingly, been drawn over one's eyes. The same applies to the theatre, for which very few new dramatists are willing or able to manipulate the rhetoric of emotion. As for current British fiction, whatever the virtues of Amis, Boyd, Barnes, McEwen and company, the characteristically cool, unsqueamish tone of their prose leaves precious little opportunity to (as they used to say) tug the reader's heartstrings. Those writers, meanwhile, who operate in a postmodern mode are unmoving almost by definition, curbed as they are by the ironies of quotation and paraphrase. (Their dilemma was lampooned in a, for once, clever cartoon in the *Modern Review*, which had the demented young woman of Münch's *The Scream* raising her two sets of fingers in a gesture conventionally expressive of inverted commas, thereby wittily 'quoting' her own *angst*.)

Does it really matter? *Is* pathos bathos and vice versa? In attempting to distinguish them, do I run the risk of defending sentimentality? Very well, I defend sentimentality. For what I have also come to realise is that a tolerance of sentimentality is something one grows *into*, not *out of*. It may be, paradoxically, one of the natural attributes of maturity.

For as long as I can recall, I have unreservedly loved the work of a trio of artists whose names are commonly associated with the cause of sentimental humanism: Dickens, primarily, and two of his multifarious posterity, the filmmakers Chaplin and Capra. When I was younger, however, I willingly deferred to the received wisdom that, if each was supreme in his own field, it was in spite rather than because of an incorrigible inclination to sentimentality – or, as it was often called, mawkishness. I unthinkingly accepted that Dickens's true genius lay in his scathing portraiture of humbug and hypocrisy, Chaplin's in the subversive power of his slapstick routines and Capra's in his satire of rapacious Yankee capitalism. Now, more mature as I am, or as I affect to think I am, I would give all of Dickens's Pecksniffery for the unmourned death of Jo, the poor homeless crossing-sweeper of *Bleak House* ('Jo moved on'); all of Chaplin's sight gags for the naïvely uplifting speech made by the little Jewish barber in the closing sequence of *The Great Dictator*; and all of Capra's comically bloated bourgeoisie for the climactic moments of *It's a Wonderful Life* in which James Stewart is reunited with his family – on Christmas Eve, even!

Perhaps my 'heart' has been expanding over the years until it has become as outsized as Cyrano's nose, or perhaps I am simply advancing into senility, but it is moments like these, moments when I feel for the characters almost as though I were in the book or film alongside them, moments that would require from contemporary artists a commitment to emotional candour that few of our cold and unforgiving performers seem equipped to command, that I find so cruelly wanting in our culture.

It is so easy to be hard, so hard to be soft! Yet softness of texture is, I believe, a quality that should be as prized in art as it is in life (in furniture, in clothing, in the human body). And, *pace* Oscar Wilde, I find I can now read of the death of Little Nell *without* bursting into laughter.

Notes

1 Curiously enough, those critics who turn their noses up at the pathos of Chaplin's films tend to be the same who positively wallow in the pathos of Keaton's life: his alcoholism, his wife's desertion, the fact that his career was ruined by the talkies, etc.

On special effects

What makes American films different?

If that recalls the question put by Fitzgerald to Hemingway in the twenties, 'What makes the rich different?', it is because the answer is in both cases the same: 'They have more money.' It is, I know, a very partial and faintly jaundiced answer, but most of the more specific differences between American and European films – that the former tend to be industrial, extroverted and spectacular, the latter to be artisanal, introverted and (if often out of commercial necessity rather than aesthetic predilection) much less preoccupied with pure spectacle – can probably be regarded as subdivisions of it. And another subdivision is the most recently manifest difference between the two: that American films tend to contain special effects and European films not.

I am in two minds about special effects. On the one hand, I do enjoy them; on the other hand, I usually do not enjoy the films in which they are prominently featured. On the one hand, it depressed me that the trailer for Coppola's *Dracula* was exclusively concerned to promote its special effects, as though it had been assumed that nothing else in it, neither the cast nor the plot nor the love interest nor the armed-to-the-teeth protagonist himself, would hold anything like the same fascination for the public; on the other hand, I cannot deny that it was by dint of those (gorgeous) effects that the film, for all its ripe, gamey dreadfulness, was tolerably amusing and watchable throughout. On the one hand, I tell myself that special effects constitute a perfect symptom of what I view as the cinema's current decline; on the other hand, I immediately remind myself that the medium, as initially perceived, *was* a special effect: the first spectators of the Lumières' *L'Arrivée d'un train en gare de La Ciotat* back in 1895 responded to the image of the oncoming locomotive with the same gawping incredulity that modern audiences have reserved for shots of descending spacecraft in Spielberg's films.[1]

But there is a subtler argument to be used in their defence. Verne aside, I am no fan of literary science-fiction: if ever, on the printed page, my eyes alight on an expression like 'time warp' or 'parallel universe', they instantly glaze over. I have always had a weakness, however, for the same storylines in the cinema, perhaps because film renders realistic, or at least illusionistically credible, what is fated in literature to remain strictly conjectural. Yet, watching low-budget science-fiction films in the terrestrial planetarium of my local fleapit in the fifties (it is only since Stanley Kubrick's *2001*, the exact cinematic equivalent of the 1969 moon landing, that extravagant budgets have become standard for the genre), I remember dreaming of an *ideal* science-fiction film, one that would have been freed from the technical imperfections of which I was even then aware, one in which the physical, spatial and logical dislocations proper to such a narrative would have become seamless. Well, as anyone who has seen *Close Encounters of the Third Kind* or *Total Recall* or *Terminator 2* will confirm, that dream has at last been realised. After these films, it is possible to conceive of different kinds of effects in the future but difficult to believe that there might be substantively better ones.

Why, then, even as I am astonished, is there some part of me which resists the seduction? Why is my astonishment so shallow and unreverberative?

Some easy answers suggest themselves: the fact, as I have intimated, that special effects in the cinema have almost always had a futuristic coloration and that nothing dates more swiftly than the future (no word has a more passé ring to it than *futuristic*); the sheer imbecility, on a psychological level, of all but the finest science-fiction films; the preclusion, by the presence onscreen of special effects, of the deployment of a rich and expressive *mise-en-scène*, since complex camera movements and angles, already awkward to bring off in a film whose images are only truly finalised in the laboratory, would risk distracting from the technical accomplishments which are often the film's *raison d'être* (in this respect, *Dracula* represents something of a breakthrough, as its barrage of special effects does contrive to coexist with a flamboyant, if occasionally laughable, visual style); the fact, too, that the textures of our own workaday lives have themselves been enriched by vertiginous special effects. Relative to that last argument, consider the computer on which I typed this very essay and whose screen I can organise as I please, enlarging, contracting and switching fonts, shuffling documents every which way, even doodling on it as idly as on a notepad. Such aptitudes are scarcely less miraculous than the multiple metamorphoses of *Terminator 2* – and I am of course exploiting only a fraction of my computer's resources.[2]

Finally, though, I have come to realise that my dissatisfaction derives primarily from another dream I have long had, the dream that cinematic special effects might for once be deployed by a genuine *auteur*, an artist of the first order, a Godard, a Rohmer, a Kiarostami (or by the best of their younger contemporaries), to personal, autobiographical and unpopulist ends. And I can imagine one way at least in which they could be so deployed. Think of such an *auteur* filming himself now, in 1997, instigating one half of a conversation (about what? That would be up to him); then waiting twenty years, until 2017, before filming his older self engaging, across the millennial abyss, in the other half of the same conversation; then invisibly stitching the two halves together. Now that *would* be a special effect.

Notes

1 There is also the fact that the cinema's first genuine stylist, Georges Méliès, a conjuror by profession, was equally its first maestro of special effects.

2 Recently, seeing Kubrick's *The Shining* again, for the first time since its release in 1980, I was confounded by the likeness of the giant Overlook Hotel in which it is set to a kind of word-processor that barely existed when it was made. The hotel's various empty suites and rooms resemble so many unopened files and documents; its miniaturised maze resembles the hard disk symbol which materialises in the top-right-hand corner of the screen; and the hyperflexible Steadicam camera, giddily scooting round its corners and along its corridors, could serve as a metaphor for the intoxicating liberty of a computer mouse.

On the theatre

In 1992 the *Guardian*'s theatre critic, Michael Billington, felt impelled to 'spring to the defence', as he put it, of the medium to which he has devoted his professional life. What prompted this plucky initiative was a series of journalistic articles anathematising the theatre over the last few years, one of which happened to be by yours truly. And since, inevitably, his arguments were mainly subjective, even solipsistic, they tend to elicit no less subjective refutations.

Thus he declared that, for him, the theatre possessed 'a greater potential than any other medium to rearrange one's consciousness'. It may be that I have not understood what those last three words were intended to imply; but if they do mean what I think they mean, I have to say that I have found my own consciousness far more radically rearranged by, say, the novels of Kafka and Proust, the paintings of Cézanne and Picasso, and the films of Buñuel and Godard (since the cinema has always been the implicit archrival in this debate), than by practically anything I have seen in the theatre.

Then, too, he stated that the theatre 'has an almost unique capacity for inducing ecstasy'. I trust that, even for Billington, the operative word here is *almost*, given that one might mention the music of Mozart and Wagner (music, surely, is *the* ecstasy-inducer among the arts), the poetry of Rimbaud and Rilke, the paintings of Piero and Vermeer, the films of Murnau and Mizoguchi. (Neither of the latter two directors is, I realise, a household name, but they are both very great artists for all that and therefore – a *therefore* too frequently elided even by those who profess to love the cinema – among the creative giants of the century.)

His third postulation, that the theatre's pool of performers has been systematically plundered by the contemporary cinema (he names Anthony Hopkins, Gary Oldman and Daniel Day-Lewis), is irrefutable, except that, apart from revealing his philistinely Anglocentric conception of film, he seems never to have thought of turning his thesis around and asking: Why do so many actors systematically up and leave the theatre in the first place?[1] In fact, I would suggest that the most valuable function of the cinema in this (mostly one-way) traffic is to *expose* the theatre – to expose all its vain speechifying rhetoric. Billington cited David Hare's *Racing Demon* as one of his modern 'consciousness-rearranging' plays. Yet Hare's work in the cinema as both director and writer (*Wetherby*, *Strapless*, *Paris by Night* and the scenario of Louis Malle's preposterous *Damage*) has laid bare a hollow, spell-it-all-out-so-that-no-one-will-miss-it literalism which makes one wonder whether 'theatre' and 'subtlety' are incompatible terms. And one could say the same of the uniformly undistinguished films of Tom Stoppard, Richard Eyre, Peter Hall, Christopher Hampton, etc.

What the theatre has enjoyed in this country, and for too many years now, is a spurious *prestige*; whereas the cinema was, as we know, raised on the wrong side of the tracks and has never quite managed to lose its *lumpen* accent. (The theatre was born in ritual, the cinema in relaxation.) That prestige is gradually being eroded, but it hovers about still, just in the way, for example, that the theatre's devotees talk. Have you noticed how such devotees always ask if you have *not yet* seen a new play, as though there were just two permissible states of being for any literate individual: having seen a play and having *not yet* seen it? It never occurs to them that there is a whole other world out there, a world in which, without giving it too much thought, one simply does not go to the theatre.

Nor is it just a question of how they talk but of how they *laugh*. This is a fiendishly elusive notion, not easy to communicate in print, but let me try anyway. Think of the last time you were in a theatre. Think of the sense of occasion that you experienced, the sense that, for once in your life, you were doing something exceptional. You bought a programme, you took your seat, you removed your overcoat, you positively rustled with expectation. Then the lights dimmed . . . Now it is unimportant whether the play was a comedy or not, whether it was by Shakespeare or David Hare or someone you had never heard of, when one of the characters on that stage said something that was even mildly amusing, you laughed. At Shakespeare's feeblest puns, puns a thousand times overtaken by the three centuries which separate him from us, you actually found yourself laughing aloud – as loudly as you would laugh at the boss's jokes during an after-dinner speech or the best man's at a wedding reception. You laughed, in short, because it would have been *rude* not to, because the person making the joke was standing in front of you. In the cinema, by contrast, where there is seldom a sense of occasion, where the public just hunkers down and patiently or impatiently bides its time through the supporting programme, and where there is nothing in front of you but images on a screen, you laugh when, *and only when*, the film strikes you as genuinely funny. Is it not so?

There you have a minor but symptomatic instance of how the theatre *exploits* its prestige, while the poor, hardworking, unprestigious cinema is obliged to *earn* an audience's goodwill. And it is true not only of bad jokes but of good ones. What is the difference between an epigram (in a Restoration comedy) and a one-liner (in a Woody Allen film)? The accent, basically. It does not matter that a film like *Annie Hall* can claim more and, for the most part, sharper witticisms than a play by Farquhar or Wycherly; it does not matter that even Wilde nodded (if his best paradoxes are almost Nietzschean in the dazzling manner in which they, shall we say, rearrange our consciousness, his weakest are nothing but platitudes performing handstands): nothing matters but the fact that theatrical wit is enhaloed by a prestige rarely if ever accorded to the cinema.

Not, though, for too much longer. That there is a progressive disaffection from the theatre cannot be doubted (even Billington has had to concede the fact), and I predict that the more theatres endeavour to lure the public in, a youthful public in particular, the more determined that public will be to stay away. As Groucho Marx once said – or, rather, as the foppish hero of some Restoration comedy might have said – 'Fie, Lady Sneerwit, 'twould vex me sorely to join a club that would have me for a member.'

Notes
1 I refuse to believe that money is the only inducement.

On fame

'No close-ups,' murmurs Jean-Luc Godard on the soundtrack, during a brief but unendurable sequence of Holocaust footage in his documentary film *Histoire(s) du cinéma*. 'No close-ups. Pain is not a star.'

If only it were true. But, alas, as we know, pain *is* a star, a bigger star than Madonna, than Arnold Schwarzenegger, than Princess Diana. Pain, in the modern world, is top of the bill. Open a newspaper and what you are guaranteed to read about is pain – pain in Bosnia, pain in Iraq, pain in Somalia, pain in Britain. Go to the cinema and what you are (all but) guaranteed to see is pain – pain, usually, of the picturesque, bone-crunching, head-first-through-a-plate-glass-window brand. Whatever might have been one's doubts about Michael Medved's book *Hollywood vs America,* whatever might have been one's concern about his readiness to support his thesis with incompatible and even contradictory statistics, there is no doubt that, when he dealt with pain and violence as the staple of mindless upbeat entertainment, to be consumed along with popcorn and Coke, he spoke the real, timely and salutary truth.

What Medved did not sufficiently insist upon, though, was the *meaninglessness* of much of that violence, which has become merely another excrescence on the already scabby surface of most (not all) of the films he censured, devoid of significance in itself and therefore capable of assuming any significance which the director, as well as the complicitous spectator (and critic), elects to attribute to it. In this respect, it is now, in the context of the filmic image, the equivalent of the word 'fuck' in speech, deployed indiscriminately, unreflectingly, to plug ever-growing gaps of ignorance and illiteracy. And it can be argued, as I would argue (admittedly, with no statistical evidence), that a direct correlation can be drawn between the rise of violence in speech and that of violence in action.

For violence is also a star in life – with a few of its victims receiving, as in Warhol's dictum, their statutory fifteen minutes of fame. Little Jamie Bulger, for example.

Is it possible to write, as a 'cultural' critic, of the murder of an infant? The categorical answer to that question is no. There are methodologies equipped to apprehend and comprehend such an event – moral, sociological, psychoanalytical – but the cultural is not one of them. Why, then, should someone like myself write about it at all? To that I would reply that, apart from my despair when faced with such a crime, and my attendant sense of the futility of rattling on about books and films and plays, it *is* possible to write culturally, if not about Jamie's death itself, then about the unprecedentedly demoralising effect it had on the entire nation. Given how his death occurred, there should be no mystery to that effect, except that infants die violently all the time, all over the globe. Why did this one prove to be so haunting?

There is, in the first instance, an inevitable element of social and racial isolationism involved. For the average Briton a Somalian child just does not 'count' in quite the way a British one does; likewise, a plane crash in India has never made the headlines of a British newspaper (unless the plane turned out to have British passengers aboard). For all that the world has become a global village – one in which, via the international media, whatever happens somewhere, happens simultaneously everywhere else – we persist in being most affected by that which happens closest to home.

Then there is the matter of numbers. Numbers numb. The more they pile up, the less they signify. It is as though, when ten thousand Kurds die, one death has to be divided among ten thousand people, each of them with a claim to only a fragment of death. A single individual, named, identified, his photograph published – a child, moreover, too small to know, as we grown-ups know, what a horrible place the world really is – shares his death with no one.

Finally, and most 'culturally', there is the existence of video footage of Jamie being lured out of a shopping mall. Everything, even crime, now finds itself filtered through a screen. That in itself need offer no cause for protest: if it could not save Jamie himself, the footage was at least instrumental in the identification of his murderers, a small mercy for which we must try to be grateful. There can be no question, however, that it also constituted a very special kind of torment for the rest of us, that our despair was intensified by the fact that we were able to watch the crime being committed and unable to do anything about it.

And I find something disturbingly symbolic, too, about that video footage. Not only because we associate screens with stars, and Jamie Bulger was not just another star, a ten-day wonder to be dropped on the eleventh day. And not only because, on the screen, he was little more than a *blur*, just as, in time, the memory of a loved one's face must fade and eventually become a blur. But also because of what it has to tell us about the real nature of fame.

Notwithstanding the numerous and characteristic ironies with which he distanced himself from the subject, Warhol clearly thought of fame as a wholly positive, desirable ambition, with the sole drawback that it had come to be so ephemeral a state that most of us would be able to enjoy it for only fifteen minutes. Yet it is worth recalling that, for whoever is subjected to its attentions, fame is, outside of the context of show business, almost always a profoundly negative experience, paid for with pain, distress and violence, and that media stardom is something one would not wish on one's worst enemy, let alone on a child. *May you become famous* – there is an appropriate curse for the times we live in. For think of little Jamie Bulger. He has had his fifteen minutes of fame – his fifteen minutes of life.

On nostalgia

Has there ever been a decade as low and dishonest as the nineties?

The phrase 'low, dishonest decade' was of course Auden's, and he was referring to the thirties, but I am not the first to have noted a startling symmetry between the two decades. Each has been marked by the same deep, enduring recession (which in the thirties, in some respects a less dishonest decade than ours, was called a Depression); the same governmental sleaze; the same high rates of unemployment (rates which were judged then to be unacceptable and are now treated as more or less normal); the same rise of racism, fascism and anti-Semitism on the continent of Europe; the same successive tidal waves of refugees (refugees now, as distinct from then, unlikely ever to be granted refuge); the same warring factions in the Balkans; the same urban drabness and decay; even, uncannily, the same Royal Family in disgrace. Odder still is the fact that similar correspondences can be mapped between the two immediately preceding decades, the twenties and the eighties. I might cite the same fixation on style at the expense of substance (with 'high-tech' design, the eighties' *art déco*, destined to epitomise the period for future nostalgists); the same obsession with material well-being; the same mania for novelty in the arts; the same wild, freebooting fortunes made, spent and squandered; the same prevailing euphoria (in some quarters); and, uncannily, the same dénouement in a stock market crash.

Does history repeat itself? Or have we become so conscious of decades, of the decimalisation of the recent past, that we cannot help but be sensitive to such analogies? This is certainly the century, so to speak, of decades. Throughout the nineties, for example, BBC Radio 3 has been broadcasting a series, 'Towards the Millennium', chronicling the twentieth century's musical history, decade after decade, one a year, right up to 1999. The Barbican recently housed an exhibition titled *The Sixties Art Scene in London*, with works by Hockney, Caro, Hodgkin, Riley and Pauline Boty, a promising young artist who did not survive the decade of her revelation. And, on a more frivolous but still relevant note, A. J. Cronin's *Doctor Finlay* returned to the television schedules: relevant because the series, which, when last seen in the sixties, was set in the twenties, found itself, for the nineties, 'updated' to the forties.

According to the show's producer, Peter Wolfes, the reason for the switch was that the twenties had become 'history'. 'We needed to update it to the immediate postwar period to get the sense of a time just back down the road.' Fair enough. But, if that statement reflects a producer's pragmatic thinking on the issue, the fact is that, as the curtain descends on the twentieth century, each of its ten decades has been made fashionable again in turn. Each, too, in this its second manifestation, has been able to lay claim to less than half its original running time – three or four years, at most, of fashionableness. And in the context of that nostalgic replay the twenties are over. They have had their vogue. They have become history *a second time around*.

Like a drowning man reliving his life's chronology before submerging for the third and definitive time, we have spent the last two decades idly flipping through the eight which preceded them. First off the starting block, the turn-of-the-century itself enjoyed a nostalgic revival (Edwardian memorabilia; Visconti's film adaptation of *Death in Venice*, with its demure yet also come-hither bathing costumes; Merchant Ivory's reinvention of E. M. Forster); then the century's teens ('ah, that last glorious summer before the First World War!'); then the twenties (Scott Joplin's rags; Robert Redford upstaged by his own shirts in *The Great Gatsby*); the thirties (gangsterism in pinstriped suits; the fad for the Bloomsberries); the forties (Glenn Miller and the Big Band sound; the chic Nazism of *The Night Porter* and chic Fascism of *The Conformist*); the fifties (Hawaiian beach shirts, bakelite wireless sets and hideous molecular furniture); the sixties (the comeback of the miniskirt; the belated film version of *Hair*; more recently, such biopics as *JFK* and *Malcolm X*); and now, apparently, the seventies (flares, platform shoes and the Abba craze).

As far as the late twentieth century is concerned, Marx was only half-right: if history has repeated itself, it has been once as tragedy, once as *style*. And observers alert to the trend must be starting to wonder where it will all end. Is the serpent going to consume its own tail? Are we going to mimic the decade we are living through even as we live through it? But how can that be, since, with all our busy serial mimicry of the past, what can there be *present* to mimic?

The question has, I believe, two answers.

The first is that, when the point of saturation actually was reached, when the memorialised past actually did threaten to catch up with the present, probably at some time in the late eighties, then that past was simply dehistoricised. Its chronology – which in the minds of the stylologists never had been all that secure – ceased altogether to be respected. Different decades were flung together pell-mell. Transformed into a monstrous free-for-all, a pot-pourri of fashions, tastes, conventions and myths, they entered the public domain, to be looted indiscriminately by film directors, fashion designers, commercial artists, advertising copywriters and even politicians (Thatcher's Victorian values, Major's invocation of Winnie the Pooh). You could take what you wanted and leave what you didn't need. History's copyright had expired.

The second answer is of greater import. This essay opened with an extended comparison of the thirties and the nineties. Naturally, I am aware that such an analogy can be invalidated by the just as many dissimilarities between the two decades (not all of them to the advantage of the present), but it seems to me, on general lines, to hold up nevertheless. And my point is that, this time around, the referents are just as much *for real*. The Orwellian deprivation is for real. The unemployment *à la* Käthe Kollwitz is for real. The Steinbeck-like hopelessness is for real. The Groszian beggars are for real. Even the peaky-faced infants one has started to see in the streets, evocative as they are of those prewar Ealing comedies set in the East End of London, are for real. Nostalgia *is* what it used to be.

On sweets

There is no one a newspaper columnist resembles so much as Scheherazade. Week after week, month after month, he (and, of course, she) must come up with a brand new tale to divert the Caliph (which is to say, the Reader). And if the fate awaiting him were he ever to exhaust the finite kitty of these tales is less parlous than that reserved for Scheherazade (it is his job, not his head, that he risks losing), he has one problem with which she never had to contend: the fact that, nowadays, there are in the national press as many Scheherazades as there are Santa Clauses in Oxford Street during the run-up to the Christmas holiday, all of them competing for the Caliph's fidgety attention.

The goal, then, is to discover a subject on which no rival has as yet alit, a subject of some small but real significance in the texture of all of our lives but which, ideally, has never been written about – a scoop, in other words. Well, I fancy I have now found such a subject, one whose most intriguing feature is precisely the journalistic conspiracy of silence surrounding it. The subject I refer to is sweets.

Why does no one ever write about sweets? I mean the humble confectionery stocked by ordinary newsagents, Rolos and Polos, Picnics and Yorkies, fruit pastilles and liquorice allsorts, coconut ice and marzipan, the sort of sweets which monopolised our childhood reveries (remember?), which are still the object of an occasional indulgence in most of our adulthoods and which, so it has been claimed, are retailed in Britain in far greater quantities (if not necessarily qualities) than in any other country in the world. If chocolate – or, rather, the morbidly excessive craving for chocolate that has entered the language as 'chocoholism' – has received generous journalistic coverage, sweets have prompted almost no copy at all.

I should confess that my own interest in the subject is not confined to essayistic space-filling. It has long been my intention (too long now, I fear, for it ever to be realised) to write a novel about confectionery, about one individual's obsessive quest for the perfect sweet.[1] Less plausibly, I have always thought how wonderful it would be to stage Strauss's *Der Rosenkavalier* on a set contrived entirely out of chocolate, in colour-coded shades of milk, plain and white.[2] The rose which Octavian presents to Sophie would be made not of silver but of marzipan; the décor would slowly, lingeringly, melt during the final, famously heart-rending trio; and the opera would end with the Marschallin's blackamoor ('Marschallin' – how appropriately marshmallowy the word sounds!) absconding not with his mistress's discarded handkerchief but with an enwhorled scoop of Bournville. That it would be a delicate matter lighting such a set, I am well aware; as also that the production could be staged, if at all, for one performance only. But how it would finally, unassailably, establish the intimate, sensual kinship between sound and scent.

It is the nearly inexhaustible variety of sweets that makes one wonder why their metaphorical potential has been so infrequently tapped. Scientifically speaking, they invoke the molecular (Aeros, Maltesers), the geological (those chocolate bars with layered strata of fudge, nougat, caramel and peanut brittle), the topological (Polo Mints, whirly liquorice strips), the agricultural (jelly beans) and the geographical (the jaw-breakingly brutal Alpine serration of Toblerone). Within a cultural framework, they hint at primitivism (Dolly Mixtures, jelly babies), Cubism (Bassetts' little liquorice all-sorts man is practically a breach of Fernand Léger's copyright), Op Art (old-fashioned candy-striped humbugs), Pop Art (lollipops, *passim*) and pure abstraction (what could be closer to Carl Andre's much-derided installation of bricks in the Tate Gallery than a bar of Cadbury's Dairy Milk?).

Sweets are interesting for other reasons, too. As much as toys, they familiarise children with the quirks of material shapes and textures. They have an infallibly Proustian capacity for calling up the spirits of one's own childhood, dating one – or me, at least – in the generational sense (on the very rare occasions when I buy sweets for myself, I inevitably remain faithful to those which I recall from my formative years, having no truck with Lion or Dime Bars or any of that newfangled rubbish). They operate as a vivid signifier for a long-vanished Britain, a Britain of corner shops with shiny copper weights and small white paper packets which the shopkeeper blew into to open and enormous glass jars which had to be fetched down from the topmost shelf with a stepladder and whose lids were devilish hard to unscrew. And, of course, they offer a precocious foretaste of the pleasures of oral gratification indulged in, like unreproductive sex, for its own sake. Sweets are consumed for themselves (the last thing one feels like eating, if really hungry, is a quarter-pound of wine gums). They are gratuitous, futile and injurious to dental hygiene. But they are also dense little aspirins of contentment – momentary contentment, it is true, but not much more momentary than many more elevated manifestations of that elusive state.

In one of his *Fictions* Borges wrote that he could not imagine the universe 'without the interjection of Edgar Allan Poe, "Ah, bear in mind this garden was enchanted!", or without the *Bateau ivre* or the *Ancient Mariner*'. Yes, yes, all true enough. But just as, where memory is concerned, it is not the things one expects to remember that one invariably does remember, I cannot imagine modern Britain without Bountys or Mars Bars or the interjection, 'Don't forget the Fruit Gums, Mum!'

Notes

1 As it happens, there already does exist at least one novel in which sweets play a central role, *Le Salon de Würtemburg* by Pascal Quignard, the author of *Tous les matins du monde*. And a brief section of Adam Thorpe's *Ulverton* contains a humorous vignette of village sweetshop life on the day in 1953 that rationing ended.

2 This is the Strauss who also composed the score for the ballet *Schlagobers*, or 'Whipped Cream'.

On silence

Whatever happened to silence? Ours is, in every respect, a hypergar-
rulous society, but I am thinking of silence as a specifically cultural
factor, as an aesthetic parameter, as the predominant characteristic
of late high modernism – silence, paradoxically, as a buzz word. And
the question was prompted by a revival of Pinter's *No Man's Land*,
an emblematic product of the modern movement in its dying throes,
a play whose characters – striving to free themselves from the primal
magnetism of silence as laboriously as certain 'incomplete' sculp-
tures of Michelangelo seem to dredge themselves up out of the form-
less, inarticulate stone from which they have hatched – are defined
as much by their silence as by any line of dialogue.

Like nature, the postmodern world, the world in which for better
or worse we currently live, abhors a vacuum. Its most representative
artefacts, whether films, plays, novels, magazine articles or conceptual 'installations', tend to come complete with their own inbuilt critical apparatus. They annotate themselves as they go along; their
textures and trappings are specked with signposted references and all
too public private jokes; creators who would once have sweated to
conceal the casual borrowings they had made from an older generation of masters are now eager to foreground them, with a candour
designed to leave no one in the dark as to where, in the familiar
phrase, they are coming from. And we have all grown so accustomed
to this incessant babble, to this nonstop running commentary, to what
the French social historian Marc Fumaroli termed *la rap culture*, we
have already forgotten the distinctive aura of stasis and silence peculiar to the more sober, unplayful approach to the arts typical of the
period which immediately preceded that of postmodernism.

It was a period when art (or, rather, Art – the upper-case A is
apposite here) impressed as a cold, forbidding, rebarbative thing
always threatening to revert to the absolute silence and abstraction
from which it had only just, fleetingly, emerged. The French poet

Paul Valéry (who was himself famous for a silence which lasted nearly three decades) once declared that 'God made everything out of nothing; but the nothing shows through'; and, for much of the twentieth century, it was regarded as the artist's sacred duty to position himself on the very rim of the abyss, to come as close as was humanly possible to embodying that nothingness.

The cult of aesthetic austerity persisted right into the sixties and early seventies. Although, by then, Kurt Malevich's 'White on White' canvases had already gained a measure of popular acceptance, and Mondrian's colour-block grids had actually been appropriated by Yves Saint Laurent, the more extreme forms of museum, concert-hall and art-house minimalism were still guaranteed to provoke a scandalised reaction. Carl Andre's bricks terrorised visitors to the Tate with their near-autistic muteness. John Cage's *4' 33"* was a completely noteless composition whose only 'musical' substance was the nervous rustling of a public uncertain of what was expected of it. In their best-known works fashionable film directors like Antonioni and Bergman sought to communicate the alienation engendered by the silences, respectively, of the chill asceticism of contemporary urban life (in *L'Avventura*) and of God Himself (in, precisely, *The Silence*). And in the theatre, a medium which strikes us as intrinsically dependent on talk, Beckett, by a general consensus the period's greatest dramatist, was perceived in his later years to be receding into total and incurable autism, as is intimated by the very titles of his final plays: *Come and Go*, *Eh, Joe*, *Play*, *Lessness* and, finally, indeed terminally, *Breath*.[1]

To be sure, this occasionally programmatic and reductive essentialism has always had its share of detractors. Antonioni was jocularly rebaptised 'Antoniennui' and Bergman 'the gloomy Swede', Andre's bricks were used by unconvinced critics to stone their creator with, and not even the saintly, Nobelised Beckett would be spared the barbs of mocking scepticism. When he made his one film – starring, naturally, a silent performer, Buster Keaton – he named it, perhaps equally naturally, *Film*, causing the American critic Andrew Sarris to ridicule that title as 'the most pretentious in the history of the cinema'.

Clearly, when it is that absolute, silence becomes an impasse for the artist. Which explains the need, in the sixties, for the Big Bang of pixilated postmodernism. Instead of art as a nerve-racking ordeal, operating upon its public without anaesthetic, the urge was felt to make it all good fun again, the way art is fun in the films of the *nouvelle vague* and in Pop Art. (As far as the latter is concerned, it's fun all right, but is it art?) We were Beckett's tramps, except that we now knew that Godot would not turn up and we had given up waiting for him. And the time had come for another of the Irish dramatist's offspring, Tom Stoppard, to assume centre stage.

While Pinter continued to deploy silence strategically, dynamically and wittily (until, as a dramatist, he elected to withdraw into a silence of his own), what Stoppard appropriated from Beckett – in *Rosencrantz and Guildenstern Are Dead*, for example – was not the vortex of silence into which his characters would without exception be engulfed but their concurrent penchant for obsessive, neurotic, deliriously circular chatter. Stoppard's plays told us what to think of them even as we watched them. In an orgy of twittering intellectualism (or pseudo-intellectualism) their 'subtext' was jacked up to the surface for all to see and partake of, which meant that no one any longer felt coerced into *prospecting* for meanings. The same is true of the filmmaker Peter Greenaway, Stoppard's exact cinematic counterpart. In Greenaway's films ideas hum on the surface of the screen like static, like what is called 'interference'.

That silence has become anathema to the postmodern artist is all part of a historical, cyclical process, about which there is little point in complaining. But it is also possible to argue that a fear of silence is a fundamental symptom of arrested development (as is the case with those people who, when entering their homes in the evening, switch on the television set before they switch on the light) and that we may soon require an environmental health officer to monitor the decibel level of the cultural discourse. At present the individual can only retort in his own modest, private fashion. I personally recommend earplugs, *boules Quiès*, not just for sleeping with but for getting oneself through the day – earplugs as a tranquillising little Walkman of silence.

Notes

1 I remember, from the seventies, an after-dinner pastime the goal of which was to imagine the ultimate Beckett play. For example: The curtain fails to rise. When the audience has tired of waiting, it troops out of the theatre and mulls over what it has just experienced.

On boredom

I should like to propose a revolutionary new concept for the arts pages of upmarket newspapers and magazines. My idea (and I realise that it would have to be very judiciously phased in) is that, alongside the more traditional art forms – comic books, rock promos, television commercials and Arnold Schwarzenegger films – a place might be found for the coverage and analysis of such marginal but potentially interesting media as poetry, drama, opera and ballet. It is an idea, I know, which will alarm and shock the purists, who will no doubt see it as the thin end of a neo-élitist wedge, but I do believe nevertheless that a case can be argued for extending the boundaries of what we have all instinctively come to regard as the cultural mainstream.

Well, yes, all right, just kidding – matters have not yet got so out of hand. What is undeniable, though, is that the current and ongoing rehabilitation of popular culture risks transforming it into something of a Frankenstein's monster, casting its warped shadow over every serious endeavour to talk and write and think about the arts. And what is still more dispiriting is that the campaign to promote cultural populism above all other manifestations of artistic expression has had the effect of making modish again, and with a vengeance, the ancient English vice of philistinism.

Thus we are reassured that no one need be ashamed to admit to a fondness for reading or indeed writing schlocky fiction (yet 'schlock', however knowing, is nothing but a hip synonym for 'rubbish'); that a novel like *The Runaway Soul* is unreadable anyway so that any guilt one might feel about being unable to face its eight hundred pages are entirely misplaced (yet Harold Brodkey's book is not so much unreadable as unread); that operas are incredibly dumb affairs in which the soprano, the baritone and the tenor sing a jolly little trio together before stabbing each other to death (yet the finest operas of the repertoire have had librettos that are works of literature in their own right); and, finally, that if foreign films did not intimidate critics with their arty subtitles they would be dismissed as the pretentious trash which most of them are (yet films are not born with subtitles and such an attitude reflects a bigoted Anglocentrism that would have been unthinkable only a few years ago). Liberated by, as they suppose, the relativism of the postmodern era, the philistines are abroad – or rather, they are *here*.

If it is true that the rise of cultural tolerance, open-mindedness and catholicity of taste characteristic of postmodernism initially represented a salutary reaction to a hierarchical and class-bound stratification of the arts, it is now set to become, as everything eventually does become in Britain, a bit of a bad joke. And if it is true that, since the advent of Pop Art, semiology, neo-rococo architecture and the rewriting of film history in the wake of the *politique des auteurs*, new attention has been paid to what used to be dismissed as 'low-brow' culture, one additional factor should be taken into account when considering the phenomenon in Britain – our national obsession with bores. For only in Britain can the fear, the almost pathological dread, of boredom be inscribed within what might be called a tradition, a tradition which stretches from Dr Johnson to Evelyn Waugh, from Beau Brummell's 'What a bore!' (lips nonchalantly tapped in a feigned yawn) to Monty Python's 'Boring! Boring!' (intoned in an onomatopoeically monotonous singsong chant).

It is not my intention to counterpropose a defence of bores. I wish merely to suggest that an abnormally low tolerance for the boring in art is the first sign of philistinism. To dismiss a work of art as a bore is to dispense with the need for any more intimate inspection of its inherent qualities or flaws; it constitutes a virtual censorship of ambition; and, in Britain, it is now neither more nor less than a tic. In the very week, for example, in which was published Vikram Seth's *A Suitable Boy*, widely hailed as a masterpiece, Auberon Waugh (the editor, let us not forget, of the *Literary Review*) was quoted as saying of it, 'I suppose one has to take notice.' One *has to* take notice. Seth's novel is no sooner published than it is a bore.

The problem with the word 'bore', alas, is that it is so fatally, maddeningly plausible. I myself am a great admirer of Harold Brodkey. Yet, if ever I hear someone remark, '*The Runaway Soul*?

What a bore!', I am immediately assailed by the recollection that turning its more clotted pages was sometimes as wearying as lifting a barbell. 'Wagner? What a ghastly bore!' Of course not, how crass! And yet . . . the person has not been born who does not find his mind occasionally wandering in *Parsifal*. 'Eisenstein? Boring! Boring!' Again, true enough as far as it goes – no one could honestly deny the odd longueur in *Ivan the Terrible*. But the operative words here are *sometimes*, *occasionally* and *the odd*. The works I have cited are all magnificent achievements which one quits with a strange and poignant sense of divorce, of exile, of banishment, from an imaginative world which seemed for a while more powerful than the real one, and a few minutes, or even a half-hour, of tedium is a pilfering price to pay for the intensity of the overall experience. Could the same intensity ever be claimed of *Cats* or *Jurassic Park* or a Joanna Trollope novel, none of which, I suppose, can be said to number boringness among its (many) inadequacies.

At a production of *Götterdämmerung* at Bayreuth, the French man-of-letters Elemir Bourges found himself seated next to an elegant matron, who was suddenly heard to sigh, 'Yes, yes, it's beautiful – but, oh, far, far too long.' Whereupon Bourges leaned over and gently whispered in her ear, 'Perhaps, dear lady, it's you who are too short.'

On decadence

It was in Frankfurt, on New Year's Eve 1925, that a promising young Viennese composer, Ernst Krenek, attending a performance of a negro revue, *Chocolate Kiddies*, with music by Duke Ellington, conceived the then novel idea of a jazz opera. The result, *Jonny spielt auf*, whose transparently allegorical libretto centred on the theft of a priceless old European violin by a black American banjo minstrel, was an instant triumph when it was premièred two years later; and, by the end of the decade, a decade of which it would become one of the emblematic artefacts, it had received more than seventy productions, an extraordinary statistic for a new, ground-breaking opera. If it made Krenek rich and famous, however, neither his wealth nor his fame would survive the following, far less congenial decade. Early performances in the composer's native city were interrupted by cat-callers protesting at the 'outrageous introduction of Jewish-Nigger filth' into the Staatsoper, the national opera house, by this 'half-Jewish Czech' of a composer (Krenek was an Austrian gentile). And, in 1938, in Nazi Berlin, the inevitable finally occurred: Krenek was officially designated an *entartete* (or 'decadent') artist. Following which, his opera was neglected, forgotten, until a smattering of revivals were staged during the eighties, including one in Britain by the New Opera Company in 1984.

So much for the work's history. With an eye to its posterity, Decca has issued the very first complete recording of *Jonny*, in tandem with another 'decadent' opera from the interwar years, *Das Wunder der Heliane*, by Erich Wolfgang Korngold, now probably better known as the composer of some of Hollywood's most rambunctious soundtrack scores (*The Adventures of Robin Hood*, *The Sea Hawk*, *King's Row*, etc.). These two recordings have been chosen to launch a lengthy, ambitious project – named *Entartete Musik* after an exhibition organised by the Nazis in Düsseldorf in 1938 as a pendant to the infamous *Entartete Kunst* show held in Munich the previous year – a project whose goal is to retrieve a number of musical works which were either destroyed or banned during the century's various political convulsions, most notably by the Third Reich. (The catalogue of future recordings includes works, not exclusively operas, by Hindemith, Schreker, Toch, Eisler and Franz Waxman, the latter another composer to whom Hollywood made an offer he couldn't refuse.)

It is, then, an entirely admirable venture, particularly from as conservative a recording company as Decca generally is. Although neither of the two operas is top-drawer stuff, both are more than just period pieces, documents of a zeitgeist. The Krenek, even if it strikes the ear as dated in a way that Kurt Weill's operettas, to take the most obvious point of comparison, do not, is witty and astringent, and the jazz numbers, counterpointed in a delirious dialectics with a more traditionally operatic lyricism, are great fun.[1] As for the Korngold, whose peerless gorgeousness of orchestration contains pre-echoes of the soundtrack scores to come, it represents the absolute last, lush and languorous gasp of musical Romanticism.

Yet, listening to these operas (especially the Krenek), I detected a strange paradox in the seduction which they exert upon us. However unpalatable it may be, the fact is that our opinion of them today *is exactly the same as the Nazis'*. Which is to say, we continue to regard them as 'decadent' – just as we regard Weill's *Mahagonny* as 'decadent', or Grosz's cartoons, or Pabst's two films with Louise Brooks, or Isherwood's Sally Bowles stories, or the Berlin cabaret songs (I mean Berlin the city, not the composer) which Decca also plans to record. Other once so-called degenerate artists (Schoenberg, Thomas Mann) have long since taken their place within the mainstream of the twentieth century's cultural repertoire; but, to describe any work of art whose effect above all is to invoke the whole intoxicating cocktail that Germany was in the twenties and thirties, or has become for us in mythic terms, a cocktail, simplifying grossly (or Groszly), of drugs, drag and Dietrich, we still tend to have recourse to the same old word 'decadent', even if the adverb with which most of us would qualify it is 'deliciously' rather than 'degenerately'. We still consider them, obscurely, and perhaps in spite of ourselves, 'immoral'.

Are we, then, where German art and music of the recent past are concerned, secret Nazis? Hardly. For a second (enormous) paradox is that, in this context, the question of immorality turns out to have practically nothing to do with moral judgments or moral reprobation. We regard these works not, like the Nazis, as immoral (evil) but as 'immoral' (naughty). Degeneracy here has itself degenerated – degenerated into a mere style, an aesthetico-historical exoticism, reducible for most purposes to such harmless decorative accessories as monocles, garter belts and outlandishly elongated cigarette-holders.

There is a third paradox, too, which is that, sixty years on, the Nazis themselves have been invested with the same decadent aura as the objects of their lethal censure. The 'charm' of a Broadway musical like *Cabaret* is generated not by its raffish nightclub setting alone but by the juxtaposition of that raffishness with, implicit offstage, the encroaching forces of the Hitlerian night: for the charm to operate, the garter belt *needs* the jackboot and vice versa. Equally, it is possible to argue that one can only fully appreciate *Jonny spielt auf* if one hears the goose-step behind the foxtrot. To a degree that is absolutely not true of any of Schoenberg's works, say, the drumming of that unheard but nevertheless oppressively present goose-step is an integral component of whatever appeal Krenek's opera has for us today.

For many years the century's codified nostalgia was all but monopolised by the *belle époque*, by that halcyon era in which, at least as enhaloed by the shimmer of a collective memory, parasols were more common than umbrellas and butterflies more numerous than flies. Now, to tempt our more 'sophisticated' palates, palates ever receptive to a delicate *soupçon* of the sinister, we have invented, with the thirties' return to fashion, what might be called the *laide époque*.

Notes

1   What Krenek composed was not jazz at all, of course, but a cosmopolitan European's bastardisation of Jazz Age rhythms: foxtrots, shimmies and such like.

On *film noir*

Feasting as it does off the inventions and innovations of other art forms, the musical comedy is a vampiric genre. In fact, it has now reached the point where no work of literature, drama or cinema is safe from the predatory attentions of bloodthirsty and subject-hungry composers, to whom it is a matter of total indifference whether some poor defenceless original will actually lend itself to the vulgarisation (in both senses of the word) which a musical version fatally entails – as demonstrated by such monstrosities as *Rhinoceros*, *Carrie* and *Kiss of the Spider Woman*. The same charge might be levelled against the cinema, of course, except that the cinema is not a genre but an autonomous medium; against opera, too, except that opera, in musical terms an incomparably subtler and more complex form, is unfettered by the rapaciously mercantile appetites of Broadway and the West End. No, if what you are after is a not too taxing *digest* of some prestigious classic or near-classic that you always meant to get around to reading or seeing, the musical is still your best bet.

Take a recent example. *City of Angels* was a theatrical musicalisation of a quintessential Hollywood thriller of the forties, and more specifically of Howard Hawks's *The Big Sleep*, itself based on the novel by Raymond Chandler. Or, rather, it was a parody of such a thriller, its parodic intention foregrounded by the fact that the theatre audience was shown a film-within-the-play unfold (in black-and-white) as it was being written on stage by its scenarist (in colour). A droll, ingenious show, if musically very dreary (is there anything more monotonous and samey than the Broadway 'sound'?), it had uniformly wonderful reviews. And, seeking to contextualise its subject matter, every single reviewer had recourse to the same French expression: *film noir*.

What, though, is a *film noir* and why should it be fit source material for a musical comedy? I used, above, the word 'thriller'. That is, as it happens, a slightly misleading term, since many Hollywood thrillers (gangster movies, whodunits, etc.) were not *films noirs*; nor, curiously enough, were all *films noirs* thrillers. (Raoul Walsh's dark, fatalistic *Pursued* was arguably a *noir* western; Charles Vidor's *Gilda* a *noir* melodrama.) Was Michael Curtiz's *Casablanca* a *film noir*? No, it was too optimistic, too 'upbeat', an entertainment. Hawks's *Scarface*? No, it was made too soon. Hitchcock's *Psycho*? No again, that one was made too late. If, within a journalistic context, the expression *film noir*, or just *noir*, or even *noir*ish, has now become so ubiquitous and indiscriminate that all sense of its exact historical co-ordinates has been forfeited, it continues to have, for film historians if for no one else, a rigorously circumscribed frame of reference.

It would be impossible, in the space of a short essay, to do anything like justice to the visual, iconographical and psychological opulence of *film noir*: several books have been written on the subject and failed to exhaust its potential. But it might be worth drawing up an inventory of a few of the stylistic and thematic characteristics that make it so distinctive a moment in cinema history – a moment that lasted from the early forties to the middle fifties, in so far as one can be precise about so vague an abstraction.

Visually, its most indelible signifier was the nocturnal, neon-lit city street[1] aslant whose rainswept sidewalks a flotilla of shadows would cast their terrifying nets. On the corner of that street, at the still centre of a world populated by grifters, gamblers, blackmailers, show-girls, prostitutes and cold rich bitches, stood the detective (although, it should be said, not all *films noirs* have detective protagonists). Himself just on the rim of criminality, this detective was a loner who would inevitably end by being contaminated by the very corruption he was struggling to expose – contaminated, as frequently as not, by love, the most famous case being Dana Andrews's obsession with the portrait of the dead, or allegedly dead, Laura in Otto Preminger's film of that name. The Oedipus complex was never far away; nor, if such a thing exists, was the Jocasta complex, in the person of a scheming, castrating *belle dame sans merci*, as hard as the nails she would so indefatigably file and polish. And when the hero, a usually somewhat passive and oneiric presence (Dana Andrews once more, the definitive *film noir* actor and the most sheerly *indispensable* star of the postwar American cinema), had finally succeeded in unravelling the crime, when he had at last arrived at the terminus of his lonesome quest, the solution to the enigma almost never accorded, either him or the public, a cathartic, truly liberating release. Nothing, really, had changed.

These films – one might cite Fritz Lang's *The Woman in the Window*, Billy Wilder's *Double Indemnity*, Preminger's *Laura*, Edgar G. Ulmer's magnificent *Detour* (the finest of all B-movies) and Robert Aldrich's *Kiss Me Deadly* – were, in short, among the most pessimistic ever made in Hollywood. Yet, and this is the real enigma, they were also among the most entertaining. No filmgoer of the forties ever went to see a *film noir* with the apprehension that he or she was about to be submitted to a harrowing but salutary dose of existential nihilism (a nihilism, I repeat, that is not just a matter of critical interpretation but perfectly perceptible in the narratives of these films and even objectified in their visual textures) – just as no one, today, need ever recoil from watching one of them on television.

This is both the paradox and the secret of the American cinema's global popularity: that a grim Hollywood drama is somehow closer in feel to a breezy Hollywood comedy than it is to any correspondingly grim European drama. Bergman, for example, is a very great director; yet not even his most devoted admirers can deny the faint but nagging resistance that must be overcome when one is about to plunge oneself into the world of one of his films. Well, it is a resistance that no spectator has ever experienced with even the grimmest of *films noirs*.

Which is why *City of Angels* works so well on stage in spite of the apparent but ultimately superficial contradiction between subject matter (*film noir*) and genre (musical comedy). Here musicalisation is not, as is so frequently the case, the sugar to help the pill go down. Instead, it constitutes the not unintelligent acknowledgement that the pill always did have a soft, sweet centre.

Notes

1 *Film noir*: the precursor of the modern American cinema's *neon*-realism.

On craftsmanship

There are few figures in contemporary society who now strike us as
more obsolete, at any rate less fashionable, than the craftsman. The
very notion of craftsmanship as a measure of an object's value and
beauty has been seriously, possibly definitively, undermined in recent
years. If it lingers on at all, it is in situations in which it has become
a virtual synonym for 'oldness'. ('Just examine the craftsmanship,' a
dealer will comment of some antique piece of furniture, the implication being that such individual attention to detail is now exclusively
a thing of the past.) Or else in situations in which the word is felt to
carry certain kitschy overtones (Venetian glass-blowing, of appeal
solely to tourists; a bookshelf of Morocco-bound classics, purchased
en bloc as a pure status symbol and destined never to be read).

Equally, and by a bizarre paradox, craftsmanship has come to be
regarded as unfriendly to the environment, whose raw materials it
squanders on a privileged few. The mythic preconception of the
craftsman is of someone who chops down a tree in order to whittle
a single perfect matchstick out of it, then chops down a second tree
to make a second matchstick, then a third, and so on. In ecological
terms, craftsmanship is perceived as a parasitical luxury.

The word 'craft' itself no longer sits convincingly on our tongues,
hinting either at the artsy-craftsy, with intimations of dainty Olde
Shoppe horrors in Cotswold villages, or at that actorish modesty
which is all too soon revealed to be a very real and smug immodesty:
the way in which, for example, recipients of theatrical and cinematic
awards will demurely allude to their 'craft' instead of to their 'art',
as though keen to deflate the idea of themselves as being anything as
pretentious as 'artists'. (This mannerism can be bracketed with the
philistine cliché of Shakespeare as just another pro, a mummer, a
strolling player, a jobbing scribbler, who, were he alive today, would
be writing miniseries for Verity Lambert.) It might be said, in fact,
that the diminishing prestige of 'craft' has been overtaken in recent

years by that of 'design'. A bottle of Ty Nant mineral water is just as mass-produced as a can of Heinz spaghetti; but the arching Brancusi-like limpidity of its form allied to the indelible blue of its colour gives it the cachet that used to be reserved for bottles individually blown. Industrial designers – these, perhaps, are the craftsmen of today.

Yet there does exist one area in which craftsmanship has not totally compromised its original status, one area in which its image is neither kitschy nor self-consciously passéist: the manufacture of sports goods.

With the occasional exception of tennis, I myself have absolutely no interest in sport; my only regret, however, is that I thereby do not get to own, fondle and care for hand-crafted sporting equipment. I have actually fantasised about collecting sports goods without ever putting them to use – not so absurd when you think of collectors of stamps or beer mats or indeed of Old Masters languishing unseen in numbered Swiss bank vaults. Even if, like me, you are hopeless at the game, is not a croquet mallet a lovely heavy object in and of itself? A snooker cue a lovely light one? What *objet d'art* affords one a greater tactile pleasure, just being held in the hand, just being amorously fingered, than an arrow or a hockey puck or a seamless black bowling ball? A wooden golf club with a head like an outsized chestnut, like the smoothest, shiniest conker in Christendom; a cricket ball as round and red and 'natural' as an apple; an insectlike fishing rod with an attachment of flies as delicately pretty as lapel brooches; an airy little shuttlecock: these are artefacts both beautiful and functional, an ultra-rare combination these days, and, if tending to be on the pricey side, they are nevertheless within the budgets of many for whom objects of authentically antique craftsmanship have always been out of bounds.

An added attraction, too, is that most of them historically predate the now pervasive aura of the brand name. Not that the best cricket bats, footballs or fishing tackle are unidentifiable by brand; the fact is, though, that their brands are often promoted (on shirts, protective padding, sports ground awnings, etc.) with a discretion intended to prevent them from ever becoming real household names, rather as with those small, exclusive country hotels which never stoop to advertise, preferring to rely on the right kind of word-of-mouth. Everyone knows which, at any given moment, are reputed to be the 'best' trainers, the 'best' wrist-watches, the 'best' jeans, the 'best' double-breasted suits. To know which is the best cricket bat, and also why, one really has to be a professional or amateur cricketer.[1]

No less a repository of old-fashioned craftsmanship are indoor games. Think of the velvety luxuriance of a backgammon board. Think of the wonderfully knobby perfection of that archetype, that King James Bible, of modern chess sets, the Staunton. Think of the feel of a pair of ivory dice in the palm of the hand or the round-peg-in-a-round-hole satisfaction of Chinese Checkers or the wit and fantasy of that classic deck of playing cards (designed by whom?), with its four Kings enthroned upon themselves and its four Queens joined at the middle like Siamese twins. Think of the simple dimples of dominoes.

Ultimately, what is so appealing about the fabrication of games and sports equipment is that it constitutes one of the few extant spheres in which, instead of being celebrated for its nostalgic patina, to be appreciated for its own sake alone and paid for accordingly, craftsmanship is directly and infallibly generative of efficacy. The 'best' (which is to say, the most expensive) cricket bats are also the best (which is to say, the most practical). The most beautifully crafted saddles are also the ones with which both horse and rider are most comfortable. Fish rise to the most exquisite bait. Outside of sport such a mutually supportive union of form and function would appear to be, as you might say, a lost art.

Notes

1 In this, an analogy can be drawn with musical instruments. Only a harpist, say, is likely to be familiar with the brand name (which seems almost too vulgar a term for so ethereal an object) of the finest harp on the market.

On Freud

It was Nietzsche who said that the great ideas of the world arrive on tiptoe. On occasion, too, that is how they depart. Thus a conviction which I have had for some little while now was corroborated, first, by a recent visit to New York and, second, by a belated perusal of the English newspapers that had accumulated in my absence. I mean the conviction that, as theory if not necessarily as practice, psychoanalysis is at this very moment in the process of tiptoeing off the world stage; that, to put it bluntly, and to paraphrase Nietzsche (on God) instead of quoting him, Freud is dead.[1]

Actually, it was the fall of Marx, and the 'domino effect' collapse of the ideological praxis to which his name was attached, that originally set me to wondering whether Freud's days might also be numbered, whether it might soon be his 'turn'. Marx and Freud, Freud and Marx – for so long were they the twin patriarchs of modern thought that it has become impossible to imagine what might have been the life of the intellect in the twentieth century without their respective 'isms'. They managed, as though complementarily, to map the entire territory of the mind, to cover the whole waterfront, from mass to individual psychology, from the conscious to the unconscious, from political to psychic alienation, from society to self. Since what they offered was (to adapt a voguish scientific formula) a Theory of Everything, there could be no salvation for the world's intellectual communities outside of their combined oeuvres. And in certain especially intense periods of cerebral ferment – notably, the sixties and seventies – any thinker whose work was not underwritten, as it were, by their theories and methodologies, or by those of their most prestigious disciples (Gramsci, Lukacs, Lacan, Foucault, etc.), would find himself ruthlessly marginalised.

No one needs to be reminded of what happened to Marxism. It neither arrived nor departed on tiptoe, but was born, in Eastern Europe, in a convulsive revolution, and died, in Eastern Europe, in what might be described as a convulsive devolution. To be sure, even when it was known to be irredeemably corrupt as a political practice, it tenaciously clung on as an academic theory (the common fate of all great lost ideas and ideals). Yet from that lesser eminence, too, it has finally been expelled. Whether in Europe or America, next to no unreconstructed Marxist academics are left.

And Freudianism? What I discovered in New York (and saw confirmed on my return to London with newspaper coverage of an acrimonious public debate on the legitimacy of psychotherapy) was that, as one of the fundamental religions of the liberal, cultured middle classes, psychoanalysis is finished. It may seem frivolous to cite Woody Allen in this context, but the star system is as central to American life as it is to the American cinema and there is no doubt that one impression widely left by Allen's custody trial was the following: that here was a man who had been in analysis nearly all his adult life and whose psychological immaturity remained such, after all those sessions upon sessions, he could still believe that having an affair with his own teenaged stepdaughter was, at the very worst, an error of judgment.

On a more personal level, I was astonished to discover that acquaintances of mine, academics mostly, who conformed to the classic stereotype of the liberal intellectual, and who themselves had been analysands for as long as Allen, were gratefully turning to pharmaceutical therapy – to, in a word, pills. (When I suggested that this was as illegitimate a shortcut, a cheat, as it would be for a Catholic to swallow an aspirin instead of the host, I was told that, unlike analysis, *pills worked*.) Just as startling was the absence, in the burgeoning field of cultural studies, of any interesting new developments founded on Freudian dogma. Today, with the emergence and rapid expansion of minority-oriented political correctness (in the United States, from a strictly intellectual point of view, female is currently better than male, black than white, gay than straight, the Third World than the First), the psychoanalytical method, which had long provided the American intelligentsia with a model, a grid, by which to interpret the contemporary human condition, has become completely irrelevant. Although Freud's greatness, no less than Marx's, continues to be recognised, his present status is that of some statufied genius in the eternally ebbing history of ideas, like Kant or Schopenhauer before him.

A more sceptical reading of Freud can of course be subsumed in a growing antipathy worldwide to all totalising doctrines, all grand master-narratives. (*Totalising* sounds too much to our twentieth-century ears like *totalitarian* and *master-narrative* offends those same ears with a queasy-making echo of *master race*.) Notwithstanding the millennial quest for a universal Theory of Everything, it is significant that, at least as the layman understands them, no doubt superficially, many of the most radical speculations of contemporary science and mathematics have been grounded in concepts of *ambiguity*: relativity (Einstein), uncertainty (Heisenberg), undecidability (Gödel) and, most recently, chaos. As for the latest fashionable 'ism', postmodernism, it should properly be understood less as a genuine doctrine than as a ruefully ironic recognition that the whole doctrinal era has passed. The postmodernist thinker is one who accepts, as Marx and Freud could not, that his ideas are of an intrinsically *interim* nature, calculated (often very much sooner than expected) to be rendered obsolete.

This, then, is the truth with which we are confronted at the turn of our century: that the history of ideas is fatally governed by an entropic principle. If the achievements of even such giants as Marx and Freud can, suddenly or progressively, cease to mean very much to us, then there can be no advance in the realm of the intellect which it would be wise to regard as other than provisional. Unimaginable as it may strike us, even Shakespeare will one day be not much more than a museum piece, of interest primarily to scholars and specialists. For such is the axiom of axioms: however vertiginous the ascending parabola initially described, absolutely *every* idea, *every* theory, *every* form of creation, is, with the passage of time, destined to assume less and less significance. It is an axiom, moreover, whose implications, as we know from projections of the universe's own finite lifespan, do not exclude the Creation itself.

Notes

1 That the tenets of Freudian analysis continue pragmatically to serve as a therapeutic methodology I daresay is true. My concern here is solely with the once
   widespread extra-clinical applications of Freud's theories.

On transtextuality

Everyone has heard of, even if far from everyone has read, Victor Hugo's *Les Misérables*. I seriously doubt, however, whether anyone in the English-speaking world will have heard of, let alone read, *Les Miférables*, a more recent French novel whose heroine suffers from a debilitating speech defect. Jean Giraudoux's comedy *Amphitryon 38*, whose curious title was intended by the dramatist to signify that his was the thirty-eighth version of the legend in question, is still fairly often staged; more often, certainly, than a subsequent version, titled, as you might expect, *Amphitryon 39*. E. F. Benson wrote six *Mapp and Lucia* novels in the twenties and thirties. A fact of lesser notoriety is that, in the eighties, an admirer of Benson named Tom Holt appended two more to the official canon.

The technical term for such literary revisitations is transtextuality, and it is the subject of *Palimpsestes*, a fantastically erudite volume by the one French critical (more accurately, philological) mandarin never to have enjoyed an international vogue, Gérard Genette. As Genette demonstrates, transtextuality can take many forms (pastiche, parody, burlesque, sequel, the posthumous completion of a work left unfinished by its author's death, etc.) and cross not only textual but generic frontiers (a cinematic adaptation of a novel, a musical version of a straight play, a song-cycle setting of verse may all be regarded as examples of the transtextual). And it might be worth casting an eye over the phenomenon and its implications, given how ubiquitous it has become of late: Marina Warner's novel *Indigo* redevelops several of the themes, myths and characters of *The Tempest*; Emma Tennant's *Tess* is a transtextual paraphrase of Hardy; Susan Hill has written the authorised sequel to *Rebecca*; and so on.

Still the most remarkable fact about transtextuality is the deep critical disrepute in which it is held.[1] Not so surprising, you might think, in a period for which originality is the supreme literary virtue, a period in which a race would seem to be on in this country, in the face of increasingly ferocious competition from its former colonies, to write the Great British Novel. Yet I do say 'remarkable', because pastiches of every order are nearly as ancient as literature itself. Not only were Homer and Virgil parodied from the early centuries of the second millennium onwards *(Homère travesti, L'Eneide travestita, Virgile travesti)*, frequently by writers of real, if not quite comparable, distinction (the author of *Homère travesti*, for example, was Marivaux); not only was the *Aeneid* a conscious sequel to the *Iliad*; and not only did the *Odyssey* inspire one of the very greatest novels of the twentieth century (no reader, I trust, needs to be told which); but there exists a school of thought which is actually ready to attribute the invention of self-referentiality to Homer himself, in his reiteration of what are now termed Homeric epithets. Many of Shakespeare's plays were of course poetic revisions of pre-existent works, and French classical drama of the seventeenth century, reprising as it did the themes and personages of Greek tragedy, was conceived almost entirely under the sign of pastiche: Racine was, if you like, the Giraudoux *de ses jours*. As for our own literary modernity, apart from Joyce, and the neoclassical epidemic (or, as Gide called it, 'oepidemic') of Oedipuses, Antigones, Electras and Orpheuses in the theatre of the interwar years (mostly French – Giraudoux, Cocteau, Anouilh, Sartre – but one must not forget O'Neill), there was Mann *(Dr Faustus, Lotte in Weimar, Joseph and his Brothers)*, Proust *(Pastiches et Mélanges)*, Broch *(The Death of Virgil)*, Brecht (virtually all of his plays), the Wilde of *Salomé*, the Jean Rhys of *Wide Sargasso Sea*, and others too numerous for any comprehensive inventory (Eliot, Pound, Laforgue, Hoffmanstahl, Borges, Barth, Calvino . . . and would the last man please close the brackets behind him?

To those critics, then, who dismiss the pastiche as a parasitical and even cannibalistic form, I suggest that they remind themselves of this old and noble tradition. To those who claim that it has a tendency to make for dry, bookish, impersonal literature, I would argue that a writer's discovery of, and passion for, another writer of the past may be just as fascinatingly 'autobiographical' as his coming of age or his first love affair. And to those who believe it to be a lazy alternative to the rigours of originality, I would simply reply that it is easy enough to come up with the subject of a potential pastiche but extremely hard to carry it off successfully.

Consider Cocteau's celebrated monodrama *La Voix humaine* (*The Human Voice*), whose middle-aged heroine makes one last, despairing telephone call to the lover who is on the point of abandoning her. It is possible to imagine a reworking of that play that would focus instead on the other end of the telephone connection, on the abandoning lover. Nor would it strain a competent writer's powers of invention to devise some new, transtextual title (*The Inhuman Voice?*). Then that writer has to get down to the workaday chore of writing the thing, from line to line, from page to page, and the problems he confronts are liable to be just as formidable as those necessitated by a completely original scenario. The more so as he will naturally seek to avoid treading on the Master's toes.

There is, finally, another, more topical argument that I might propose. When *A Suitable Boy* was first published, it was hailed as a timely reversion to the codes and conventions of the great, premodern fictions typical of the nineteenth century and, by extension, as a conscious rebuke to the type of postmodern fiction which I have been defending in this essay. Yet, in a sense, it is the very *consciousness* of Vikram Seth's decision to turn his back on the modern movement, to feign ignorance of its existence, which makes his novel so paradoxically postmodern an artefact. Its length aside, what distinguishes *A Suitable Boy* from the majority of novels published today is not its 'innocence' but its self-awareness. It *knows* it is old-fashioned and so that is exactly what it is not; whereas most contemporary fiction does not know it is old-fashioned and so that is exactly what it is. Better, I would say, to write a witting pastiche than an unwitting one.

Notes

1   I should perhaps declare an interest here. As it happens, most of my own published fiction is (neatly rhyming with 'incestuous') 'palimpsestuous' in inspiration; and, in even the most laudatory reviews I have received, there has been detectable an implicit reproach that I have yet to embark on what might be called a 'solo flight'. 'When, oh, when,' is what I keep reading, 'will Adair become his own man . . .?'

On journalism

Here is a sentence extracted from an interview given by the philosopher Michel Foucault on the publication, in 1984, of his book *L'Usage des plaisirs*:

> It [pleasure as distinct from desire] is an event 'outside the subject' or on the edge of the subject, within something that is neither body nor soul, which is neither inside nor outside, in short a notion which is neither ascribed nor ascribable.

Although Foucault's definition of pleasure is free of jargon, and salubriously low in polysyllables in both English and in the original French, it would be idle to pretend that it presents no difficulties to the ordinary reader, for whom a tantalising hint of meaning must seem to hover above it without ever properly alighting. In actual fact, if one submits it to a little study and reflexion (and especially, of course, if one reads it in context), it is perfectly comprehensible. What it is not, and this is where the difficulty arises, is *journalistic*.

The problem is that, for many of us, the journalistic has become the primary and sometimes sole means of access to knowledge, understanding and taste. It is as though almost everything we know, everything we learn, we know and learn from journalism, from articles, features, profiles, columns, reports, leaders and reviews; and not only from print journalism but from an ever-expanding variety of electronic media; from books, too, hard covers having long since ceased to be a barrier to eligibility for membership in the all-inclusive media club. Nor is literature itself any longer able to resist the racy blandishments of the journalistic mode: an increasing number of current novels and plays constitute not much more than fictionalised *reportage*, magazine articles with plots.

This is not an attack on journalism as such, merely a reflection of one insider's concern that, in its present domination of our culture, it has usurped a role that is not its own. The purpose of journalism

– the purpose of an article, let us say, on the arts – is surely to draw the reader's attention to an achievement which might otherwise remain neglected or misunderstood, which at any rate calls for some significant degree of interpretation, in the hope that that same reader will then be tempted to explore it further for himself. But I am beginning to wonder whether that is actually how journalism currently functions for the newspaper- and magazine-mad British. I am beginning to believe that it tends no longer to open doors but close them; that, instead of proposing a useful but necessarily partial glimpse of understanding, it tends now to be interpreted as the sum total of that understanding. Which means that whenever one is confronted with a text not couched in a journalistic style – a book by Foucault, for example – one finds that one has to adjust one's whole way of thinking and reading (it is something of a wrench, I can tell you) in order to cope with a discourse in which the fixation on surface liveliness, the snappy ellipse and the facile 'controversy' (there is nothing easier in the world for a journalist than to be controversial) has absolutely no place. One has repeatedly to reassure oneself that such a book is not 'austere' or 'pretentious' or 'long-winded' merely because it is no longer hemmed in by the spatial constraints of a newspaper article and the temporal constraints of its readers' attention span. In fact, if I may be permitted a disobliging simile, I would say that a newspaper is rather like a zoo, whose inmates, or journalists, chatter away in their own separate cages, or columns. A book, by contrast, is the writer's natural habitat, in which he can stretch and run and fly and leap from tree to tree, from chapter to chapter, and through whose occasionally matted undergrowth we cannot always follow him.

Newspapers are essential things, but it might be worth reminding ourselves, both as journalists and readers, of all the phenomena (which are precisely not 'phenomena' in the sensationalist sense of the word) which simply cannot be written about in conventional journalese, of all the *invisible events* which are at least as important as those of which the journalistic discourse habitually makes such a production number. In the arts there exists what might be called a *clandestine culture* (which sounds like, but is not, a contradiction in terms). By that, I mean a culture which has never had the good or ill fortune to be topical and has therefore never enjoyed or suffered the attentions of the press, upmarket or down.

Consider Mañoel de Oliveira. Who he, the reader asks. Who cares, the trendy journalist answers. A veteran Portuguese director, that's who, and in my opinion (and not only in my opinion) one of the two or three greatest living filmmakers, indeed greatest living artists, greater, anyway, than the second-, third- and fourth-raters with whom our ears are bent back by arts journalists, day after day and week after week. Naturally, I may be wrong, but since he is, journalistically speaking, *infra dig* (and, perhaps as a consequence, only one of his films, *Abraham's Valley*, has ever been released in Britain, and a catastrophic failure it was, too), I am unlikely to be contradicted.

Or consider Pierre Klossowski, a novelist and philosopher (and, *pour la petite anecdote*, the brother of the painter Balthus), whose work, I believe, will outlast that of *anyone*, of any generation, writing in English today. Again, I may be wrong. But one has only to read the arts journalism of fifty years ago, and note what *it* judged to be of lasting value, to realise that being neglected is not the same as being negligible.

I have no desire to denigrate journalists. I am one myself and have been as glib and superficial on occasion (and probably in this very essay) as any of my colleagues. The point is, rather, that journalism is an exemplary occupation just as long as its practitioners understand that it can offer, on any topic, no more than a point of departure. It is when it starts to regard itself as a substitute for the very object of its scrutiny that it becomes a potentially dangerous one. Every 'ism', as the world has learned to its cost, eventually degenerates into a terrorism. Well, that truth applies equally, alas, to the ostensibly modest 'ism' that is journalism.

On word-of-mouth

As much as with the innate qualities of a new film, reviewers are more and more preoccupied these days with what is known as its 'career': its initial returns, the umpteen millions of dollars it makes in the course of its opening weekend across the United States, the box-office records it breaks, etc. Not only reviewers. I know film buffs capable of reeling off a meticulously detailed rundown of 'domestic' (i. e. American) grosses, as though they themselves were up for a percentage cut, and of quoting *Variety* as reverentially as though that curious publication were not just 'the Bible of American show business' (as it complacently affects to style itself) but the Bible itself. So, for once, it might be interesting to follow the career of a single film from a subjective, unabashedly first-person angle of approach – which is to say, to track just how that film 'came to me' and also how it 'left' me, to examine how such a career functions at the micro-economic, instead of at the usual macro-economic, level. And the film I have chosen for this little experiment is *Groundhog Day*.

The story starts in New York, on an exceptionally mild Manhattan spring evening, with a vague desire on my part to, as they say, 'see something'. What, though? A play, which for many would be the obvious option, is out of the question. (I have a horror of the theatre in general; a horror, in particular, of the theatre, in New York as in London, as one of the codified types of *sightseeing*.) A film, then, but which one? *Indecent Proposal*? *Benny and Joon*? *Groundhog Day*? *Much Ado About Nothing*? Ho hum. I eventually opt for *Falling Down*, but that's another story.

Back in London, a month or so later. A rash of posters of *Groundhog Day*. For me, same difference, same indifference. Why on earth should I want to see a film with a title like *Groundhog Day* – a film starring, to boot, Bill Murray, an actor I have never got the point of, and Andie MacDowell, one of those actresses I associate more with *Vanity Fair* covers than with the cinema? (Is Andie MacDowell Demi Moore or vice versa?) I don't give it a second thought. Like a household cat oblivious of the blandly animated flicker of a TV screen, I decide that *it has nothing to do with me.*

Then, suddenly, all at once, everyone starts talking to me about the damned thing – from a first, neutral 'So what did you think of *Groundhog Day*?' to an incredulous, buttonholing 'What? You, a film critic' (which I have not been for many years now) 'and you haven't seen *Groundhog Day*?' Actually, I never recommend films to others and pay scant heed to what others recommend to me. As, I suppose, an unreformed auteurist, someone who believes in the absolute primacy of the director's vision, what I look for, 'when the lights go down and all our hopes are concentrated on the screen', as Pauline Kael once prettily put it, is not a story but a *world*. But, although I have always been more or less impervious to word-of-mouth, I have never known it to be so tangible or tenacious. Grudgingly, I surrender.

Cut to the Odeon, Leicester Square, on an exceptionally mild West End spring evening. I so seldom go to the cinema in London[1] that I have forgotten how grisly an experience it can be. There is the idiocy of pre-imposed numbered seats, obliging my companion and myself, once inside the half-empty auditorium, immediately to change places. There are the usherettes patrolling the aisles, Gestapo-style, with their torches. There is the unending stream of commercials that I itch to fast-forward. There are the – as always – totally counterproductive trailers. (Sylvester Stallone in *Cliffhanger*? Yuk. Danny De Vito in *Jack the Bear*? Re-yuk.) To cap it all, there is the man beside me who unwraps a boiled sweet which then sits obscenely enthroned on his tongue like a minute, plump, well-oiled eunuch on a red velours rug. (Change places again.) Then, at long last, *Groundhog Day*.

Not bad. Not as good as its central conceit (a man condemned to relive the same day over and over again) but, no, not bad at all. Bill Murray, to my surprise, a lot more than passably amusing. Andie MacDowell sweet and sexy. I laugh out loud once or twice, my companion, as restaurant columnists say, slightly more often. No, indeed, not bad.

Afterwards, dinner together and the sort of fatuous chit-chat that time-warp films inspire. (Did the other characters also relive the same day? Since Murray was portrayed as a free agent, why did he not just alter his daily routine to see what would happen?) I put to my companion the suggestion that the film had squandered its own ingenuity, an ingenuity worthy of Resnais, and that, had it been played not as broad comedy but as Kafkaesque nightmare, it might have revitalised the whole genre of cinematic horror, weaning it away from its slavish dependence on gore, mutation and the weary stereotypology of science-fiction. He disagrees. Then we talk about something else, and about something else after that, and by the end of the evening it is as though we had never been to the cinema.

Is this a cautionary tale? Not really. *Groundhog Day* is certainly an above-average entertainment and, given that I have seen literally thousands of films, I am certainly not an average spectator. Yet if it is nice to know that a film can still acquire an audience by virtue of word-of-mouth, the paradox is of course that such word-of-mouth is a near-infallible guarantee of anticlimax. Seeing the film for one-self, after so extravagant a build-up, can only be a disappointment. (Rave reviews do not have anything like the same effect, since they represent an 'official' seal of approval which, even if one is secretly unconvinced, one is subliminally coerced into endorsing for fear of being 'excluded'.) And to those who wish to avoid that disappointment I would simply propose that they begin to take the cinema as seriously as gamblers take their bets. By which I mean that they henceforth rely, as I have always done (and in the sense in which these words are used in a horse-racing milieu), not on 'tips' but on 'form'.

Notes

1 As with art exhibitions, I prefer to see films abroad: in Paris where, no matter how 'difficult' the film, I can be sure that there is not a single spectator who does not know exactly what he or she has come to see; or else in New York, where I buy popcorn and Coke and, despite being a professional, an auteurist, some would say an élitist, settle down to watch the film 'like everyone else'.

On a theory of television

The Policy Studies Institute recently published a set of statistics to the effect that television viewing figures had declined of late in much the same proportion as radio listening figures had risen. More interesting, though, than the figures themselves was the consensual conclusion which seems to have been drawn from them: that such a transference of allegiance (if that *is* what has been taking place) is fundamentally *a good thing*. For such a conclusion suggests that, while radio continues to benefit from a sort of generalised cultural goodwill, the act of watching television has never ceased to carry a lingering connotation of the pejorative, of the antisocial. It is as though, to offer a homely analogy, radio (which some rather self-conscious traditionalists still tiresomely refer to as 'the wireless') were a nice, restoring cup of tea without which one could not be expected to get through the day, television a slug of hard liquor, addictive and intoxicating, to be taken, if at all, only in the evening, and then only in moderation. It suggests, too, that not a few formerly heavy drinkers are turning into TV teetotallers.

I have never understood the moral foundation of such a bias. I am not, myself, a radio person. I do own a radio but, except for the odd concert, never switch it on. When, in the past, I was actually obliged to listen to a radio play for professional purposes, mostly for the late *Critics' Forum*, I always felt as though I were sitting in a theatre behind a column obscuring my view; I did not know where, as it were, to 'place my face'. (Is one supposed to look at a radio while listening to it?) When I mentioned this little dilemma to friends, however, what they told me was that the supreme virtue, the genius, of radio, and what distinguished it from television, was precisely that one could go about one's domestic round without having it vacuum up all one's attention.

My answer to that is to advance a theory of television which has long since been put into practice in the United States (where many households apparently have a set in every room) but has not yet caught on over here: the theory that *television is radio*, that they are, to all (or, rather, most) intents and purposes, the same thing.

A television screen is not something one need continually look at; it is something one need only occasionally *glance* at. I do not watch much television; but, when I do, I watch it while cooking dinner, reading a newspaper, playing computer chess, even filling out a tax return. From time to time I peer up at the screen – just *to get the picture*. Since so much of television is founded on repetition (regular slots, long-running series), it strikes me as absurd that I should have to start from scratch every time I switch on the set, that I should have to pay uninterrupted attention to each successive edition of, say, *Cheers* (even good actors have only a limited range of facial expressions, with all of which one soon becomes familiar in a situation comedy) or *The Late Show* (when only one item out of three ever tended to interest me, anyway) or *Newsnight* (I now know, just by the way he sounds, exactly what Peter Snow looks like at any given moment of the programme and I certainly do not feel obliged to watch a bunch of moronically corrupt politicians lie their way out of one crisis after another). There comes a point when one feels daft sitting in an armchair and staring at a squarish box in the corner of the room.

As for the medium's strictly visual qualities, they are in my experience utterly neglible: either preprogrammed (those shows whose few settings remain practically unaltered from week to week) or flat and platitudinous (as is the case of most television drama). For there is an essential if elusive difference between a television and a cinema screen. The televisual image is in a sense *transparent*, in that we have the impression of seeing through it to the reality which it is designed to capture; whereas the textural density and saturation of the filmic image, reinforced by the anonymity-preserving darkness of the auditorium, means that we perceive the cinema screen as a wall, a dead end, an impasse. Everything that happens in a film happens on that screen; there is nothing behind it, nothing beyond it. A television screen, by contrast, is comparable to a window. We cannot rid ourselves of the sensation that we are looking not at it but beyond it – beyond it to the space from which the programme is 'going out', that space being a studio possessed of its own spatial parameters as distinct from those defined by the compositional frame of the screen. We are permitted to 'see into' the studio via the television cameras, which thus do not offer us an *image*, on the model of the painterly or filmic image, but access (if only ocular access) to an autonomous *event*. And if that event has been staged for those very cameras, it can nevertheless, as is not at all true of a film, be satisfactorily experienced without them (if one is a member of the studio audience, for example).

It is therefore preposterous to define television as an art form or argue, as is currently being argued, that it has a 'history'. Television has no history – no history, at least, in the probably intended sense of a legacy of masterpieces that it might have bequeathed to us. There are no great living works of the medium's past which can be watched today as a great film of the past can be watched or a great novel of the past read or whatever. British television may well be the finest in the world, but, oh, how abruptly punctured are our long-fostered illusions whenever it rashly revives an old Dennis Potter play or an episode of *Hancock's Half-Hour* or *That Was the Week That Was*. It is not that these have ceased entirely to be of value but that their value is of either a nostalgic or sociological nature. We watch them exclusively as documents, documents in the dossier of our shared past. And to those who did not share that past they are, I fear, almost totally without interest.

On Aids

Like the universe, Gérard Depardieu's filmography appears both infinite and ever-expanding, and among several neglected films that lie buried in its now plumbless depths is Marco Ferreri's *L'Ultima donna* (or *The Last Woman*). Such as I recall it, its neglect is well deserved, but what made it controversial in 1976, when it was originally released, was a climactic scene that had its brawny leading man emasculate himself with an electric kitchen knife. The scene itself, like the rest of the film, was mildly ridiculous, but interesting all the same for the manner in which it exposed the paradox inherent in certain too casually employed figures of speech. Depardieu, as I say, slices off his penis. In the film's narrative, however, this demonstrably *literal* act of emasculation, serving as it does as a Freudian symbol for the character's spiritual alienation, thereby acquires an essentially *metaphorical* function. Physical emasculation exists, to be sure, although it must be very rare, and even more rarely self-inflicted. But symbolic 'emasculation' (or, as it is more frequently designated, 'castration') is one of the prime constituents of social and sexual anxieties among contemporary males, which is why the physical act has been all but obliterated by the psychological neurosis for it which was appropriated as a metaphor. In the same way, the term 'schizophrenia' is often used by journalists – and, for psychologists, tastelessly misused – as a catchall term for virtually any form of disjunction and dislocation, most of them unrelated to neurological disorder. And, rather more trivially, I once heard a middle-aged acquaintance of mine described as 'going through the female equivalent of male menopause'.

One of the most insidious instances of such rampant metaphorisation involves cancer (as one might refer to 'a cancer eating away at the Conservative Party'), and it was outrage at this usage, and at its inevitably pejorative connotations, that prompted Susan Sontag to write her book *Illness as Metaphor*. Although to some degree a defence of political correctness *avant la lettre*, it was a moving and powerful work, partly because Sontag nearly died of cancer herself. *Aids and its Metaphors*, a subsequent study and a pendant to *Illness as Metaphor*, was much less successful, not only because it could not help but strike one as less personal and more pious but also because one began to realise just how doomed were Sontag's pleas for a metaphor-free world. It simply cannot be done. *Pace* Gertrude Stein, a rose is not a rose, it is a metaphor (or a simile: 'My love is like a red, red rose'). It is at least as much a metaphor, anyway, as it is a flower. Language itself is metaphor, and all one can do is keep a wary eye open for the worst of its abuses.

Take Aids, precisely. What makes talking and writing freely about Aids such an awkward business is that one finds oneself in constant conflict with those who seek to place it (like, say, the Holocaust) beyond the reach of metaphor – indeed, beyond the reach of language itself. I happen, for example, to find Cyril Collard's *Les Nuits sauvages*, one of the still very few films about Aids, quite worthless as cinema, atrociously shot (like a video promo), atrociously written (in the pseudo-aphoristic style that makes me ashamed of my francophilia) and atrociously performed (above all by the film's own director, who narcissistically cast himself as its repository of truth, beauty and wisdom). Yet when I voiced this opinion to some gay French friends, I was accused of treating Aids as though it were subject matter like any other. Aids is *different*, I was told; one should never talk about it as though it were not. (Naturally, it did not help that Collard himself was an Aids sufferer and has since died – but that fact, if tragic, does not retroactively make him a better director or actor.) Similarly, Ian Hislop, the editor of *Private Eye*, has complained of the prominence which Aids now assumes at show business functions, a prominence denied to leukemia or tuberculosis.[1] And the *Sunday Times* has come under frequent and withering attack for its persistent questioning of current speculations on the increasing threat to heterosexuals from the virus.

It is a delicate matter. On the one hand, the indignation of gay activists is understandable, given that Aids was, from the start, the object of a campaign of disgusting metaphorisation (the tabloid smear of 'the gay plague'). On the other hand, Hislop does have a point. There is something a trifle discouraging about the fact that the politicisation of the gay community has not had the effect of significantly broadening its ideological base. What a falling-off from the sixties, after all, when white Americans from the North marched against the racial segregation of schools in the South and European students demonstrated against the Vietnam War, two causes in which, respectively, they knew they were never going to be directly implicated. Nowadays, political militancy has become not much more than a higher brand of special-interest lobbying.

That said, I do believe that homosexuals are justified in making a special case for Aids, precisely because of the implicit metaphor which continues to smoulder within its public image. Of what, in the average mentality, is Aids a metaphor? *Of homosexuality itself.* In the minds of so-called 'ordinary', 'decent' folk, Aids is homosexuality finally compelled to reveal itself in its true colours, homosexuality as a virus, as *contagious*. For what is most feared in Aids is exactly that which has always been most feared, if less rationally, in homosexuality: its power to *contaminate*. If, for the so-called moral majority (and for many, too, in the liberal minority), the notion of hiring a self-confessed homosexual as a schoolteacher has always been unthinkable, it is less out of fear that he might automatically start molesting his charges than that, by just being there, in the classroom, he would somehow, subliminally, contaminate them. The metaphor is, in short, an intensely paranoid one, that of the two faces of Jekyll and Hyde: Dr Sexual and Mr Aids.

So the problem is even now, as it has ever been, a problem of the public's attitude towards homosexuality. Homosexuals are right: Aids is not a medical condition like any other and never will be. Not, at any rate, until homosexuality is regarded as a human condition like any other.

Notes

1 Then again, statistics tend to suggest that, along with homosexuals and drug addicts, there exists a *third* high-risk group where Aids is concerned: celebrities.

On titles

I collect titles – by which I mean, the titles of novels, plays, films and so on. I am fascinated by them. I am fascinated, supremely, by the radical before-and-after effect which they have on a reader or spectator, by the virtual impossibility, once a title has acquired its patina of fame and familiarity, for that same reader or spectator to appreciate just how improbable, how vulnerable, how *puny*, it must have sounded to its creator's ears at the moment of its conception. Proper name titles, especially. For most of us, 'David Copperfield' and 'Oliver Twist' are names as conjurable as those of our closest friends. Yet how audacious, when one thinks of it, to have baldly called a novel *David Copperfield* or *Oliver Twist* (and, yes, I am aware that both of these titles are handy abbreviations of longer-winded nineteenth-century originals) – more audacious, certainly, than the majority of contemporary authors would dare to be.

For there is an element of presumption, even of vanity, in naming a brand new novel after its protagonist. It is as though the author believes not merely that his work is good enough to dispense with a descriptive or merely catchy phrase-title but, with what risks passing for unseemly confidence, that the qualities of the work are such, they will eventually confer upon it a classic status capable of endowing its title, retroactively, with the evocative charge it lacked when it was first published. After all, if few literary titles are as familiar today as *Oliver Twist*, it is because the average person is likely to know a lot about the character even before (or without) reading the book of which he is the hero. And it is not by chance that one of the very few instances of a name-title in recent years was Gordon Burn's *Alma Cogan*, whose recognition value did not have to be earned. (First names alone pose no problem, on condition that they be foreign and preferably 'poetic': e. g. Michael Ignatieff's *Asya*.)

But what is it exactly that makes for a 'beautiful' title? Oddly, for someone who dislikes the theatre as much as I do, I find that the most beautiful titles of the last hundred years have been those of plays. And it might be an intriguing exercise to select a handful of my own favourites and try to figure out what, if anything, they have in common – to explore, in short, the possibility of arriving at a theory of the title.

Consider these seven titles: Oscar Wilde's *The Importance of Being Earnest*, John Millington Synge's *The Playboy of the Western World*, Luigi Pirandello's *Six Characters in Search of an Author*, Eugene O'Neill's *Mourning Becomes Electra*, Jean Giraudoux's *The Trojan War Will Not Take Place*, Tennessee Williams's *A Streetcar Named Desire* and Christopher Fry's *The Lady's Not for Burning*. Naturally, you may not agree that all of them are as beautiful as I would claim, but there can be little doubt that their respective devisers were enchanted to have hit upon them. And, very different as they are, there is nevertheless something that invests all of them with the same weird compacted force, a quality which, given what one would suppose to be the basic expositional function of a title, impresses one as somewhat paradoxical: their *ambiguity*.

With *The Importance of Being Earnest* that ambiguity resides in the dual status of the word 'Earnest', here not only an adjective but, when shorn of its 'a', the name of one of the play's characters. With *The Playboy of the Western World* it resides in the apparent anachronism of 'Playboy', a word that seems to postdate the play itself, its earliest popular associations belonging to the twenties, perhaps, and the advent of café society. With *Six Characters in Search of an Author* it is in the inscription within the title of such metaliterary terms as 'Characters' and 'Author'. With *The Trojan War Will Not Take Place* it is in the plain fact that, as every schoolboy and girl knows, the Trojan War *did* take place.[1] With *A Streetcar Named Desire* it is in the idea of any public transport vehicle being so coquettishly christened. (Since 'Desire' is the real name of the district of New Orleans in which the play is set, a more accurate if incalculably less effective title would have been *A Streetcar Named 'Desire'*.) And, with *The Lady's Not for Burning*, it is, I propose, in the lapidary quaintness of the title's phraseology (now much parodied), as though it were entirely up to the lady herself whether to burn.

If I have kept *Mourning Becomes Electra* for last, it is for the simple reason that it is, I think, the most beautiful of all, and arguably the most beautiful title in the language.[2] In this instance, the ambiguity, reinforced by an absence of articles, prepositions and connectives of any kind, derives essentially from the verb 'become', employed here in its secondary, rarer sense of 'suit' or 'fit', and from the fact that that sense is still so *recherché* we find it hard to prevent ourselves from reading the more obvious meaning first before mentally correcting it. At which point, we begin to wonder whether O'Neill did not after all intend us to read the primary meaning; whether, in his updating of the legend, the Greeks' hieratic conception of 'mourning' actually does 'become', in the sense of 'turn into' or 'is embodied by', the more approachably human, more carnal figure of his heroine. Even then, the title has not exhausted its potential for ambiguity. It is unclear, for example, whether O'Neill means 'Mourning' to be interpreted as referring to the abstract condition of loss and lamentation or else to the (sometimes notoriously fetching) black garb which is still its traditional accompaniment.

All that in a three-word title. Now think of the new plays currently staged in the West End of London.[3] *Don't Dress for Dinner. The Last Yankee. The Woman in Black. On the Piste. Ali. Arcadia. It Runs in the Family. The Gift of the Gorgon.* Not much poetic ambiguity there, except, at a pinch, for the very last.

It would certainly be ridiculous to assume that there has to be any sort of a direct correlation between the quality of a play and the beauty of its title. But the best titles are amazing little literary constructs, as capable as poems, almost (almost!), of meaningful reverberation; the history of the English theatre can claim many, many more than its fair share (*Love's Labour's Lost, The Knight of the Burning Pestle, 'Tis Pity She's a Whore, She Stoops to Conquer*, etc.[4]); and if there exist many great plays without great titles, I cannot (as I write) think of a single great title which does not have a great play attached to it. It may be, then, that, in both senses of the word, great titles *become* great plays.

Notes

1 When initially produced in English, *La Guerre de Troie n'aura pas lieu* was

bizarrely retitled *Tiger at the Gates*; bizarrely, as its translator, Christopher Fry, himself had a genius for memorable titles: *A Phoenix Too Frequent*, *The Dark Is Light Enough*, etc. Giraudoux's play is now generally staged with its original (easily translated) title intact.

2 *The Iceman Cometh, A Moon for the Misbegotten, Long Day's Journey into Night* – O'Neill had an extraordinary way with titles. It might even be said that he put his genius into his titles and only his talent into his plays.

3 This essay was first published in 1993. A glance at any newspaper's West End theatre listings will confirm that what I wrote then still goes.

4 Each of these, you will note, conforms to my theory of titular ambiguity: the overly dense, almost tongue-twisting alliteration of the Shakespeare; the puzzling conceit of a burning pestle and the equally puzzling proposition that it might have its own knight; the in-your-face crudity, to modern ears, of the word 'Whore' following immediately on from the Elizabethan gentility of ''Tis Pity'; and the more conventional paradox of a conquest obtained by stooping, not rising.

On event freaks

If you recall, the first complete performance of Alban Berg's opera *Lulu* was staged at the Paris Opéra in 1979. The conductor on that occasion was Pierre Boulez, the director was Patrice Chereau and the taxing title role was sung by Teresa Stratas.

I, for one, do recall it, vividly, since it was the very last production I saw at the Palais Garnier before resettling in London. I recall how excited I was at the prospect of at last seeing and hearing the fabled final act (reconstructed from the composer's notes by Friedrich Cerha) of Berg's unfinished masterpiece, which had always been performed and recorded in a truncated two-act version. I recall, too, that my excitement was matched by that of an acquaintance of mine who had never seen the truncated version, had never shown much interest in Berg as a composer, had, indeed, almost never been to the opera, any opera. In short, although more or less indifferent to *Lulu*'s first two acts, he could not wait to hear the 'new' third!

His excitement stemmed essentially from the fact that, whereas *Lulu* had once been an opera – which is to say, just one opera among many others – its third act transformed it into an *event*. And it was while reflecting on such a transformation that I was alerted to the existence of a contemporary sociocultural type, a 'character' in the sense intended by the seventeenth-century moralist La Bruyère in his classic anthology of portraits, *Les Caractères*.[1] The type in question is, to employ an inelegant formula, the event freak.

Consider the annual men's championship match at Wimbledon. The event freak is someone who religiously watches that match year after year and who is heartbroken if he should chance to miss it – in spite of the fact that he has paid next to no attention to the run and tenor of the tournament of which it is the culmination. The event freak is someone who automatically purchases a ticket to a silent film provided that it is accompanied by a live orchestra conducted by Carl Davis in the theatre pit, but to whom it would never occur to go and see the same film if screened at the National Film Theatre with a perfectly serviceable piano accompaniment. The event freak is someone who feels that he just *has* to have the Booker prizewinning novel, even though there may well be another title on the shortlist (or yet another not even shortlisted) with which, all else being equal, he is more likely to have an affinity. (Cocteau notes somewhere that, even as late as in the thirties, *A l'ombre des jeunes filles en fleur*, the one volume of Proust's *Recherche* to win the Goncourt Prize, continued to sell significantly more copies than any of the others – of what is, its multivolume status notwithstanding, a single novel.) The event freak is someone who, if he has been unable to visit some major exhibition at the Tate or the National Gallery in its opening week, when it is still an event, would never think of paying a visit to it in subsequent weeks, when it has reverted to being merely an exhibition. The event freak, finally, is someone who claims to be fascinated that a proof has been discovered for Fermat's Last Theorem, even if he heard of the proof before knowing that the theorem existed and has only the fuzziest notion, anyway, of what makes that proof an event in the first place.

Events, events. In the seventies, when Buster Keaton's films enjoyed an international revival for the first time since they had been made (Keaton himself survived just long enough to savour his elevation to eventhood), I watched *The Navigator* in a Paris cinema and laughed so loudly I was asked by the spectator in front of me to pipe down. When I protested that the film was a comedy, he hissed at me, 'It's not a comedy, it's a classic!' In other words, an event.

These days, moreover, events are not just happenings – they can also be people, people to whom the event freak finds himself in perpetual, febrile thrall: to take only the most flagrant cases, Michael Jackson and Madonna, Diana and Fergie, are all living, breathing events. There are those, too, who, after enjoying a brief period of eventhood, eventually and irreversibly subside into that circle of Hell specifically reserved for non-events. Stevie Smith, for example.

Do you, as I do, remember a time when Stevie Smith seemed to be *everywhere*, a time when one could not open a newspaper or a magazine without stubbing one's fingers, so to speak, on her quaint spinsterish eccentricities, her Thurberesque, *faux-naïf* scribbles and her inevitable 'not waving but drowning'? Where, as they say, is she now?

Ours is a culture of events – from novels whose length renders them eligible for the *Guinness Book of Records (A Suitable Boy)* to films which 'have to be seen' even if they turn out to be million-dollar schlock (*Jurassic Park*). And the joke is that the *real* events of that culture (those, I mean, which posterity will judge to have been actually *seminal* of something) are taking place somewhere else altogether, in a totally different time-frame – they are, like certain bombs, delayed-action events. As for most of those which strike us as so unmissable now, why, we are all going to have a good laugh about them when we are in our graves.

Notes

1 The tradition of the 'character' as an ironic paradigm of human ethics and behaviour was instigated by the Greek philosopher Theophrastus (c. 372–c. 287 BC), but compilations like La Bruyère's were still common in both England and France until the early eighteen-hundreds. Although the fables and foibles of our own society would appear to offer a fertile seam of satiric inspiration, the sole recent instance of the form of which I am aware is Elias Canetti's *Earwitness*.

On style

What is the primary defining trait of popular fiction, or at least of that seasonal subdivision of popular fiction which is usually classified under the vague generic rubric of 'holiday reading'? Style, surely. Be it a novel by Danielle Steel or Jeffrey Archer, be it a designer-label bodice-ripper or a thick-ear thriller of the New World Order, the reader is guaranteed a cast of characters who dress with style, travel in style and, dependent on the genre, stylishly make either love or war.

The style I refer to is, of course, synonymous with affluence (no one on holiday wants to read about poor people) and founded on an unsophisticate's idea of sophistication. Its *donnés* can be directly traced back (via Ian Fleming's James Bond novels) to the now close-to-unreadable Edwardian romances of Michael Arlen, Ouida and E. Phillips Oppenheim, for whom style was a question above all of accessories, of brandy snifters and Havana cigars, flawless dinner jackets and diaphanous evening gowns, shooting lodges in the Tyrol and so-called 'great' metropolitan drawing rooms with cabinet ministers warming their buttocks at the Adam fireplace. In the work of their contemporary avatars, the accessories themselves may have changed, but the settings are still the *loci classici* of high-style lifestyles: mansions in Bel Air, penthouses in Manhattan, villas in Tuscany and white wedding-cake hotels on the Riviera. Style is everything, and it scarcely seems to matter that the only person bereft of it is the author.

But then, style as an indelible authorial presence, an absolute linguistic uniqueness – style in the sense which we inherited from Flaubert, the first writer on public record for whom literary composition was an *agony* – has never had a high priority for the sort of holiday reader who, on the *plage*, will sport only the most stylish beachwear but is perfectly content, where his or her chosen reading matter is concerned, to settle for nondescript, off-the-peg prose.

Literature-wise, the public which insists on only 'the best' in life is quite happy to travel steerage.[1]

Nor, nowadays, is such an attitude confined to holiday reading. A lot of fiction is published in Britain, and some of it is good, but rare is the modern novel whose style is widely held up as the truest measure of its excellence. Or, if ever it is, if ever a reviewer refers, as reviewers are wont to do, to its author writing 'like an angel', and quotes a sentence or two in support of such a claim, the quotation invariably centres on some cute, ingenious metaphor which one cannot help suspecting has been plucked from the otherwise doughy consistency of the novel's prose like a shiny sixpence from a Christmas pudding. Anything more enveloping, more all-encompassing, is likely to be dismissed as 'mannered' or 'self-indulgent', as though a real style were a filmy gauze with an exasperating tendency to obscure the essential – which is to say, the story.

I have often fantasised about how literary style at its most uncompromising might be rendered palatable to the general reader. Let us imagine that one is reading a novel by a writer with an arduous albeit instantly identifiable style, a writer of the order of a Proust or a Henry James. One dutifully ploughs through the first fifty pages, and then on the fifty-first page one is suddenly brought up short by an author's note: *Congratulations, dear reader, on having persevered this far. Now, look, since you know I can do it and I know I can do it, why don't we just forget about the whole damn business of style and get on with the plot.* At which point one discovers that the novel's remaining two hundred-odd pages are written in an accessible, unobtrusively neutral idiom.

My little fantasy also has a converse variation. This time it is the novel's first fifty pages which are couched in the above-mentioned neutral idiom. And this time the author's note which the reader then encounters is as follows: *Admit it, dear reader, you're hooked. You're eager to learn more about these characters of mine and the predicament that they've got themselves into. This, then, is the ideal moment to turn on my style full blast.* Naturally, the following two hundred pages would manifest all the linguistic density traditionally associated with the writer in question.

But to return to the question of holiday reading: if I have absolutely no patience with those writers who shrug off their stylistic incompetence by professing to aspire 'only to be a storyteller' (an infallible sign of literary nullity), it is less out of any puritanical distaste for the chic lifestyles which their books depict (Proust, after all . . .) than because I find them simply, mortally, unreadable. A poorly written novel is like a poorly painted picture, neither more nor less. It is like a musical composition full of ugly, wrong notes. It is a novel which has been written, but not rewritten. As Flaubert knew, however, writing makes a book *possible* but only rewriting makes it *good*.

Nor can style ever be reduced to what the French term a 'signature effect', as a certain infamous chapter in Ian McEwan's *The Innocent*, in which two of his characters are obliged to dismember a third, was a signature effect, designed primarily to remind the reader, who might otherwise have forgotten, that it actually was an Ian McEwan novel he was reading. Such a reductive conception of style always makes me think of the late French filmmaker Albert Lamorisse, the director of *The Red Balloon*, *Voyage in a Balloon*, and so on. Lamorisse's 'touch' was certainly recognisable: there was always a balloon in his films. And for more than one critic that balloon was itself enough to constitute a distinctive Lamorissian 'style'.

No, style is very much more than that, very much more than 'stylishness', than 'fine writing'. It is a mysterious, metaphoric and metamorphic investment of self in a text and it may carry almost erotic implications for both writer and reader. Ultimately, indeed, the beauty of a literary style is to the act of reading what the beauty of a face is to the act of making love. Although, as one proceeds in either situation, one's attention is liable to be more and more urgently solicited elsewhere – towards one's partner's body or else towards the novel's plot – the appeal of that 'elsewhere' will always remain contingent on the beauty, facial or stylistic, by which one was attracted in the first place.

Notes

1 At Mahe airport, in the Seychelles, I once chatted to a wealthy American businessman who told me that he read very little but that 'when I do read a book, it's got to be the best there is'. Whereupon, to drive his point home, he brandished a copy of the latest Stephen King.

On conceptual art

It was in 1887, in the arts journal *Fors*, that John Ruskin published the celebrated diatribe against Whistler's *Nocturne in Black and Gold* which included this often-quoted (and, at the time, libellous) passage: 'I have seen, and heard, much of Cockney impudence before now; but never expected to hear a coxcomb ask for two hundred guineas for flinging a pot of paint in the public's face.'

Ruskin was of course in error, not only legally (although Whistler's victory in the consequent trial was strictly symbolic: he was awarded damages of a farthing) but also historically. Whistler has endured as an artist, an artist whose figurative studies of a foggily abstract London proved to be instrumental in preparing the recalcitrant public eye for true abstraction, an artist who, as one might fancifully put it, was the first (with Turner) to think of looking not *through* the fog but *at* it. And yet . . . For many of us, Ruskin's fulmination is still relevant to certain prevailing modes of artistic abstraction, so much so that it is possible to imagine some contemporary artist setting up a gallery 'installation' which would consist of his or her, at specified times of the day, quite literally flinging pots of paint in the faces of the visiting public – and doubtless asking substantially more than two hundred guineas for the privilege.

If such an installation did exist (dread word, that, 'installation'), it would likely be categorised as conceptual art – art, in short, whose privileged moment of creation was that of its conception, not its execution. Which is precisely where the problem lies. I believe it fair to say that abstract, non-figurative art no longer provokes much of a scandal. Ordinary people may not really like art without 'meaning', they may not 'understand' it, but they have on the whole got used to it, got used to encountering it in hotel lobbies and bank managers' offices if not necessarily in museums. In some quarters, it has actually come to be appreciated for its therapeutic virtues: the Rothko room in the Tate instils even in those who are more or less indifferent to the artist himself a strange inner serenity and calm, a definite feeling of well-being towards the world, exactly as does the gallery of the Orangerie in Paris in which hang Monet's series of *Nymphéas*. (In both cases, perhaps, it is the room itself which is the masterpiece rather than any individual painting exhibited in it.) No, what is calculated to winkle out the Ruskin lurking in even the most enlightened among us is the aggressively minimalist quality of much contemporary painting and sculpture. The scandal is no longer the absence of meaning but the absence of *labour*.

To illustrate an article by Kate Bernard on the 1993 Turner Prize, the *Sunday Times* published photographs of the contending works by the four shortlisted artists. Aside from a (I am almost tempted to say) 'traditional' abstract painting by the already well-established Sean Scully, these consisted of a plaster cast of a mattress, a photograph which had been printed on canvas then mounted on to a panel, and an installation entitled 'Neon Rice Field', which, to be fair, was not too visible on the page but certainly looked minimal enough. Now I would not presume to *judge* these works on the sole evidence of four minuscule snapshots, but I am prepared to go as far as to harbour the vague suspicion that, with each of them, the conception, the original idea, mattered more than the execution. Naturally, the artists themselves would argue that the two processes cannot and should not be separated, exactly as Whistler, in response to Ruskin, argued that what mattered was not the two days it took him to paint his *Nocturne* but the experience of a lifetime that the painting distilled. Well, I may be as much in error as Ruskin, but (as a writer, as someone who *writes*, therefore *works*, for a living) I have to say that I demand from a painting a whiff of *sweat*, a sense that labour has been exerted, just as much as I would from a novel or play or film. An idea is not a work of art.

Mine is a sentiment, I fancy, that is widely shared and may help to clarify a number of otherwise inexplicable cultural prejudices. The apparently paradoxical fact, first of all, that the general public tends to reject the notion of photography as an authentic art form while contriving to admire as art any painting so meticulously fashioned as to *resemble* a photograph. Here, again, the issue at stake is surely that of labour. No matter how exquisitely lit and composed, a photograph of a crowded street scene would seem to preclude the need for any extended exertion on the photographer's part, whereas a hyperrealistically detailed painting of the same scene wears the painter's manual dexterity, not to mention his stamina, on its sleeve. Or take the lasting appeal, mostly to visitors of provincial galleries, of the works of the nineteenth-century academics, the enormous, 'well-made' paintings (as one says 'well-made' plays) of Lord Leighton and Alma-Tadema. Or indeed the undimmed popularity, in the face of universal critical disdain, of the Royal Academy's Summer Exhibition. Photorealists, academicians, Sunday painters – these are artists who, good, bad or unqualifiably inept, do at least give the impression of having *worked* at their art.

This is, I realise, a somewhat perilous path to find oneself on, for it may well terminate in the philistine attitude which accepts Picasso as a true artist only, and grudgingly, because he could paint proper – which is to say, naturalistic – pictures when he wanted to (an attitude that always reminds me of those parents prepared to approve their offspring's desire to become an actor or a writer only on condition that he complete his studies first, just in case . . .). Yet if we can all have ideas (I myself have had lots of ideas that would make wonderful Magrittes), we cannot all paint, and there is something galling to the layman about the commercial success of a professional 'artist', a Jeff Koons, let us say, who has never been able to bridge the abyss between the (fairly amusing) idea and the (horrible) execution.

Degas, a great artist, also aspired to be a poet. As he confided to his friend Mallarmé, however, he had somehow never succeeded in writing a good poem despite having had good ideas. 'That,' Mallarmé replied, 'is because poetry is made not with ideas but with words.'

On art movies

I have always been on the side of the art movie. As a critic, I have defended as an endangered species (which, alas, it is these days more than ever) what I would call the cinema of special causes rather than special effects and excoriated the commercial imperatives to which it now has to pay obeisance (the creeping Hollywoodisation of the international festival circuit, the systematic, even routine, co-option into the mainstream of film directors whose most congenial niche is on the margin, the ever more populist programming of repertory houses up and down the country). As a spectator, I came of age in the sixties, the last halcyon era of the art movie (I might cite, *entre autres*, the *nouvelle vague*, Fellini, Antonioni and Visconti, Bresson, Bergman and Buñuel) and I can recall, in the Paris of the following decade, actually having had to *queue up* to see films as abstruse as Miklos Jancsó's *Red Psalm* and Glauber Rocha's *Antonio das Mortes*. Even now, I know few anticipatory pleasures as acute as that of waiting for the curtains to part on a new film by a real *auteur*. On this matter my credentials are, if I say so myself, unimpeachable.

Yet, watching Jane Campion's *The Piano*, a *bona fide* art movie if ever there was, the laureate *ex aequo* of the 1994 Cannes Film Festival and a work apparently without a single public detractor, I found myself oppressed beyond words by the dead weight of its relentless, meaningless formalism. I have had a similar experience with recent films by Wenders (*Until the End of the World*), Rivette (*La Belle Noiseuse*), Carax (*Les Amants du Pont-Neuf*), Kieślowski (*The Double Life of Véronique*), Greenaway (not only *Prospero's Books* but the nauseating *Baby of Mâcon*), Lynch (*Wild at Heart*), Bertolucci (*The Sheltering Sky*), Potter (*Orlando*) and von Trier (*Europa*), etcetera, etcetera, etcetera, as Yul Brynner used to say in *The King and I*. And I ask myself what has happened to the art movie – or what has happened to me.

What, to start with, I object to in these films is the calculated man-

ner in which they *bully* the spectator into submission. Not, I hasten
to add, by the spectacle of mindless violence, as in the average
Hollywood blockbuster, but by strictly formal conceits. There is the
current vogue, for example, for outlandish running times (Wenders's
three hours and Rivette's four – but, beware, if a film is too long it
gives the spectator time to enumerate its faults). The concurrent
vogue for grotesquely overdetermined soundtracks (a match struck
in *Wild at Heart* sounded like a retroactive rocket being launched,
the squeak of a door being opened in Kieślowski's *Blue* was as grating on the ear as would be the scraping of a piece of chalk across a
blackboard). There is the directorial dependence on excessively
sumptuous costumes and sets in lieu of any real visual style (the
bewigged and beribboned folderols of Greenaway and Potter). And
there is, most deplorably, the nerve-wracking formal virtuosity by
which one has come to recognise a director's fraudulent pretensions
to modernity. In *The Piano*, notably, one had the feeling that
Campion was petrified by the thought that, were she to relax for
even an instant, she might compromise the dourly unremitting wizardry of her *mise-en-scène* by selecting a camera angle that failed to
impress even the doziest of spectators as startlingly new and unexpected. Thus a character in her film cannot stir a cup of tea without
the camera at once reverting to a direct overhead shot, thereby letting the drifting spirals of liquid assume pseudo-cosmic connotations. It is an aback-taking image all right (the primary ambition of
all of these directors is to take aback), but, for crying out loud, it *is*
only a cup of tea being stirred![1]

In the second place, there arrives that inevitable moment, in practically every new art movie, when the characters' behavioural patterns simply lose all contact with identifiable human conduct.
Current instances of such a tic are too many and various to list here,
but everyone will know the sort of thing I mean. A woman is slapped
on the face and instantly embraces the man who slapped her. A couple amble with dreamy unconcern past a horrendously bloody car
crash. A connoisseur holds a priceless vase up to the light then nonchalantly lets it slip from his fingers. As L. P. Hartley nearly said, the
art movie is a foreign country. They do things differently there.

As for the third aberration, it is related to the myth that the specificity of film as an art form resides in its capacity to do what no other medium can do. It is a myth to which I myself, as both critic and spectator, long subscribed, but which I now find impossible to accept. I believe, rather, that the finest films are those which do what the other arts do just as well, if necessarily according to their own lights.

Consider *And Life Continues*, a magnificent film by the Iranian director Abbas Kiarostami. It was shot in the immediate aftermath of the 1990 earthquake and centres on a filmmaker who, with his son, motors through Iran's devastated hinterland to discover whether the two young leading actors of one of his earlier films have survived the catastrophe.[2] In one scene, the filmmaker meets an ancient, bent crone who solicits his assistance in removing a carpet from the ruins of her already tumbledown house. After cursorily inspecting the situation, he declines to help on the grounds that the carpet is too tightly wedged under rubble for the two of them alone to extricate it. The narrative continues on its way until, some ten minutes later, while the focus of our attention is directed elsewhere, we observe, in a corner of the screen and out of the corner of an eye, that the old woman has after all succeeded, with unimaginable determination and labour, in dragging the carpet outside by herself.

It is a sublime moment of cinema, all the more so because it refuses to bully us into interpreting it as a statement on 'human resilience in the face of adversity'; because it is simply and sparely shot, with a total absence of vain directorial curlicues; and because, being about *more than the cinema*, it does not matter in the slightest that its essence could equally well have been captured in print. Not art cinema, perhaps, but cinema art.

Notes

1 What has happened to *stasis* as a parameter of filmic imagery? Is there no one among the younger generation of directors capable of producing visuals of a genuinely passive, contemplative quality, a quality which would allow the spectator to reach out towards the screen rather than recoiling from it – that quality, in short, which characterises the work of Godard, Rohmer, Oliveira, Iosseliani and Straub, the true masters of the modern art movie?

2 This earlier film is clearly one of Kiarostami's own, *Where Is the Friend's Home?* (1987).

On critics

Many years ago I was invited to a theatrical first night – my first first night – by an acquaintance of mine, the theatre critic of a national newspaper. By British standards it was quite a 'glittering' première, and I spent most of the interval shamelessly gawping at celebrities, real and imagined. But my friend the critic, who had decided to give the bumpkin that I was a running commentary on the event, had his own priorities. 'Don't turn around,' he would murmur in my ear, 'but that man over there with the goatee? That's Irving Wardle, the critic of *The Times*. And the small but perfectly formed fellow standing beside him? Jack Tinker of the *Mail*. And . . .' 'But look,' I tried to interrupt, 'isn't that Noël Coward talking to – why, surely it's Maggie Smith?' He gave them a perfunctory glance. 'Yes, I suppose so,' he said shortly, before rewarming to his theme. 'Notice the elderly man leaning on his walking stick? Well, that's Harold Hobson of the *Sunday Times*. And . . . and . . . and . . .' And so it went.

A severe case, obviously, of professional deformation. There comes a time in the existence of every socioprofessional body when its attention is irrevocably diverted from the activity which is, or ought to be, its fundamental *raison d'être* and towards the collective dynamics of its own tight little community. Or, to be specific, if there's one thing that interests theatre critics more than the theatre, it's other theatre critics.

That remark is applicable, of course, not only to theatre critics. I myself was a film critic for several years and I can vouch for the truth of what I have just written where that specialisation, too, is concerned: it has, as I say, a relevance to well-nigh every social or professional caste, whether connected with the arts or not. Nor am I referring exclusively to the prurient, gossipy curiosity about one's colleagues' affairs, about their spouses and salaries, that is, I imagine, a universal human trait. The real professional deformation affecting critics (and it is a fact of which the general public is probably unaware, given that it *zaps* newspapers and magazines just as it does television channels) is that they write as much for one another as for the ordinary readers at whom their reviews are ostensibly targeted. Even I, writing this essay on the whole phenomenon, am disproportionately preoccupied with what my fellow critics are likely to think of it – disproportionately, that is, if one considers how very few of them there are in relation to the potential readership of either an article or a book.

Is it simply a truism that I am stating here – that critics, like politicians, actors, lawyers, dons, vicars, homosexuals, engine-drivers, social workers, trainspotters and doubtless candlestick-makers, like the members of any profession, of any special-interest body, are indefatigably fascinated with themselves? Not entirely. In the first place, journalists enjoy a unique opportunity (an opportunity of which few of them shy from availing themselves) to air and disseminate their self-fascination. Books about newspapers can depend on getting reams of coverage on the books pages of other newspapers, scandals involving newspaper tycoons are invariably blazoned across huge banner headlines: every newspaper in Britain is, to a certain extent, a trade paper. More significant, however, is the relationship of critics to the uninformed public. I think, analogously, of the employees of HM Customs and Excise. Like customs officers, critics intervene primarily at what might be called the point of entry, the entry of, in their case, a new work of art. Like customs officers, what they are paid to ask of this new book, film, play or painting is 'Have you anything to declare?' And, like customs officers, once they have examined its intellectual baggage, so to speak, and stamped it (or not) with their approval, they generally lose all interest in the object of their scrutiny. While the public which they serve is still coming to terms with the work in question, they have already moved on to the next applicant.

Yet it is easy to forget that the living culture of a country is an inextricable tangle of the brand new, the extremely ancient and the middling recent. We read books from virtually every period of literary history, only a handful of which have just been published. We watch old films on television, or newish films on video, rather more frequently than we take in the very latest films in a cinema. We listen to a wider and much more heterogeneous range of music on radio or record than would ever be possible in a lifetime of concert-going. And even if its influence remains steady enough at, precisely, the point of entry, journalistic criticism has ultimately little to do with the way in which most of these choices are made.[1]

Paradoxically, then, where once it was the artist who wrote for Stendhal's 'happy few', now it is the critic. Where art for art's sake has long been a discredited ideology, criticism for criticism's sake is thriving. And the risk inherent in such mandarinism (such *relative* mandarinism – let us not exaggerate) is that the critic, aware that he is writing principally for 'his peers', as award-winners say on Oscar night, may end by letting his own discourse take precedence over that of the artist he is supposed to be writing about.

Such a tendency, alas, although ever more prevalent in the British media, amounts to nothing more than mere vain self-glorification. Even brilliant, a critic is still only an interpreter, a go-between, an importer-exporter, not a creator. An artist, after all, may discover America. All a critic can hope to discover is Christopher Columbus.

Notes

1 This explains why, in recent years, one has seen a consistent decline in conventional reviewing practices. Only in the case of the theatre, topical by definition, has straightforward critical coverage remained the norm.

On pop music

Let me start this essay with two terrible words: I smoke. I am a smoker. I inhale a toxic substance into my lungs and exhale it through my nostrils. I am what is known as an addict.

Being an addict, though, does not mean that I solicit or expect indulgence from anyone not so afflicted. I acknowledge that smokers differ from alcoholics, say, or drug abusers in that we pollute the air about us; hence that, in public places and *a fortiori* in their own homes, non-smokers are entitled to ask us, although surely politely, to stub out our cigarettes (which I for one will instantly do). Where smoking is concerned, I am not at all a 'libertarian'. For me, a chain smoker (which I myself am not) is a smoker in chains, and I do not believe that limiting either his or my opportunities to smoke in public represents the curtailment of one of humanity's fundamental freedoms, the thin end of any wedge. I am, I think, a rational addict.

However (and you had probably already guessed that there was a 'however' hovering on the horizon), I have never really understood why we smokers should be singled out as if we were the sole polluters of air that would otherwise be of a crystalline purity. Speaking exclusively for myself, I can think of at least one other form of air pollution which is just as noxious as smoking but to combat which no concerted action has ever been taken: pop music.

In Britain today, as is no longer the case with cigarette smoke, pop music is everywhere. Step into a men's clothing shop to buy a shirt and you are bombarded with pop music. Should a car drive past you with its top down and its radio on at full, earsplitting blast, it has to be pop music. Live in a large block of flats, and at any given time of the day (or night) someone somewhere will be playing pop music. Stand in line at the Post Office – pop music. Eat in some not necessarily trendy brasserie – pop music. Take a taxi – pop music. Switch on television – as likely as not, pop music (the same gestural tics, the same flashy camera movements, the same garish filters – the *mise-en-*

scène of televised pop, of a quite extraordinary poverty of invention, has not budged in thirty years). Go see a film – chances are that, from the opening to the closing credits, its soundtrack will be dominated by the nasal, repetitive whine of pop music.

Nothing, to be fair, is as subjective as a tolerance of trash. If there does exist, more or less, a canon of artistic greatness, there is no such thing as a Pantheon of the pits. I myself, for example, can watch almost any Hollywood film released between 1929 and 1955 (except, no Abbott and Costello, no Shirley Temple, no Tarzan, etc.), and I accept that others might want to scramble *their* brains with an unadulterated diet of pop music. My objection is not to its existence but, as is the case with the less paranoid of anti-smoking campaigners, to its public ubiquity. In an ambience of deafening pop music I feel as physically nauseated as others do in a smoke-filled room. I struggle in vain to plug my ears against the cretinous lyrics and non-existent melodic line. I object, in short, to being made a *passive listener*.

Pop music is, after all, just one type of 'cultural' expression and I can find no good reason why it should so predominate. No one has ever been coerced into listening to amplified readings of Mann's *Buddenbrooks* or Heidegger's *Sein und Zeit*. Nor, for that matter, to performances of Berg's Violin Concerto. Yet, even in one's own home, it is practically impossible to escape the pervasive aura of pop. It is a bit like the fairy-tale of the Princess and the Pea: so seemingly loudly does pop music have to be played that, three or four floors up, while the melody itself has all but evaporated, there is still the nagging pea of that thud-thud-thud bass beat to keep one awake.

I am certainly no historian in these matters, but my feeling is that the rot began to set in during the late forties and early fifties when the word 'popular' dropped its last four letters, when 'popular music' yielded definitively to 'pop music' and set about targeting an exclusively youthful, not to say adolescent, audience. Prior to that period, popular songs had been written by such composers as Gershwin, Kern, Rodgers, Berlin and Porter, songs which even now have not, as the French say, acquired a single wrinkle. In the period, moreover, since the initial shift from 'popular' to 'pop', the problem has been compounded by the fact that the adolescents of forty years ago are the adults of today, many of whom have not merely not out-grown their own teenage tastes but have obliged their offspring to inherit them as though pop music were the only natural, normal aural environment in which to mature. Theirs is a prejudice which in its turn derives from the common philistine assumption that no one really enjoys listening to classical music. I mean, that no one *really* enjoys it – as witness all those corny film musicals of the sixties in which a classical concert is suddenly interrupted by some lone, pop-oriented saxophonist . . . and in a flash all the snooty dowagers and their snoozing hubbies are tapping their toes to his irresistible beat. It is high time, surely, that that particular canard was laid to rest.

Understand me. Although, to a non-initiate like myself, pop music is not just trite and monotonous but actually stupefying – it is, in my opinion, one of the many current cultural manifestations which make Britain an increasingly *stupid* country – I am not proposing a ban on its circulation. I do not, as a rule, believe in censorship. What I *would* like is for one simple, constructive proposal to be made legally enforceable. That, in future, on every pop record issued in Britain, there should be printed this warning from the Surgeon-General: *Pop Music Can Seriously Damage Your Mental Health*.

On Mae West

Of late, for a few American superstars, life has been no sinecure. Arnold Schwarzenegger's *The Last Action Hero* could hardly have been a more conspicuous flop. Woody Allen's Hitchcockian comedy thriller, *Manhattan Murder Mystery*, was so tepidly received by press and public alike as to suggest that he is now in danger of becoming, for all but his unconditional devotees, just another and in no sense exceptional filmmaker. Michael Jackson's trademark 'weirdness', long perceived as reassuringly *sui generis*, has at last come under close and specific inspection.[1] And then there is Madonna, who, only recently, was all over the place at once, descending upon her fans with the miraculous aplomb of her celestial namesake. What further and, as I write, unimaginable stops is she going to have to pull out in future when she has already exceeded most of the admissible bounds of the raunchy and the outrageous?

As it happens, I recently found myself reminded of Madonna when reading of the various retrospectives held across America to commemorate the birth of the woman who has always struck me, rather than Marilyn Monroe or any of the usual candidates, as her true model, Mae West – Mae West, who was apparently born in Brooklyn a century ago, on 17 August 1893. (If I write 'apparently', it is because the reference work which I myself consulted has her born in 1892. Yet the celebrations have indeed been held this year,[2] raising the possibility that her birthdate was, typically of Hollywood stars, what you might call a movable feast.)

Even aside from the odd superficial coincidence (Madonna was born on 16 August, not 17 August; the title of her first book, *Sex*, was also the title of West's first play), the two women have a great deal in common. Like Mae West before her, Madonna has evolved an obliquely feminist attitude towards female sexuality through a calculated exploitation of her body which remains respectful of the most blatant stereotypes of male desire while simultaneously contriving,

by that very brazenness, to resist its ultimate possession and coloni-
sation by the male voyeur. (Monroe, for her part, was perhaps ill-at-
ease inside her fabulous body and silently screaming to get out.) Like
Mae West, another Babe in Toyboyland, Madonna has flaunted her
taste for the company of male bodies rather than of men. Like Mae
West, Madonna has publicly flirted with deviant forms of eroticism.
(West's second play was entitled *Drag*.) And if the image of an *elderly*
Marilyn Monroe would have been so unpalatable it was probably
fated never to come to pass under any circumstances,[3] there is no
compelling reason, at least in terms of her public persona, why
Madonna, like Mae West, should not survive into her eighties, a
tough, leathery old filly.

In one crucial respect, however, they could not be more dissimilar:
in their relationship to *nudity*.

Paradoxically, a nude, or even a semi-nude, Mae West was always
inconceivable. Because, in the classic Hollywood cinema, the human
body was rigorously masked, she was never permitted to bare very
much of her own; but one cannot believe that, even in a more
enlightened climate, she would ever have cared or dared to. The
epitome of knowing sex appeal, West did not actually possess very
much of that indefinable quality herself, certainly by current standards but even, I suspect, in her heyday. Rather like that of a trans-
vestite, her supposedly irresistible allure was a pure simulacrum, a
wholly stylised fabrication, female sexuality as reflected in a funfair
mirror.

Yet it really did not matter all that much, since she patently understood that the subtlest of the body's erogenous zones is the head; for
Madonna, by contrast, the head would seem to be not much more
than something to prop up the face, to hold it in position. Thus,
while Madonna has had recourse to ever more frantically extreme
measures to preserve her trademark aura of sexual liberty (turning
her naked body practically inside out, jingling her metallically plated
breasts at the camera the way one might jingle a pocketful of small
change), Mae West, who had the wit to realise that sex is the short-
est distance between the sublime and the ridiculous, achieved precisely the same effect with no more than a flutter of false eyelashes
and a well-timed *mot*. ('It's the story of a girl who lost her reputation

and never missed it.' 'When a woman goes wrong men go right after her.' 'Between two evils I always pick the one I haven't tried before.')

And there, if you like, is the essential difference between them. Madonna has a sexy body – and, in fifty years or so, when her fame will almost certainly have evaporated, that body, as displayed in yellowing second-hand copies of *Sex*, will have become just a body, just another body, anybody's body. Mae West, on the other hand, had a sexy brain.

A late aunt of mine, it used to be said in the family, looked just like Ingrid Bergman. Which was true, except that the resemblance was not mutual: Ingrid Bergman looked nothing at all like my late aunt. Similarly, if Madonna reminds me of Mae West, Mae West does not in the least remind me of Madonna. If she reminds me of anyone, it is of Oscar Wilde. Where else, after all, save in snapshots of Wilde, have I seen that odalisque's languor, that matelot's rolling gait, that corseting and that rouge? West's wisecracks are to Wilde's epigrams what a wad of chewing gum is to an iridescent soap bubble. If the *deus ex machina* of Wilde's disgrace was the odious Marquis of Queensberry, the Queensberry of boxing's Queensberry Rules, it was Will Hays of the notorious Hays Code who presided over West's tragicomic comeuppance. And if genius, finally, is probably not what she would have had to declare to a customs officer, the basic structure of Wilde's celebrated riposte would not have needed much in the way of alteration.

Happy birthday, Mae.

Notes

1 I do not know whether Jackson is guilty or not of child molestation, but his astonishing appearance – like that of a creature from some fabulous bestiary or from an illustration to Mario Praz's *The Romantic Agony* – would certainly provide an ingenious alibi, a 'front', for almost any criminal perversion.

2 This essay was originally published in 1993.

3 The same conjecture might be made about a sixty-year-old Michael Jackson. What in heaven's name will *that* look like?

On ordinariness

The Americans, it would seem, are currently indulging in their inter-mittent but immemorial national pastime of 'Brit-bashing', thereby placing us 'Brits' in the designated role of the 'queers' or 'Pakis' (heretofore almost the sole repositories of such concerted 'bashing') of the ebbing 'special relationship'.

Forgive this excessive rash of inverted commas (excessive even for me), which I would justify by the fact that what is at issue are con-notations, not denotations, mythic values rather than real ones. The Americans in question appear to be confined to a few prominent East Coast journalists (the *New York Times*'s William Safire, the edi-tors of *Time* and *Spy* magazines), along with the odd, haphazardly interviewed tourist in the street. As for the Brits under scrutiny, they have been culled, as ever, from the two outermost extremes of our demographic constitution, lager louts and the Royal Family, yobs and nobs, as though there were nothing in between.

It is, though, precisely what *is* in between that concerns me here; and, in at least one aspect of this latest assault on our national sen-sitivities, I detect a first faint hint that the penny may finally have dropped elsewhere. For the purposes of its 'Brit-bashing' issue *Spy* concocted an only partially caricatural representative of contempo-rary British society, one Johnny Applegate, described as living in a dreary bedsit in Hackney. Now I believe it true to say that, for many of us, the name of virtually any district of New York, no matter how uncherished by that city's own inhabitants, has an irreducibly exotic ring to it – Brooklyn Heights, Columbus Circle, SoHo, the Battery, the Bronx, etc. I believe it true to say, too, that most of us have always imagined that such a phenomenon is reversible and that there must therefore be something exotic for Americans in a name like Clapham or Camden or Soho or indeed Hackney.[1] Hackney, the real Hackney, the Hackney of snug, smug terraced houses, of laundrettes and takeaways, of pavements littered with junk food wrappers and streets eternally strung out with traffic cones like so many dunces' caps, *that* Hackney (or Clapham or Camden or wherever) was, we were convinced, *our secret*. Let the Americans rant on about Diana and Fergie, about punks and hooligans, about losing an empire, not finding a role and is there honey still for tea; just so long as they never discover the real truth, the awful truth, about Britain – its indelible, apparently incurable *ordinariness*. Well, from the evidence of the article in *Spy*, they have.

Is there any other country in the world which so creaks under the dead weight of the ordinary, the humdrum, the norm? Is there any other country which is so parodically ordinary that its very place-names have become jokes? Is there a French Romford? An American Neasden? An Algerian Wigan? A Japanese Balham? ('Balham, gateway to the South!', as Peter Sellers once rhapsodised in a cod-travelogue.) What is it that, despite the heroic efforts of trendy magazine editors, whiz kid television producers, record sleeve designers and the like, makes modern Britain so fatally unsleek a country, so strangely 'provincial' in the global scheme of things?[2]

Obviously, being neither a historian nor a sociologist, I can do no more than speculate on the sociohistorical precedences which have brought us to where we are at present. And my own subjective (and, as I myself would admit, crudely determinist) hunch is that our native ordinariness can ultimately be traced to the fact of Britain's geographical location in Europe – not quite north enough to be 'northern' nor quite south enough to be 'southern', but an ill-defined somewhere in between. Certainly, this would help to explain why, although exquisite British faces do indeed exist, our national physiognomy, when seen *en masse*, tends to be dispiritingly unprepossessing, as bereft of the honeyed blondness of Scandinavians as of the olivy smoothness of Latins: it was Truffaut who cited the uninspiring quality of the British face as one of (several) reasons why, for him, every British film was a born loser.[3] It might explain, too, given the country's notoriously variable climate, why British pleasure-taking often strikes one as such a melancholy affair (our food, our clothes, our resorts, our beaches, our sport, our famous warm beer) and why the British landscape, when divested of its artistico-literary mystique, is, who can deny it, less beautiful, less spectacular and less untamed than that of practically any other country we know?

Whatever its source, the fact remains that, in a cultural context, there can be sensed an increasing estrangement from the national environment, from its mythologies and iconographies. I think of the nasal cod-American twang now routinely assumed by rock singers and radio disc-jockeys. I think of the struggle of British filmmakers to transform London into a gleaming, cosmopolitan metropolis, one utterly unrecognisable to those of us who live in it. I think, above all, of the endeavours of a whole generation of young or youngish British novelists to *transatlanticise* the experience about which they are condemned to write, novelists who are clearly more at ease alluding to 'K-Mart', let us say, than to the nerdishly British 'Tesco', novelists for whom there exists a whole new U and non-U syndrome: one feels them positively chafing with frustration at having to write *favourite* instead of *favorite* and *behaviour* instead of *behavior*.

There is, to be sure, an obvious answer to these charges, which is that the glory of Britain has always resided precisely in its moderation: no revolutions, no tidal waves, not too much of this, not too much of that and not too much of the other. What I would counter-propose, however, is that moderation in everything is *moderation to excess* and that what our country badly needs is, for once, a little real excess. Excess in moderation, of course.

Notes

1 The exotic potential of English place-names is immeasurably intensified if one transposes them into a foreign language, as in this (slightly truncated) sentence from a novella, *La Nuit de Putney*, by the French chronicler of *les années folles*, Paul Morand: 'Nous laissâmes à notre droite Putney Common et son gazon usé par les matches de cricket du samedi et que les moteurs dévissés avaient souillé d'huile.'

2 It is an odd fact that the word 'provincial' is never used with reference to the United States. Neither Detroit nor Philadelphia has ever been called a 'provincial city'.

3 More modestly, Stephen Frears once claimed that what made it hard to shoot a convincing thriller in Britain was the silly shape of policemen's helmets.

On set-pieces

I sometimes experience a frisson on seeing the word 'famous' in print. Not, I should make clear, when it is used to describe a celebrity, in which case it tends to be either pointlessly tautological or else paradoxically self-negating. (If someone has to be referred to as 'the famous yachtsman' or 'the famous cricketer', it can only mean that he is not quite famous enough to dispense with the label.) It occurs, rather, when, reading a record's sleeve notes, I chance upon a reference to 'the famous melody in the second movement' of some symphony or other. In this latter sense, I take the word to mean 'on listening to the melody, you will instantly recognise why it has become famous', and the frisson I allude to is generated all over again when, during the said second movement, I hear the opening bars of a tune which already strikes me as unforgettable even though I may never have encountered it before, a tune which I know beyond any possible doubt to be 'the famous melody'.

It is a sensation which is induced not by music alone. Several years ago, I finally caught up with a film which I had for long, forlornly, longed to see, Hitchcock's *Young and Innocent*, primarily because of how often I had read of its 'famous tracking shot'. Since there were, as I knew, many brilliant tracking shots in Hitchcock's work, what, I wondered, was specifically 'famous' about this one? Well, in spite of a number of false alarms along the way, when I would systematically imagine that each of the film's tracking shots must be 'the one', I knew it when I saw it. Frustratingly, it makes its appearance when the narrative has almost run its course and when, having tracked the murderer (whose sole identifying feature is a nervous twitch in one eye) to a seaside resort, the *ingénu* and *ingénue* stand, uncertain what to do next, on the threshold of a hotel ballroom in which a chintzy *thé dansant* is taking place. Suddenly, detaching itself from them, Hitchcock's camera starts to traverse the entire room until, like a Patriot missile, it zeroes in on a single member of the hotel's blackface minstrel band, the drummer, whose eye, at that point, and only at that point, begins uncontrollably to twitch.

The scene is, I suppose, what is usually called a set-piece or a *morceau de bravoure* or a *morceau d'anthologie* (or even perhaps, given the metaphysical overtones that certain French critics have claimed to detect in Hitchcock's films, a *morceau d'ontologie*), of which Hitch was one of the supreme cinematic masters: e. g. the Dalinian dream sequence of *Spellbound*, the fairground climax of *Strangers on a Train*, the plane dusting crops where 'there ain't no crops' of *North by Northwest*, the shower murder of *Psycho*, to list but a handful of the best known.

It was, moreover, a subsequent set-piece, one that did not quite come off, which signalled the ultimate decline of Hitchcock's imaginative powers. In his very last film, *Family Plot*, an aimless, amiable comedy thriller, there is a scene in which a bishop is kidnapped, in full view of a bizarrely passive congregation, while conducting High Mass. The conceit is superb: that it does not work, alas, in the strictly filmic terms by which Hitchcock always insisted on being judged, is confirmed by the scene directly succeeding it, a scene in which, when he enquires why no one in the congregation reacted, the puzzled detective is informed that the solemnity of a cathedral Mass would have had the effect of precluding any too precipitous act on the part of the faithful, no matter that a crime was being committed before their very eyes. He is, as I say, 'informed'. The set-piece was an archetypically Hitchcockian one, except that its ingenuity had to be spelt out in dialogue, whereas *North by Northwest*'s crop-dusting scene communicated *its* ingenuity by uniquely visual means.

For the youthful French critics and directors-to-be of the fifties who reinvented him – most notably, Truffaut, Rohmer and Chabrol – Hitchcock was exactly what Edgar Allan Poe had been for his French poet-translators, Baudelaire, Mallarmé and Valéry, a century before: a visionary artist whose imagination was so rich and strange it had a cathartic effect on an artistic tradition that ostensibly could not have been further from it. For Anglo-Saxons, by contrast, he has remained the 'Master of Suspense', his influence enormous but superficial. Apart from a slavish (and feeble) imitator like De Palma, mention might be made of the seminal impact of *Psycho* on the whole contemporary horror genre as also on *Fatal Attraction* and *Basic Instinct*; of *Suspicion* and *Notorious* on such erotic thrillers as *Someone to Watch Over Me* and *Sea of Love*; of *North by Northwest* on *In the Line of Fire* and *The Fugitive*. Yet what is missing from all of these latter films, and from the current American cinema in general, is that absolutely crucial component of the set-piece, of the 'famous' scene, an *idea*.

The thriller, Hitchcock's own chosen genre, is ubiquitous these days; and Hollywood, with the stupendous means at its disposal, regularly manages to come up with ever more macabre killings, ever more extended chases, ever more spectacular orgies of mass destruction. But that is both the point and problem. More, more, more – the principal is that of inflation, inflation for its own sake, inflation deliberately designed to camouflage the absence of any real invention. In one scene of *The Fugitive*, for example, Harrison Ford, attempting to elude his pursuers, finds himself caught up in a noisy, colourful St Patrick's Day march in Chicago. One thinks, inevitably, of Hitchcock and of what he could have done with such material. All that happens in *The Fugitive*, though, is that, for about a minute, Ford weaves in and out of the fancy-dress revellers, then sneaks out of sight. That's it. End of scene. For all that it mildly engages the attention, no one is ever going to reminisce about 'the famous St Patrick's Day scene'.

Appearances to the contrary, American films are considerably more primitive now than when Hitchcock himself was alive. I would suggest, indeed, that they have actually regressed to that pre-idea, turn-of-the-century, Nickelodeon period when the filmgoer's choice was essentially between *The Great Train Robbery* (alias *The Fugitive*, *In the Line of Fire*) and *What the Butler Saw* (alias *Basic Instinct*, *Sliver*). And, given the triumph of *Jurassic Park*, it is worth recalling, too, that the first ever film made for children was a 1909 cartoon by Winsor McCay titled *Gertie the Dinosaur*.

On stereotypes

Initially I had quite a problem with David Mamet's play *Oleanna*. My problem was that, if he was not the most appetising of characters, the college professor protagonist (played in the London production by David Suchet) had nevertheless been lavishly endowed with 'life' – which is to say, with all the psychological attributes of standard theatrical humanity – whereas the disturbed young student (Lia Williams) who is responsible for his second-act comeuppance struck me as less an autonomous personality in her own right than the pure objectification of male professorial anxieties, an Identikit portrait of political correctness in its most terroristic guise.

After seeing the play I was prompted to think again by two revelations, one of them public, the other entirely personal. First, the apparent fact that a fair proportion of Mamet's audience (exclusively its women?) regarded the student as something of a heroine and the play's nightmarish development as a vindication of their own views. Second, the definite fact that, on a trip to France just two weeks after *Oleanna* opened in London, I met her. I met Mamet's character. She was not, as it happens, a student but a professor, a hellish Hellenist who taught in some obscure Californian university. During the first act (as I could not help thinking of it) of our encounter around a dinner-table in Paris, she was blandly, articulately amiable. By the second act, though, the likeness had become uncanny, simply hallucinatory, the discourse almost verbatim, the air about her just as unbreathable.

Oddly enough, the basic premise of her argument, that 'political correctness' (her quotation marks) was essentially a ploy by the Right to trivialise, undermine and ultimately discredit the Left's current agenda, and that most of the more ridiculous euphemisms circulating in its name had never been employed outside of a debunking right-wing context, was one with which I more or less concurred.[1] Where the conversation took a truly vicious turn was in her utter refusal to concede that free speech and thought had *ever*, for whatever motivation, been stifled by the Left, to concede that there had *ever* existed what, to her teeth-gnashing chagrin, I referred to as left-wing fundamentalism. When I brought to her attention a case of PC harassment of which I was personally aware (a friend of mine, a lesbian academic in New York, was ordered by something called a Gay Student Council to be more overtly homosexual in her teachings – or else), her answer was that my friend was undoubtedly paranoid. And so it continued. I had assumed, as one does, that I was knocking on a door, but the door turned out to be a wall.

Since Mamet seemed to have caught the type perfectly, my opinion of his play was at once upwardly revised. But then I thought to ask myself another question: was my encounter with this woman an argument or just an anecdote? By which I mean, did the existence of this one person justify Mamet's ferocity (as I saw it, but there were those, I repeat, who interpreted his play very differently)? After all, considering that it takes all kinds to make a world, there must live, somewhere on the planet, at least one individual who conforms absolutely to the anti-Semitic stereotype of the sly, usurious, hook-nosed Jew. If I had happened to have dinner with him, would I then have been willing to condone Céline's repulsive anti-Semitic pamphlets and the infamous Nazi film version of *Jew Suss*? Or what about homosexuals, whose case is only slightly less clear-cut? Do gays, and particularly gay actors, writers and filmmakers, have a monopoly of gay stereotypes, just as, so we all believe, only blacks have the right to use the word 'nigger' about themselves? Does the existence of flamboyant, campy and effeminate gay men – an existence which, as distinct from that of stereotypical 'Jews', cannot be dismissed as merely conjectural – mean that any such portrayal of a homosexual in a film or play may be excused as reflecting at least a partial reality? Or, to turn the argument upside-down, does the presence of one flamboyant homosexual in a film *necessarily* mean that its director and writer suppose such a characterisation to be true of all homosexuals? If not, and short of their covering themselves with a credit-title disclaimer, is there any way the distinction can be made? And am I myself pandering to a crude negative stereotype by placing a woman, a militant feminist to boot, at the centre of my own personal tale of political correctness, even though that is what she was?

These are all awkward questions, questions of representation, generalisation and extrapolation, to which no answers are immediately forthcoming. Nor does skirting them altogether offer more than a short-term solution to the contemporary artist. If, feeling inhibited by the pressures of positive discrimination, a straight, white, male filmmaker chooses to focus exclusively on his own kind, he is still likely to come under fire – for portraying no women, blacks or gays in his films.

Notwithstanding all the journalistic fuss and ado about political correctness, the real debate has yet to get going. As no more than a tentative start, I offer the following proposition: that works of art, works of fiction, which is all I am concerned with here, are possessed of their own values, codes and practices, and that it is therefore in those that a solution should be sought. To the question, therefore, of whether an artist has the right to project a negative image of Jewishness, I would reply that the stereotype I describe above is as much a cliché as it is a libel, an offence to art as much as to humanity, and that any artist who has recourse to it is not only a moral idiot but a hack. On the other hand, a Jew portrayed negatively, even very negatively, but in a manner *that is not a cliché*, not an anti-Semitic stereotype, is surely now possible in a work of art without arousing the wrath of the Jewish community. (Why the character has to be Jewish at all is another matter, of course, but it is not difficult to think of various legitimate reasons.)

In this context, then, as perhaps equally in others, stereotypes must be avoided not merely because they are dangerous but because they are hackneyed.

Notes

1 The best test of these euphemisms is one of efficacy. Hence, if the term 'crippled' has effectively been replaced by 'disabled', it is because the later word, although certainly less blunt, is no less straightforward than its predecessor. It is unthinkable, by contrast, that a phrase like 'vertically challenged' will ever trip easily off anyone's tongue, so that attempts to impose it, if they genuinely do exist, are foredoomed to failure.

On actors

A funny thing happened to me in the theatre, at the first night of Pinter's *Moonlight*. An hour into the play, during a scene with Ian Holm, Anna Massey and Edward de Souza, I suddenly realised that I had not the faintest idea what the actors were doing. I do not mean to imply that their performances were in any way poor or unfocused. Quite the contrary. It was, instead, as though I had been staring at them for so long (the theatre is the only place in the world where it is regarded as impolite *not* to stare) that, collectively, they had started to resemble the sort of word, a word as elementary as 'word' or as rarefied as 'rarefied', which, when peered at for any length of time, dissolves into a meaningless configuration of squiggles.

It was as though I had to learn all over again what acting was; as though this inexplicable lapse of mine were alerting me to the fact that, while I understand perfectly well what writers do (I ought to, being one myself), and am able to transfer that understanding to the diverse if arguably kindred practices of directing and composing and painting, I have never really known what it is that actors do, I have never really grasped the precise nature of the internalising process which enables them to arrive at that organically convergent cluster of external effects that we call a performance. Although, mercifully for me, my aberration, my little epiphany of disorientation, lasted no more than a few seconds, I found myself asking afterwards, for the first time in my life, a few rudimentary questions relative to the art of acting (questions which may well be addressed and answered in the writings of the great theorists of that art, Diderot, Stanislavski and Artaud, none of which, to my shame, I have ever read).

The most elementary of my questions is this: Who does an actor 'think he is' when he is standing on a stage? Himself? The character he is playing? Or an inextricably interfused combination of both?[1] When, in *Moonlight*, Ian Holm turns to address Anna Massey, is it

'Anna Massey' whom he sees or is it 'his wife' (her role in the play)? If it is not the latter, how does he manage – how do they both manage – to keep a straight face? Might it be claimed that actors are under hypnosis – hypnotised by the director, hypnotised by the text, hypnotised, paradoxically, *while still conscious*? And why, finally, when they talk about their 'craft', is it so often a calamity?

That last question is the only one I, a non-actor, a layman, would dare to try to answer. For it seems to me that, for an actor, talking about acting must be like, for the rest of us, articulating two experiences which, however intensely and ecstatically experienced by the speaker, generally meet with incredulity and indifference from the listener – sex and dreams.

Sex, first. It is possible – offensive, even libellous, but nevertheless possible – to compare actors to prostitutes. Like prostitutes, after all, actors have to put not only their minds but their bodies on the line, which may be at least part of the reason for their notorious vanity and insecurity. (To criticise an actor for a performance is not at all equivalent to criticising a writer for a single text, since the criticism calls his whole being, physical and mental, into question, rather than just one facet of it.) Like prostitutes, actors are paid to flesh out the fantasies of others, fantasies which may well be, and increasingly are, sexual in nature. (More than ever these days, they are required to take their clothes off on stage or in film.) And, like prostitutes, actors retain scant personal control over the final *mise-en-scène* of those fantasies. Indeed, despite the fact that actors are almost never as bad as the writers and directors with whom they collaborate – *if certain films were as badly acted as they are written and directed, they would be simply unreleasable* – they have remarkably little influence over their own professional destinies.

Dreams, now. There is a wonderful scene in Buñuel's *Le Charme discret de la bourgeoisie* in which virtually all the main characters, seated around one of the several smart dinner-tables of that droll chronicle of interrupted meals, are startled by the raising of a red curtain behind them to reveal an auditorium full of rows and rows of expectantly upturned faces. They are on a stage in front of an audience. Panic. Paralysis. Then cut – to one of the characters sitting up in bed, drenched in sweat. He has been dreaming. He has had a dream with which many of us are familiar, a dream not unlike the classic nightmare of finding oneself naked in a public place. And if we are honest, if we conjure up a mental picture of our own physical presence on a theatrical stage in the middle of a performance, that surely is what such a fantasy represents for most of us – a bad dream, a nightmare, a scaffold, a pirate ship's plank, the Raft of the Medusa.[2]

So how can we be expected to understand actors, understand individuals who actually *long* to mount that scaffold, to walk that plank, to be marooned on that raft, night after night after night? How can they hope to communicate to us what it is that motivates them? For all their own insufferable gush about how different they are from us poor commoners, they truly are, they truly must be, a race apart.

I like the race of actors. It has given me much pleasure over the years and probably disappointed me less than that of any other species of artist. Yet, as Nabokov once said of St Petersburg, a city he loved, *there is something wrong with it*. And, at the risk of indulging in pop psychology, I sometimes wonder if what actors seek from drama is not exactly what the rest of us do, only much more intensely – an evasion out of their own lives. I wonder, in short, if what we call 'escapist' films and plays are not only escapist for the audiences which watch them but also, and possibly above all, for the actors who appear in them.

Notes

1 I myself acted once; more precisely, twice, in a couple of French films, one of them, Hugo Santiago's *Ecoute voir . . .*, starring Catherine Deneuve, the other, Edgardo Cozarinsky's *Les Apprentis sorcier*s, starring Marie-France Pisier. I was awful in both of them, mostly because I could not stop thinking: 'I'm acting.'

2 It is the fears of just such a nightmare that are played on by Barry Humphries when, as Edna Everage, he/she lures members of a theatre audience up on to the stage.

On avant-gardism

On 10 October 1993, I wrote the very last word (for the record, it was the word 'conclusion') of a literary folly with which I had been living on and off (fairly substantial periods off) for all of four years: an English translation of Georges Perec's metaphysical whodunit *La Disparition*.

I had briefly, if unseriously, toyed with the notion of naming it *All About E*, as the peculiarity of *La Disparition* is that there is not a single 'e' in the text, an omission which has, as you might imagine, the effect of making the reader infinitely more conscious of that letter than if it had been sprinkled evenly across its three hundred pages. Finally, though, I hit upon *A Void*, which is both a loose paraphrase of Perec's original ('The Disappearance', unusable in English for obvious reasons) and a declaration of his book's intentions. For Perec's novel is what is called a lipogram, a text which dispenses with one or more letters of the alphabet. And although by no means the first such experiment, it is certainly the lengthiest and most ambitious.

When I was asked, as I frequently was during those four years, what in heaven's name the point was of such a demented exercise, I had two stock answers.

One, that it had been Perec's belief that contemporary literature was *trammelled by its own freedom*, trammelled by the absence of those inhibitions and constraints (from the Aristotelian unities to the sonnet form) which, in past centuries, had been vital to the shaping and sculpting of a writer's personal expression; and that, since there no longer existed any such formal orthodoxies, it had become the writer's duty to invent them.[1] So, apart from *La Disparition*, he also published a collection of poems, *Alphabets*, composed in more or less strict accordance with the principles of Schoenbergian serialism, as well as a palindrome running to five thousand (repeat, *five thousand* words.

Two, that because the French pronunciation of the letter 'e' is indistinguishable from that of the word 'eux', meaning 'they' or 'them', and because the Jewish Perec lost his mother in Auschwitz and was ever after haunted by her martyrdom, it could be argued that what has allegorically disappeared from his book is 'they', the doomed Jews of the Holocaust, as though the Hitlerian Final Solution constituted a monstrous attempt to eradicate a letter from the human alphabet.[2]

These, as I say, were my public responses to the head-shakings of disbelief and even pity which I received over the four years of the book's gestation. As *La Disparition*'s translator, however, as someone who knows it better than any other individual on earth (the more so as it is a text which, uniquely, prohibits its translator from nodding for a single instant, lest a 'the' slip past, or a 'he', or a 'they', or a 'one', or any regular past tense ending in 'ed', all of whose French equivalents Perec himself was allowed to employ), I have since found another justification for having embarked upon such an adventure. Despite all the little jokes I devised as a means of preserving my sanity – jokes about saving up my unused 'e's and, when the translation was done, screaming 'Eeeeeeeeeeeeeeh!' in relief – what I was actually astonished to discover, once I had got into my stride, was *just how easy it is to get by without them.*

Towards the end of his life, when he was beginning to lose his teeth, his hair, his eyesight and his memory, the poet Paul Claudel remarked on how unexpectedly little he missed them. That was, if in quite a different register, exactly my own experience with the 'e's of Perec's novel. As time passed, and the translation advanced, the English of *A Void*, stilted and stylised as it, shall we say, unavoidably was, turned out to be a language like any other, possessing its own semantic principles and, I trust, its own potential for beauty. By the last hundred pages, indeed, I had become so adept at manipulating that language that, whenever I had to follow an extended bout of translation with the composition of a journalistic article, the article would, I am convinced, contain far fewer than its normal quota of 'e's. In addition, my growing accommodation to the quirks and quiddities of 'e'-less English would lead me, in my own mind, to the belated acceptance of what I had always imagined to be one of the more misguided coinages of political correctness. At the outset, the language I had to contend with seemed to me frankly 'crippled', as though, in losing all its 'e's, it had lost several seriously major limbs. Then, as I started to feel more comfortable with its warped angularities, I became inclined to regard it less as 'crippled' than as 'disabled', diminished by its loss of limbs, to be sure, but still capable of living, as we say of the disabled, a rich and full life. Then, finally, it struck me that the only proper term for it was the PC (or cod-PC) 'differently abled', in that, although there were things such a language simply could not do, it had gained all sorts of other marvellous capacities to which access was barred to any normally constituted 'e'-ful English.

On the whole, the British literary establishment is indifferent, when not downright hostile, to novels of formal experimentation: commissioning a traditionalist critic to review an avant-gardist fiction would be like commissioning a bull to review a red rag. Yet the English language can lay claim to a few of the greatest ever written, *Tristram Shandy*, *Ulysses*, Lewis Carroll's two *Alice* tales and Nabokov's *Pale Fire*. Some of the more interesting modern European or American novels, moreover, belong in the same category: Calvino's *The Castle of Crossed Destinies* (a novel in the form of a Tarot game) and *If on a Winter's Night a Traveller* (a novel about what it means to read a novel), Milorad Pavic's *Dictionary of the Khazars* and *Landscape Painted with Tea* (novels in the form, respectively, of a dictionary and a crossword puzzle), Walter Abish's *Alphabetical Africa* (a novel in alphabetical order), John Fowles's *The French Lieutenant's Woman* (a novel complete with its own critical apparatus), Martin Amis's *Time's Arrow* (a novel in reverse chronology), etc. And having realised, as I say, that one can write as well (if differently) without the letter 'e' as with it, having realised, too, that conventional, linear, 'e'-replete fiction is just that, a convention like any other, although certainly very much more tenacious than any other, I can see no good reason why the titles cited above should fill an average reader with terror. A novel in the form of a crossword puzzle? Why not? Didn't Lewis Carroll write a still popular classic in the form of a chess game?

It is all a little like sex. What else is the reader and the book but the beast with two backs? And most of us would admit, would we not, to a taste – even, eventually, in a long-term relationship, to an absolute need – for sexual experimentation. Why, then, where fiction is concerned, do we continue to insist that our novelists confine themselves to the missionary position?

Notes

1 It was a belief he shared with his fellow members of OuLiPo, meaning 'Ouvroir de Littérature Potentielle' ('ouvroir' is French for 'workshop'), a group of writers, theorists and mathematicians whose best-known adherents, Perec himself excluded, were Queneau, Calvino, the Paris-based American novelist Harry Mathews and the poet Jacques Roubaud. OuLiPo continues to meet regularly.

2 It should be said that Perec himself never publicly sanctioned the legitimacy of such an interpretation. The concordance of 'e' and 'eux' may therefore, for once, be coincidental.

On Tintin

I remember, during a French tutorial at university, being asked to explicate a short and relatively uneventful scene in *Le Malade imaginaire*, one of Molière's slighter comedies of monomania. Having done my homework, I plunged in. 'When the scene begins,' I said, 'we smile sympathetically at the embarrassment in which . . .' (Here followed a specific textual reference which I have now forgotten.) 'All too soon, however, our sympathy turns to anxiety when we . . . At which point we feel genuine pity for . . . Pity that is immediately replaced by cynicism, even horror, as we realise that . . . Yet underlying all of these reactions is a deep sense of futility . . . Our final impression is of unendurable pessimism, the pessimism of a dramatist who clearly . . .' And so forth.

At the end of this little filibuster my professor stared at me for an instant before speaking. Then he said, 'Well, Gilbert, I believe you've covered every conceivable exit. And I found it all extremely pertinent – except for just one thing.'

'What was that, sir?' I asked brightly.

He screamed at me so loudly I could almost feel my hair, like that of a cartoon-strip character, wafting back in the slipstream of his exasperation.

'You exaggerate!!!'

I tell this story because, no matter how obnoxious I was as an undergraduate, I remain convinced that exaggeration, *controlled exaggeration*, is a crucial component of all criticism with aspirations beyond the prosily pragmatic and programmatic, of all criticism that contrives to *take off* from a work of art instead of merely crawling over its surface like a fly traversing a tabletop. I tell it, too, because I am now about to adopt, in relation to another artist and his work, no less hyperbolic a tone. For I come to celebrate Tintin.

Where Hergé's most celebrated creation is concerned, one is either a Tintinophobe, a Tintinovice, a Tintinophile, a Tintinologist, a

Tintinophage or, once one has attained the ultimate state of enlightenment and beatitude, a Tintinolater. (One can be totally ignorant of Tintin, of course, but, knowing him, not neutral.) As a Tintinolater myself, as someone who has passed in turn through each of the aforementioned stages (including the first: incredible as it strikes me now, I initially found the Belgian school epitomised by Hergé sorely lacking in the energy and crackle of American comic books), I am in wholehearted support of the view expressed by the French philosopher Michel Serres on the occasion of Hergé's death in 1983. The twenty-three Tintin albums, claimed an unflinching Serres, represented a 'chef-d'oeuvre' to which 'the work of *no French novelist* is comparable in importance or greatness'. (My emphasis, as if Serres needed it.) He also compared them – favourably, as it happens – to the Tibetan Book of the Dead. He exaggerates? Very well, he exaggerates. But that exaggeration contains a truth to which no haggling pragmatist could ever have mined his way.

There is much that is deserving of conventional praise in the Tintin albums: the extraordinarily vivid draughtsmanship, its famous *ligne claire* the comic-strip equivalent of some elegantly legible, unshowy prose style; the consistently droll dialogue; the lively nucleus of recurring characters (Captain Haddock, Tintin's bluff and blustering companion-in-arms; Thompson and Thomson, the spoonerising pair of detectives; Bianca Castafiore, the 'Milanese nightingale'); and, of course, Tintin himself, who, with his upswung quiff of hair, his lapel-badge facial features and his baggy plus-fours, is the most convincing and unmawkish personification of moral goodness in the whole of contemporary culture. These qualities would be enough in themselves to make Hergé an authentic artist, however ostensibly 'minor' his chosen medium. Yet his true greatness, the importance to which I believe Serres was referring, resides elsewhere.

Before I discovered Tintin, I had often thought what an intriguing project it might be to write a *mythological* history of the twentieth century – which is to say, a history which, without eschewing factual chronology, would focus primarily on the century's fads, fashions and folk myths, on its scandals and slogans, on its dreams and dance crazes, on all the poetic and platitudinous and sometimes pernicious connotations which have attached to its 'narrative' over the years. Then I discovered Tintin, and I realised that such had been precisely Hergé's achievement.

As though it had been his creator's intention from the very outset of his career to *exhaust* the mythological encrustations of the history which was about to unfold before him, Tintin has, from album to album, confronted such emblematic phenomena of that history as the Russian Revolution, 'darkest Africa' in its lengthy colonial phase, gangsterism in Chicago, the twenties' vogue for Egyptology and the curse of Tutankhamen's tomb, the 'Yellow Peril', banana-republic politicking in Latin America, the Loch Ness monster, the eternally disunited Balkans, the oil-glutted emirates of the Middle East, the hydrogen bomb, lunar exploration (a folk myth before it became a reality), the treasure-laden temples of the Incas, the slave trade, the Yeti (remember the Yeti?), the fifties' obsession with UFOs and, in the sixties, the ascension of the 'guerrilla' as the quintessential politico-cultural hero. This, I should add, is a far from comprehensive list, but it would take a whole book to do justice both to the wealth of Hergé's invention and Tintin's own uncanny capacity, not unlike that of Graham Greene, for being in the right place at the right time.

Hergé was a master of archetypes matched by no contemporary novelist (save Kafka) and very few contemporary filmmakers. The world as he envisaged it, the world of Tintin's globetrotting odyssey, was of a paradigmatic perfection unclouded by ambiguity. It was a world of what might be called, after primary colours, primary animals (lions, tigers, elephants, etc. – nothing as taxonomically *outré* as a vole or a pangolin), a world in which national costumes were worn as casually as jeans and T-shirts, a world in which clocks were always set at the hour, a world, finally, in which the Second World War was somehow invested with the 'legendary' resonances of the Trojan War. It was a world of pure myth, in the sense intended by Cocteau when he defined history as a truth that eventually becomes a lie and myth as a lie that eventually becomes the truth.

Actually, by employing the word 'odyssey' as well as making a passing allusion to the Trojan War, I find I have already tipped my hand. What I am trying to say, in short, is that Hergé was our Homer.

On clichés

What is a cliché? In her very brief, somewhat too brief, Author's Note to *The Methuen Dictionary of Clichés* (which was originally published in the United States under the breezier title of *Have a Nice Day – No Problem!*), Christine Ammer does not trouble to formulate a definition, presumably on the assumption that her readers will know one when they see one. In 'Quiet Days in Cliché', a preface written for the British edition, Frank Muir offers this: a cliché is 'a short expression that by being brilliantly illuminating or perhaps just fun to say is so useful that it becomes over-used'. In my own turn, I would propose the following: a cliché is a type of Chinese whisper whereby a common and frequently repeated idiomatic expression is eventually drained of meaning not by undergoing alteration but by remaining exactly the same.

Dictionaries are unfailing sources of idle diversion, and Ammer's is no exception (if you will pardon my cliché or, as I believe Eric Sykes used to say, my clitch). She has traced the origins and elucidated the meanings of over three thousand hackneyed verbal formulae; and even if it is difficult to imagine for precisely which constituency of reader such a reference work is intended (who, after all, needs or wants to look up a cliché?), she does furnish lots of inoffensive and instantly forgettable amusement for those who enjoy trawling through or just dipping into this sort of book.[1] For reviewers, too, there are enough faintly moot entries in it to query in their reviews. Ammar, for example, attributes the expression *one's name is mud* to British parliamentary idiom of the early nineteenth century, whereas I have always understood it, probably erroneously, to be a corruption of the name, Samuel Mudd, of the luckless doctor who received a life sentence for having ministered to the wounded John Wilkes Booth in the aftermath of his assassination of Lincoln.

Ammer is not dogmatically anti-cliché. 'Clichés are fine,' she insists, 'provided that the user is aware of using them.' There, alas, is the snag. The very first cliché in her dictionary – the aardvark of clichés, so to speak – is *an about face*. Now, I ask you, is that really a cliché? And *to come to blows*? *To run riot*? *To sit tight*? *To run its course*? *To steer clear of*? *To compare notes*, for Heaven's sake? Is there really any point in designating these as clichés? For if they are, then 'Is there really any point in . . .?' is itself a cliché and 'for Heaven's sake' is a cliché and it all risks spiralling out of control. After reading this book, everything I found myself saying began to sound mortifyingly hand-me-down, from 'Have you the time?' to 'Pass the salt, please' and 'What on earth were you thinking of?' and 'It doesn't make the slightest bit of difference'. And it was then I set to pondering whether in fact a single word could be a cliché, a word like 'brilliant', maybe, for a critic or 'brill' for a teenager or 'sincerely' for a politician? Could a unit of punctuation be a cliché, like the three suspension points in 'You mean the murderer is . . .' of the classic English whodunit? Might even silence itself be considered potentially a cliché – silence at least as it has been schematically deployed in certain post-Pinterian plays?

The abyss, as one can see, becomes a bottomless one, from which all light will eventually be extinguished, and it is not to be plumbed by anyone who has to engage with words on a day-in, day-out professional basis. If language did not run on rails for most of its course, communication would be rendered impossible. Ultimately, there exist only two termini to the absolute avoidance of cliché or repetition or second-hand usage: autism and *Finnegans Wake*.

What is most curious and intriguing about clichés, however, is the paradox of perspective to which they give rise. The older they are and the hoarier they sound, then (so one would expect) the more desirable is their avoidance. Yet, bizarrely, it never seems to happen like that. Especially ancient clichés like *a finger in every pie* (apparently traceable to Shakespeare's *Henry VIII*) and *a pig in a poke* (already proverbial by the time John Heywood cited it in his collection of commonplaces in 1546) are vivid and rather lovable coinings which have a lot of life in them yet (as does that cliché itself). Ammer also quotes a slew of expressions used by writers as various and distinguished as Milton (*adding fuel to the flame*), Dickens (*apple-pie order*) and Shaw (*ask me no questions, I'll tell you no lies*) which were clichés for several centuries before being pressed into such distinguished service. Still others may be hijacked by caption writers or film reviewers and accorded a whole new, albeit parodic, lease of life: e. g. *a prostitute with a heart of gold* could well be paraphrased, should occasion arise, as 'a prostitute with a heart of guilt'.

Surprisingly, it is *new* clichés which tend to prove the most grating and intractable. It is new clichés which lovers of the language avoid, yes, like the plague – such horrors of the eighties and nineties as *a knock-on effect* and *the bottom line* and *at this point in time* and that particular bane of freelance writers, *like yesterday*, as in:

'When do you want me to deliver this essay on clichés?'

'Like yesterday.'

Notes

1 On occasion, alas, Ammer flies perilously close to dry-as-dust pedantry. On *to wear a long face* she writes: 'It no doubt came from the elongated look resulting from the mouth being drawn down at the corners and the eyes downcast.' No doubt about it at all, I would say.

On video

Once, on a lazy summer afternoon, I read (if 'read' is the word for it) one of those bizarre books written for adolescents, usually in a sword-and-sorcery mode, which offer the reader what might be described as multiple-choice fiction. 'If you wish to venture into the lair of the Great White Serpent,' I was advised, 'go at once to page 46. If, however, you prefer to engage in mortal combat with the Black Knight, turn to page 51.' It was sort of fun in a daffy way and so intriguing a test of the potentialities of classic narrative I began to wonder whether the principle might also be adaptable to the domain of proper literature. Proust, for example. 'If you wish to attend the Guermantes' *soirée*, go at once to page 645. If, however, you prefer to spend the night in a male brothel with the Baron de Charlus . . .' And it suddenly struck me that such a facility does exist, if not with literature, then with film. This facility is video.

Much is currently made of technological interactivity, of the (eternally imminent, eternally deferred) possibility of not just watching television but 'interfacing' with it, choosing the programmes we ourselves wish to have screened and even influencing their *dénouements*. Yet, with the increasingly widespread use of television as an adjunct to video rather than vice versa, interactivity is already a reality. Even if the sole, timid liberty taken by most owners of video recorders is that of watching a programme when *they* please and not when the programmers dictate, there exists a whole range of diverting and instructive little experiments to be performed.

I recall watching a video of *Bringing Up Baby*, Howard Hawks's celebrated screwball comedy with Katharine Hepburn and Cary Grant. During one scene in which Grant, playing a gawky, bespectacled palaeontologist, is followed along a hotel corridor, unbeknown to him, by the Baby of the film's title, an unhousebroken leopard, my telephone rang. Pressing the pause button on my remote-control unit, I went to answer it. A few minutes later, I returned to the television set and glanced at the still frozen image – to my stupefaction, no leopard! There was the hotel corridor, there was Cary Grant, arrested in a quintessentially Cary Grant posture, but Baby had disappeared.

As I stared uncomprehendingly at the screen, the image abruptly reactivated itself. Lo and behold, as in Sam Loyd's famous missing Chinaman puzzle, there was the leopard again. And it was then I realised that, back in 1938, when *Bringing Up Baby* was made, two quite separate strands of film had been spliced together to create the illusion that a major Hollywood star was sharing the same space as a dangerous carnivorous beast, an illusion whose mechanics can only be understood if one has access, as does anyone in possession of a fairly sophisticated video recorder, to the original film's frame-by-frame continuity. Since when, I have amused myself by exploring the technology of other, similarly laboratory-processed films, from the stop-motion cinematography of *King Kong* to the special, spatial effects of *2001*.

All kinds of possibilities are opened up once one has discovered the licence of video. I once saw a thriller, *Warning Shot*, whose hero, played by David Janssen, accused of murder, protests that, since he was not carrying a gun at the time of the crime, he could not have committed it. Simply by virtue of video's rewinding capacity, I was able, as with a detective novel, to 'turn back the pages' of the narrative and verify whether he had indeed been armed. Then there is the Vincente Minnelli musical, *Meet Me in St Louis*. Film buffs have long debated whether, during Judy Garland's best-known number, 'The Trolley Song', a voice can be heard on the soundtrack, off-screen, presumably from behind the camera, calling out, 'Hi, Judy!' (From such trivia is fanatical cinephilia born.) Well, I can now reveal, with the aid of video, that the legend is, for what it's worth, authentic. Or consider another musical, *Gold Diggers of 1935*, which contains one of Busby Berkeley's kaleidoscopic routines, 'The Words Are in My Heart', constructed around the typically Berkeleyan conceit of revolving grand pianos. If one freeze-frames the video image during this scene and peers closely at the television screen, one will see something that apparently no one ever noticed in a cinema auditorium. Beneath each piano, clad in a black masking body sock, crouches a little man (probably a midget) responsible for its rotation. Once seen, these little men become naturally impossible to ignore – yet no one ever saw them before.

That last example illustrates the strangest paradox of video and, more generally, of the much-maligned televisual reproduction of feature films. One sees *less* of these films, to be sure – not just less of the original cinematic image (often trimmed for television and, in the case of wide-screen formats, drastically 'panned and scanned') but less of the information that it was designed to convey (through the far weaker definition obtainable on video) – yet, on another level, one actually ends up seeing *more*. For it is only since I started watching films regularly on video that I have been made aware of mismatching cuts (when eyelines fail to coincide from shot to shot), of ugly and patently unpremeditated cutaways in the middle of dialogue exchanges (because the director was forced, for whatever reason, to truncate a scene *in extremis*), of conspicuous continuity flubs (an actress wearing gloves in one shot but not in that which follows, etc.) – been made aware, that is, of all the errors and lapses and fluffed lines and microphone shadows, all the visual 'literals' with which I now learn, to my amazement, that the Hollywood cinema, reputed to be the most technically advanced in the world, has always been riddled.

Is such an awareness a good thing? For the critic and historian, incontrovertibly. For the ordinary spectator, why not? The cinema is not a mystery, not a miracle, and it is perhaps time, now that its centenary is upon us, that it be viewed with eyes unclouded by the bogus 'magic' with which it still affects to enhalo its products. With its huge screen, its Dolby sound system and its engulfing, seance-like obscurity, a modern cinema auditorium tends to be conducive more to awe than to honesty. What the unblinking, domestically scaled-down candour of video offers us, by contrast, is posterity in action.

On portraiture

The celebrated portrait by Titian of young Ranuccio Farnese, now hanging in the National Gallery of Washington, is a painting I have always thought to be one of the most beautiful and mysterious in the world.

That it is or is not beautiful is a claim open to argument; the proposition that it is to any degree mysterious may strike the reader as somewhat mystifying in itself. What, after all, is so very strange about this portrait of a no doubt pampered Italian princeling, a portrait in which the investment of artistic mediation, beyond the manifest fact that it had to be painted in the first place, impresses one as so self-effacing as to have become almost invisible? Even a total philistine would find it difficult to deny that it is a more than competently painted image, to put it mildly, and no one would have the slightest problem 'deciphering it', figuring out 'what it means'.

That is precisely wherein its mystery resides. The placidly handsome Ranuccio communicates to us from across the abyss of four hundred years without the need of interpretation on either the painter's part or our own. With his closely cropped black hair, his candid, liquid eyes and his slightly protruding ears, and without the telltale period details of his doublet and lacy ruff, he might be some ordinary schoolboy living three doors down on one's own street, kitted out in the regulation jeans and Nikes. This is a portrait which does not remember being painted; even when seen 'in the flesh', so to speak, it gives the impression that Titian's brushstrokes, so vividly present to the naked eye in his allegorical tableaux, have simply melted away to leave one with, of the child who is their subject, not so much a reproduction as a regard, serene and self-sufficient. For all the mental adjustment one is obliged to make, it might have been painted yesterday. Yet it was not, and could not have been, painted yesterday. And the question is, why not?

Something queer has happened to the art of representation during the last four hundred years. The common assumption is that, since the invention of photography in the nineteenth century, when it usurped the role of painting as a 'transparent' recording agent of reality, artistic representation has become almost a synonym of stylisation, of formalisation, of the codified refraction and perversion of the objective world. Yet, when you think of it, things have gone very much further than that. Little Ranuccio, of whom Titian's portrait is a perfect likeness (how I know that it is, I could not say, but I do know it nevertheless), is as pretty in oils as he must have been in life. If, by contrast, he were painted today, his portrait would be a good likeness only in the sophistical sense that it would resemble other portraits by the same painter. No self-respecting artist of note would dare to serve him up as limpidly, as *legibly*, as Titian did. He would be erotically sensitised (by Balthus), made biliously fleshy (by Freud), transmuted into a cartoon of himself (by Lichtenstein) or mawkishly prettified (by any one of a hundred fashionable portraitists). His image would become the offspring of a union between the artist and the model – and it would probably 'take after' the former rather more than the latter.

Representation, in fact, as we currently understand the concept, does not so much heighten, stylise or pervert reality as systematically *reverse* its values. What, for example, are the most beautiful things imaginable in life? Let us say: a sunset, a newborn babe, a butterfly, the city of Venice. What, now, are the kitschiest things imaginable in a painting? I would suggest: a sunset, a newborn babe, a butterfly, the city of Venice. Again, what in the popular imagination is the (by now almost parodic) emblem of scenic beauty? The Taj Mahal, undoubtedly. Yet it is unthinkable that any serious contemporary artist would ever consider painting the Taj Mahal – not, at least, without rendering it squalid or sinister or caricatural.

The situation has now reached the stage when, from an aesthetic point of view, for a portrait to be disliked by its own subject is actually a good sign; were he or she to be pleased with it, one would shudder to think what it might be like. (So it is that, when painting one or other of his wives or girlfriends, Picasso had to uglify the poor woman in order to make her portrait beautiful.) And such is the current primacy of the artist's sensibility in the appreciation of a work of art, such the current negligibility of the subject, that, when we look at a statue by Rodin, what we really see is a statue *to* Rodin, a monument to *his* genius, to *his* eminence and ultimately to *his* existence. If we want to know what Balzac, say, truly looked like, we have to turn to some humble, little-known lithographer.

Which is not to say that there no longer exist painters determined to engage (and engage the spectator) directly with the real world. In fact, what originally prompted these musings of mine was the unveiling of an official portrait of John Major, a portrait which is, or aspires to be perceived as, in a direct line from those of Titian. It is, I have to say, a horror, a painting so ugly that the friction set up between its imagery and our eyes can only be compared to that produced between a blackboard and a piece of chalk: our eyes *scrape* the canvas. But it is a horror not only because of the artist's inadequacy (to put it kindly): the very idea that a portrait of John Major, or of any present-day politician, could be some kind of a masterpiece is a complete mind-boggler, beyond the imagining of man. Nor is it a horror only because of its subject-matter. The same criticism could be levelled at portraits of the Princess of Wales.

Diana! Only think what Titian might have made of her, or Velázquez, or Gainsborough, or even Sargent! But, alas, like Ranuccio Farnese, she is just too pretty for a modern artist to come to terms with – I mean the kind of artist for whom *beauty has no need of beauty*, for whom, indeed (as someone, already a long, long time ago, once said, but who? Carlyle? Nietszche? Chesterton?), 'Nothing is beautiful except that which is not.'

On running times

I recently watched, on video, George Stevens's 1959 film version of *The Diary of Anne Frank*, recorded from the American Movie Classics (AMC) television channel by an acquaintance in New York. Although inevitably heartbreaking, it is a mediocre film, based less on the diary itself than on a slick Broadway theatrical adaptation. And, my, does it wear its high-mindedness on its sleeve like a Star of David! In its cast, for example, there is an unexpected absence of big names for what was, after all, a superproduction of sorts (the only player whose name still means something today is Shelley Winters); its black-and-white cinematography is just a tiny bit too self-consciously austere (the more so as, when the film was shot, colour had long since become the norm); and its insistent, irritatingly insinuating sound-track score is bloated by (surely inappropriate?) filchings from Wagner. There is, above all, the question of length. Not only does *The Diary of Anne Frank* last 170 minutes, but it protracts this already exceptional running time with a symphonic 'overture', an intermission (complete with musical interlude) and, during the closing credit titles, a four-minute medley of self-styled 'exit music', all lovingly preserved in the usually lightweight AMC presentation.

These excrescences were not really necessary, since the film's very length could not help but contribute to its 'meaning', altering not just the way in which it was commercially exploited (as an 'event', with at least two fewer screenings a day than would normally be the case) but also that in which it was received, and continues to be received, by the individual spectator (with a perceptible little supplement of respect). And considering the present spate of films with running times of up to three and even four hours (Spike Lee's *Malcolm X*, Jacques Rivette's *La Belle Noiseuse*, Martin Scorsese's *The Age of Innocence*, Chen Kaige's *Farewell, My Concubine*, Robert Altman's *Short Cuts*[1]), I would like to offer a few random reflexions on the phenomenon.

(1) In the first instance, it is worth recalling that the outlandish

running time is almost as old as the cinema itself. D. W. Griffith's *The Birth of a Nation* lasted just under three hours, his *Intolerance* just over, and that in a period, the teens of the century, when the durational norm of a film tended to be barely half what it is now. With Griffith was posited a naïve equation which has held good to this very day: 'longer' equals 'more significant'. When works like Edgar Reitz's *Heimat* and Claude Lanzmann's *Shoah* are excluded, as having been conceived primarily for television, the longest film ever released remains Masaki Kobayashi's *The Human Condition*. Clocking in at around ten hours, it could hardly have had any other title.

(2) In this context, however, the word 'long' is ambiguous, and 'length' should not be confused with 'longness'. What exactly does one mean when one says that a film is long? Unless referring to the kind of objectively long film cited above, one means that it is *slow*. Just as a novel's length might more fairly be judged not by the number of its pages but by the time it takes one to read it, so there are films which are long in startling disproportion to their measurable length.

(3) A long film in this sense already 'feels' long after fifteen minutes.

(4) It would be interesting to study the current bias against slowness in the rhythms of narrative art in general and of the cinema in particular; to examine the widespread prejudice that, where the fast/slow dichotomy is concerned, the former is intrinsically superior. Do we feel that slow films *keep us waiting*?

(5) Adair's First Axiom (unprovable, like all axioms): A film which runs, let us say, three hours and twelve minutes will invariably strike us as almost exactly twelve minutes too long, whereas another film which runs, let us now say, two hours and forty-eight minutes will invariably end about twelve minutes before we expect it to. Such a hypothesis is not, I submit, merely a whimsical fancy on my part but a function of our internal, intuitive sense of time, the same function which prompts us to wake up in the morning a few seconds before the alarm clock actually rings.

(6) The effect of cutting a long film so that it might conform to the standards of orthodox theatrical distribution is frequently, paradoxically, to render it even 'longer' (e. g. Rivette's *Divertimento*, a sluggish two-hour version of his four-hour *La Belle Noiseuse*).

(7) Although most of the conventional genres have lent them-

selves to extended running times – the biblical spectacle (*Ben-Hur*), the western (*Heaven's Gate*), the multigenerational family saga (*Giant*), the war film (*The Longest Day*), the biopic (*JFK*) – there is one which has always defied them: comedy. No less appetising sub-genre exists than epic slapstick (*It's a Mad, Mad, Mad, Mad World*, *1941*, *The Blues Brothers*). Even more than of wit, brevity is the soul of broad knockabout farce.

(8) Strange to say, though, an outstandingly lengthy running time is not in itself incompatible with the concept of narrative brevity or fragmentation. As its title intimated, Altman's *Short Cuts*, which ran three hours, was based not on some roomy *roman-fleuve* but on a collection of short stories by Raymond Carver, stitched together patchwork-fashion by Altman and his screenwriter. For all its virtu-osity, the result was nevertheless akin to reading a year's subscrip-tion to the *New Yorker* at a single go. It loomed over the spectator like a veritable monolith of slightness.

(9) There are long films which are interminable; others which zip by in less than half-an-hour. And what ultimately makes a long film feel long, the question of individual talent aside, is how closely it approximates to *real time* – which is to say, how often in the film it takes as long to carry out an activity as it would in life. The most rad-ical case of filmic time mimicking real time was Chantal Akerman's *Jeanne Dielman, 23 Quai du Commerce, 1080, Bruxelles*, much of whose 225-minute running time was spent by its eponymous protag-onist, played by Delphine Seyrig, performing those household chores that are familiar to most women but are either elided or simply omit-ted on the cinema screen: cooking, dishwashing, bedmaking, etc. To any male spectator complaining that such scenes were excruciatingly tedious and, above all, *too long*, the feminist Akerman would have replied that that was precisely the point.

(10) Adair's Second Axiom (born of, and borne out by, weary experience): Most films are far too long anyway.

Notes

1 These titles, naturally, date the essay. Yet today, as I write this footnote (in the autumn of 1996), the trend has if anything intensified; and it is hard to believe that, as you find yourself reading it, the situation will have significantly changed.

On the Imp of the Integral

I tend at first to be faintly churlish when confronted by advances in domestic technology. Notably, for a variety of sensible reasons, I long resisted purchasing a word processor, a video recorder and a compact disc player: the first, because I had little faith in its value as a 'creative' support for a writer; the second, because I simply could not believe it was going to catch on; the third because I initially, and for many months thereafter, found the bland and conservative classical CD repertoire an unacceptable impoverishment of that of LPs. Now, of course, I can hardly imagine how I ever managed to get by without all three of them, which is where the churlishness comes in.

The word processor, for example. A dream machine, or so it originally impresses one. Then, all too soon, one begins to chafe at how awkward it is to switch from one application to another or how unconscionably long it takes to print out a document. In other words, it needs only a few minor, perfectly tolerable shortcomings for the user to forget how infinitely superior a computer is overall (perhaps especially in those areas of greatest contention) to the equipment which it supplanted. Likewise with the video recorder. Why must it take such a diabolically long time to rewind, I mutter to myself, drumming my fingers in impatience and again conveniently forgetting that, without it, I would almost certainly have missed what I had been recording, a film which I had waited all of twenty years to see but which had been screened on television at 3 p.m. As for compact disc players . . .

Well, no. There, I have to confess, I cannot detect a single disadvantage (save, no doubt, their allegedly inflated retail prices). The sound definition is unequivocally superior to that of vinyl recordings. The discs themselves, with their delightful hint of credit card iridescence, are sexy little artefacts. And, in only fifteen years of existence, the repertoire is already richer by far than that of the LP's entire history.

Take Hyperion, unquestionably one of the most adventurous

record labels in the world, its catalogue boasting, as a *Hi Fi Review* critic put it, 'more desirable recordings than any other I know'. What makes these recordings so desirable is not solely the quality of individual performances, award-winningly high though that often is, but the fact that the policy behind the company's choice of projects is predicated on the (in my opinion, unassailable) assumption that record buyers belong to a completely different breed from that of concertgoers, more stimulated by discovering an unfamiliar work than by wallowing anew in a familiar one and increasingly bitten by the bug of 'completism', increasingly under the spell of what might be called the Imp of the Integral. Thus Hyperion specialises in editions of 'complete works': the lieder of Schubert; the hundred-plus symphonies of Haydn; the jolly, roisterous chamber music of Malcolm Arnold; the symphonies and chamber works of Robert Simpson, a contemporary British composer neglected by all the mainstream record companies; and, most spectacularly, the solo piano music of Liszt, played in its entirety, in a feat of heroic specialisation, by Leslie Howard. These latter CDs encompass an extraordinary range of compositions, from the relatively well known, the Waltzes, Ballades, Legends and Polonaises – to such flamboyant *bizarreries* as the transcriptions of all nine Beethoven symphonies, the pianistic 'reminiscences' of operas by Mozart, Wagner, Weber, Glinka, Tchaikovsky, Donizetti, Bellini and Verdi, the Fantasies on National Songs and Anthems. And, in Howard, they have found a masterful interpreter of Liszt's peculiar brand of morbidly ecstatic virtuosity.

Such a project, however, does not just cater, by virtue of a fetishistic conflation of Lisztomania and listomania, to the collector's obsessive fantasy of plugging every single gap in his idol's oeuvre. What is uniquely interesting about the set is the fact that, when Liszt transcribed for piano the orchestral or operatic works of his fellow composers, it was already in a proselytising spirit, his goal being to disseminate music which in the nineteenth century could not easily be heard in its proper context. Nowadays, precisely because of CD recordings, that same music *has* become widely available. It is, paradoxically, Liszt's paraphrases which are the unheard rarities.

But there is an even more dizzying implication. Given that this is the first time many of the more obscure of Liszt's piano compositions have ever been recorded, it is possible to argue that, when the edition is at last complete (in, it is hoped, the year 2000), no one, not Lisztian scholars (who, in many cases, would heretofore have had to confine their encyclopaedic attentions to printed scores), not non-professional pianists (for Liszt is categorically out of bounds to amateurs), no one at all, I repeat, *since Liszt himself*, will have been in a position to hear so much of his piano music. And even he, conceivably, may not have played every note he ever wrote.

I will go further. We have a tendency to view the posthumous career of an artist as a specifically (and, in Liszt's own case, in view of his penchant for the poet in question, appropriately) Dantean type of afterlife, complete with its Paradiso, its Purgatorio and its Inferno. Yet if, by facilitating the propagation of works that would otherwise have enjoyed far fewer public airings, the advent of the mechanical reproduction of sound has already altered the whole course of musical appreciation, the expanding CD repertoire, salvaging from what must have seemed like definitive obscurity (from, in a word, Hell) a number of marginal but nevertheless beautiful and affecting compositions by both major and minor musicians, constitutes a significant subversion and even negation of the Darwinian process by which we have always imagined that time sifted out the greater from the lesser, the enduring from the ephemeral. One meaning, then, of the pluralist, hyper-relativist postmodern moment that we are all currently living through – allied to the reproductive technology without which that moment could not be sustained – is the gradual dissolution of historical hierarchies and the virtual abolition of a *judgmental* posterity.

On poetry

I should like to add, if I may, a brief postscript to the debate triggered off several years ago by a harmless aside made on television by the playwright David Hare, to the effect that Keats was, objectively, a greater artist than Bob Dylan.

Let us think for a moment about the first of the two artists cited. Why was Keats chosen by Hare?[1] Probably (it was, I repeat, a passing remark) because he seemed a representative figurehead of high culture rigorously uncontaminated by the populist taste to which he has always tended to be set in diametric opposition. Let us, however, look at the choice more closely. Keats was the English Romantic poet *par excellence*; and, in the English cultural psyche, the Romantic poet is the Artist *par excellence*, complete (indeed replete) with all the hackneyed attributes which have traditionally attached to so paradigmatic an image: the squalid garret; the willowy facial beauty; the notion of a gift for poetry as a symptom, almost a *clinical* symptom, of consumption (or vice versa); the premature death. Hence, by endeavouring to confound, or merely hold the line against, the professional levellers and demystifiers of culture – those for whom value judgments have ceased to be an indispensable factor in aesthetic appreciation – with what is essentially a *lowbrow* stereotype of highbrow art, Hare found himself paradoxically deferring to that populist sensibility whose irresistible rise he was concerned to thwart.

Consider now Bob Dylan. At a first, casual glance, the most intelligent response to the debate was that of Julian Barnes, quoted as proposing, Solomonically, that Keats was the better poet, Dylan the better musician, and there was an end to it. Would he, though, have arrived at the same turn of phrase had it been Keats versus, say, Liberace? There, too, it can be stated without fear of contradiction that Keats was the better poet and Liberace the better musician – yet one cannot help wondering how many people, if asked which of the two, Keats or Liberace, was the superior artist, would continue to observe such a scrupulously logical partition of incompatible categories. In effect, with Dylan's name as with Keats's, the dice were loaded. For Bob Dylan is, is he not, an unusually 'noble', 'principled', 'uncorrupted' rock singer, his wispily dishevelled appearance even hinting at that of a nineteenth-century Romantic poet, his very surname that of a celebrated twentieth-century poet. He is scarcely a typical pop icon.

I was not asked for my opinion on the matter; if I had been, I would simply have answered that *of course Keats is better than Bob Dylan!* The very idea that there should be all this solemn huffing and puffing over such a ludicrous question, with various pundits prepared to betray their most intimate convictions lest they miss the latest bandwagon (but bandwagons are like London buses: if you miss one, there'll be another along in a minute), is positively grotesque. And it was, in any event, never the ambition of any serious champion of popular culture to dismantle one canon only to erect another.

For many people, of course, the basic problem is poetry itself. They just don't get it. They haven't read it since they were at school or college. With an odd, and not very conclusive exception (the Liverpool poets, Wendy Cope), poetry would seem to be unwilling to meet a, shall we say, middlebrow sensibility halfway. In a *Private Eye* column, ostensibly a review of *The Forward Book of Poetry 1994*, the columnist, the anonymous 'Bookworm', castigated what he or she referred to as 'that frightful silliness, that sprightly fatuity, that stops almost everybody from reading poetry after adolescence' and offered a lengthy inventory of 'everything awful you remembered about poetry', from 'dreadful poems about being a poet' to 'atrociously forced findings of significance', from 'winsome comparisons' to 'excruciating rhymes', from 'poncey words' to 'preening poeticisms'.

All good clean fun, I daresay, and Bookworm's derisive quotings of chapter and verse, notably from the work of the award-laden Carol Ann Duffy, are plausible enough out of context ('I give you an onion/Its fierce kiss will stay on your lips/possessive and faithful/as we are/for as long as we are'). But are these easy anathemas, echoed by Auberon Waugh's campaign in the *Literary Review* for Real Poetry (as one says, Real Ale), truly all that can and need be said about modern English verse?

Three significant problems, I believe, arise with poetry as a living cultural form, two of them obvious, one less so.

One, the fact that poetry is genuinely untranslatable (by a self-defeating paradox, the only readers properly equipped to judge the quality of a translation are those who are already fluent in the language of the original) means that the lover of poetry, unlike that of fiction or drama or film, is necessarily trapped within the confines of his own culture, and the twentieth century, unfortunately, has not been a vintage one for English (as distinct from American or Irish or Scottish or Welsh, not to mention European) poetry.

Two, the nebulous concept of the 'poetic' has been so thoroughly appropriated by the critical discourses surrounding the other art forms (as in 'a poetic novel' or 'a poetic film' and the like) that the 'real thing', in verse and all, has come to strike many of us as redundant, self-conscious and risibly overdetermined.

Three (and since this particular problem is the most consequential for me, but may not be for the reader, I shall shift gears now to the active tense and the first person singular), I find more and more that, while I am quite content (even at times *relieved*) to read a minor novel or watch a second-rate film or listen to an opera I know is not exactly the best the repertoire can offer, I *cannot* read poetry of less than the absolute first rank. I cannot see the point. I regard it as an utter waste of time, mental effort and nervous energy. If it is not great poetry, it is, for me, not poetry at all.

Notes

1 I am aware, to be sure, that both 'Keats' and 'Dylan' are essentially brand names, pure emblematic values, which can be discarded, all but ignored, once the polemic they have prompted has got into full swing.

On rape

Rape. Rape. Rape. There's no getting around it. 'Rape' is a short, sharp shock of a word. It reverberates like a slap in the face and carries much the same emotive charge as the cluster of four-letter obscenities with which, one imagines, the act it defines is usually accompanied.

I ought to make it clear from the outset, though, that it is the word, not the act, which is the subject of this essay. Since I would never dare to stray into the (literal) no man's land of internecine feminist squabbles, my remarks here are intended to be read as mere marginalia to the debate on rape, date-rape and sexual politics in general that is being conducted on both sides of the Atlantic. And what specifically prompted these remarks was a recent mini-*cause célèbre* in the United States.

At its centre was Catharine MacKinnon, a prominent feminist and anti-pornography campaigner, whose book, *Only Words*, proposed the theory that, where rape is at issue, there was no difference between the thought and the deed. *Only Words* was reviewed in *The Nation*, a journal of irreproachable liberal credentials – its editor is Victor Navasky, the author of *Naming Names*, a classic study of McCarthyism – by the critic Carlin Romero, who elected to express his dissent from MacKinnon's premise in an extended and somewhat convoluted hypothesis. I shall try to summarise it as lucidly as possible.

Believing as he does (or says he does) that he can test MacKinnon's theory of the equivalence of thought and deed only by actually going ahead and raping her, but fearful of the consequences, Romero confines himself to fantasising about raping her and, at the same time, fantasising about writing a violently pornographic review of her book. Then, realising that he has failed to engage with the legitimacy (or not) of her theory by backing off from its ultimate implications, he pretends to sub-assign half of his review to another critic, the transparently pseudonymous 'Dworkin Hentoff', who indeed proceeds to rape MacKinnon before writing his half. (This is all taking place, I repeat, inside Romero's head.) Both Romero and 'Hentoff' are subsequently arrested, whereupon Romero protests that he had only hypothesised raping MacKinnon, thereby demonstrating, as he sees it, the crucial distinction between thinking about rape and committing it.

Mercifully, things now started to accelerate. MacKinnon's response to Romero's semantic jiggery-pokery was predictable enough. The article, she said, deliberately sought to demean and degrade her: it was just another, and outrageously public, species of rape. Romero's rejoinder was equally pithy. 'She's gone from saying pornography is rape to saying book reviewing is rape. Catharine MacKinnon's mind is one long slippery slope.' Navasky backed his reviewer, while the psychoanalyst Jeffrey Masson, who happens to live with MacKinnon, threatened Romero with what certainly sounded like physical violence and the formidable MacKinnon herself alluded unpleasantly to holding him 'accountable' for his offence. Since I found *Only Words* unsalvageable drivel from start to . . . well, to whichever page of the book it was on which I gave up in exasperation, I am a trifle surprised to find myself taking her side, but it does seem to me that in this particular exchange MacKinnon was right. And the reason for that is the faintly sinister power which has been invested in the very word 'rape'.

Words exist which are more than words. Words exist which are also covert acts, which, in the last resort, cannot be contextualised for they will always contrive to transcend their context. 'Rape', for better or worse, is just such a word. It is what grammarians call a 'performative', a word which acts as it defines.

There is a widespread belief that it is only since the current wave of militant feminism that the word 'rape' has been accorded such a status. Not so. In my childhood, it was almost a dirty word, one never to be pronounced in the presence of parents or teachers. When, in a Latin class, I was taught about the rape of the Sabines, the word itself was invariably replaced by such desexualising euphemisms as 'abduction' or 'ravishment'. Even way back then, the offence it described was held apart from other crimes, most notably murder. No one, not even MacKinnon, I trust, would dispute that murder is a more terrible offence than rape; then as now, however, 'rape' was a more offensive term than 'murder'.[1]

Why so? Perhaps because what distinguishes a verbal reference to rape from a comparable reference to murder or any other kind of physical violence is that it calls immediate attention to the victim's genitalia. Say the word 'rape' and you instantly, perhaps no more than subliminally, think of female genital organs. Write the word 'rape' with reference to a specified, identified victim, *even if only a hypothesised victim*, and the reader instantly (and again, perhaps, only subliminally) thinks of her sexual organs.

Which is surely why MacKinnon felt demeaned, degraded, publicly denuded, by Romero's overly sophisticated endeavour to catch her in the mousetrap of what he regarded as her own meretricious sophistry. And it is why I share her belief that his approach to the polemic did represent a form of rape – or, at the very least, if one were to define rape as 'making hate' rather than 'making love', that it exposed, on his part, a personal, *physical* repugnance which ought to have had no place in a serious journal.

It is worth noting, finally, that 'rape' is not the only word that works in this way. Many years ago, arguing a similar point with an acquaintance, I attempted a little experiment. I told my acquaintance I was about to make a statement to him which was absolutely false, which I absolutely did not mean to be taken at face value but which included a word I believed to be so emotive it would prove to be more powerful than its context. I was even prepared to give him advance warning of the word, which was 'loser', and reiterated several times that I was using it *solely to make my point*. Amused, bemused, he nodded agreement. I paused for an instant, then said calmly, 'Michael, you're a loser, a pathetic loser.'

He went white.

Notes

1 Unimaginable would be a version of Cluedo in which one had to figure out who *raped* Miss Scarlet in the library.

On the future

I have this fantasy. I go to bed on the night of 31 December 1999, in a London barely distinguishable from what it is today. Then, on the morning of 1 January, in the year 2000, I wake up, I draw the bedroom blinds up and, hallelujah, what confronts me outside my window is an airy metropolis of globular monorails, tall, thrusting crystal towers and immaculate heliports on which alight sleek, streamlined space-buses. 'Hey, come and see, you guys!' I feel like shouting to a still somnolent world. 'The future's here! It's finally here!'

A fantasy, as I say. Whatever we may once have believed of the future, we know it is not going to happen like that. *That* future, bequeathed to us by umpteen science-fiction novels and films, has proved to be as elusive as a white Christmas. We have already overtaken a handful of its red-letter dates, specifically 1966, the year in which H. G. Wells's *The Shape of Things to Come* is set, and of course 1984;[1] we are, as I write, hurtling towards the once no less mythic 2001; and yet we continue to find ourselves immovably (and, where the dystopian visions of Wells and Orwell are concerned, gratefully) mired in the present. For many of us, the approaching *fin de millénaire* holds fewer and fewer hopes or terrors. With 2000-plus dates already commonplace on mortgage contracts and insurance policies, the millennium is gradually being assimilated into the most humdrum textures of our lives.

What has happened to the future? In part, its manifest failure as a sociocultural ideal stems from the fact that it cannot ever be analysed, only prophesied; equally, from the related fact that the curse of prophecy is that it is self-*un*fulfilling. Prophesy something, in short, *and you make it that much less likely to occur*. Such prognostications, moreover, are usually infected by a covertly prescriptive bias. Prophets have a habit of foretelling the futures they either most desire or most fear, futures either uniformly utopian or dystopian, and they have been markedly less skilful at extrapolating from the more promising and significant co-ordinates of the present. In addition to which, the future is an idea as old as the hills, and its history has been overlaid, like that of many another abstract concept, with a now somewhat mouldy crust of clichés and conventions. A typical premonitory vision tends to be contingent less on an evolving set of technological, architectural and geopolitical determinants than on a cursory updating of other, earlier visions. In science-fiction films, for example, much play is still made of automatically sliding doors, even though banks and museums and supermarkets the world over had them installed decades ago. More generally, the cities of the future, as imagined in these same films, almost always turn out to be preternaturally autonomous structures, without a trace of that more or less harmonious cohabitation of architectural styles (sometimes dating back to the Middle Ages) that, certainly in Europe, distinguishes the modern metropolis.

Something else, too, has contributed to the death of the future as the last frontier, the last great hope, of questing humankind – the just as patent failure of the End of History. Proclaiming the definitive and irreversible triumph of democratic capitalism, and stamping George Bush's rash declaration of a New World Order with a neo-Hegelian seal of approval, Francis Fukuyama's *The End of History and the Last Man* was published to real *éclat* a few years ago. What, though, has happened since?

While it is inconceivable that anyone might now really have the impression that history has in some sense 'ended', a momentous *structural* change has nevertheless taken place. What has (for the moment) come to a halt is not history as such but the dialectic by which its progess has immemorially been articulated, that of 'before' and 'after'. It used to be that history would lurch from one (occasionally planetary) upheaval to the next – from the First World War to the Second, from the Russian Revolution to the fall of the Berlin Wall, from the sinking of the *Titanic* to the assassination of John Kennedy. Gruesomely sanguinary as most of these turning points were, they did at least, in the course of their respective aftermaths, allow for a convulsive renewal of spirits, for a period of (relative) grace in which the world could take stock and recharge its batteries.

In 1945 Europe was a disaster area; it was also a *tabula rasa*. Now, since the disintegration of one of the two superpowers that, for seventy years, sat hunched over the geopolitical stage as over a chessboard, we are permanently stuck in 'after' gear, in 'post'-everything mode, incapable of escaping from the present's unending rut. Nothing – not in Bosnia, not in Iraq, not in Ireland – ever manages to draw to a genuine and satisfying conclusion. It all just meanders on and on and on, violently and bloodily, and appears destined to do so for years to come. The sole key to planetary imperialism is henceforth economic, and the ultimate deterrent, the Doomsday Machine, is the Big Mac. Like one of those little cylindrical wheels that one places in a hamster's cage in order to delude the poor creature that it is actually going somewhere, this spinning planet of ours has become a treadmill.

Doubtless the state of affairs I am describing is a perfectly normal product of millennial frets and fevers and will not last for ever. But it has also subverted once and for all the ancient and hallowed cult of the future as an infallible, because inherently untestable, repository of our profoundest hopes and fears, the future as a foreign country, if I may again parody L. P. Hartley, where they do things differently. At the very least, it has made traditional science-fiction, if not less credible (it was never 'credible'), then less viable; at the very most, it has taught us that the future, too, is a *historical* concept, one which, like so many so-called 'eternal' values, may have passed its sell-by date.

So forget postmodernism. Ours is the era of postfuturism.

Notes

1 A thought: for first-time readers of Orwell's novel today, is its narrative still set in the future, or else in the past, or even in what might be regarded as the *conditional*?

On the critical faculty

Recently I joined a few friends for dinner. They had just been to see Martin Scorsese's *The Age of Innocence*, a film they had uniformly adored and about which they were already *reminiscing*, recalling, a matter of minutes after the closing titles, its most memorable moments in that glow of shared recollection that, rather than the film itself, is probably the high point of every communal excursion to the cinema. Assuming that, as a frequent commentator on film, I myself had seen it, they asked me what I thought.

I replied as follows (not altogether impromptu, I have to admit): that if Scorsese's own self-confessed reference, Visconti, seemed to me a crushing one for both him and his film, that if another trademark name which had been bandied about by the critics, Merchant Ivory, was equally misleading, there could nevertheless be detected in *The Age of Innocence* the (possibly unwitting) influence of a pre-existent model: *Gigi*. After all, like *Gigi*'s director, Vincente Minnelli, Scorsese had made no attempt to feign jaded, born-with-a-silver-spoon-in-his-mouth familiarity with the society portrayed in his film. Like Minnelli's, his camera's ecstatically swooping, zooming movements down on to lavish fashions, fittings and furnishings resembled so many visual gasps of delight, so many rapturous squeals of 'What about that!' and 'God, would you get an eyeful of this!' On a more trivially anecdotal level, Winona Ryder and Daniel Day-Lewis were dead ringers for Leslie Caron and Louis Jourdan, and even Miriam Margolyes and Alec McCowen, as the arbiters of elegance and propriety along turn-of-the-century Park Avenue, succeeded in evoking fond memories of Hermione Gingold and Maurice Chevalier. Significantly, too, the Place de Furstemberg, celebrated as the most exquisite little public square in Paris, was a setting common to both films. Furthermore . . .

My voice petered out. I realised from the collective glazing of my companions' eyes that I had committed a major social solecism. I had become (with, as newspaper cartoonists say, apologies to H. M. Bateman) the Man Who Offered a Detailed Critique of a Film in Polite Company. It would not have mattered if I had dismissed *The Age of Innocence* as a piece of crap and left it at that – that, anyway, would have been a straightforward, no-nonsense opinion. It was the fact, goddamn it, that I could not stop being a critic, that I could not stop being what the French charmingly call *un empêcheur de danser en rond* (literally: someone who prevents others from dancing in a ring), that I could not stop being a spoilsport or, rather (to coin a neologism which, even as I coin it, I can tell is not going to catch on), a 'spoilart'. I recognised the syndrome as one encapsulable in that eternal squawk of the paying customer: why can't critics just sit back and enjoy the film like the rest of us?

Well, why? Why *can't* we critics just sit back and enjoy the film?

Speaking only for myself, I decline to offer the disingenuous riposte that that is exactly what I do, since, if I am honest with myself, I am obliged to acknowledge that it is simply not so. Yet what tends to be forgotten in such an argument is that film critics choose to be film critics not because they love criticism but because they love films. It is their love of the cinema which enables them (most of them) to retain their sanity while exposing themselves, week after week, to the tripe which it hurls at them. And it is, so I would argue, precisely the critical faculty, to the degree that they possess one, which keeps that love intact.

I can best explain what I mean by taking an example, curiously, from the theatre. Years ago, in the early eighties, the National Theatre staged a series of revivals of neglected modern English-language plays. Of those plays, I remember, in no particular order, Maugham's *For Services Rendered*, Hecht and MacArthur's *The Front Page*, Ben Travers's *Plunder*, Lillian Hellman's *Watch on the Rhine* and a Rattigan double bill of *The Browning Version* and *Harlequinade*. I had never seen any of them before and they are by no means all of the first rank. The Hellman is unsalvageable junk, the Travers salvageable in a brilliant production (which it got), the Maugham sentimental and creaky but still fairly affecting, the Rattigans the sort of thing you will like if you like that sort of thing, the Hecht and MacArthur indestructible. But there I go again, you will grumble – comparing, contrasting, criticising. Not just sitting back and enjoying. The truth, though, is that I *did* enjoy them, all of them, pretty much equally. I enjoyed them, first of all, for their respective qualities, or what I believed were their respective qualities. But I also enjoyed them *irrespective of their respective qualities*. I enjoyed them because, in the lucid, almost hallucinatorily intelligible stagings which they received, I felt that I was seeing them *as in fact they were*, seeing them in their objective reality, warts and all. I had heard of all of these plays before experiencing them at first hand – now, I told myself, I knew at last, as a critic, as a spectator, what they were worth. And the acquiring of that knowledge was, in itself, a source of enjoyment.

To return to the cinema – I loathed Jane Campion's *The Piano* and, even more so, Krzysztof Kieślowski's *Blue*, which, not to put too fine a point on it, I regard as one of the most imbecilic films ever made. In a very real, unsarcastic sense, however, I *enjoyed* loathing them. I enjoyed at least discovering what I thought of them, discovering once and for all what (yes, yes, in my opinion) they were worth. To be sure, I would have enjoyed them a lot more had I also admired them, had I been able to surrender unreservedly to their imaginative worlds. But whenever that has happened – as, say, with a film which I consider to have been one of the most underrated in recent years, Clint Eastwood's *A Perfect World* – the fact that I could not help endeavouring to analyse it even as I watched it, that I could not help trying to figure out why it worked for me when it obviously did not for others, actually added to rather than detracted from, or distracted from, the pleasure it afforded me.

Here, then, is the fundamental paradox of the critic: that, at the deepest level of his being, of his professional identity, *he enjoys everything*.

On 'liveness'

Life is hard, yes, it is true, life is as hard as it ever was. But life is easy, too, easier by far than it has ever been. Just how easy it is now, at least in a cultural context, was brought home to me when I returned from a trip to Paris with a three-cassette box set of *Les Vampires*. To explain: *Les Vampires* is a marathon silent serial shot in 1915 by the pioneering French filmmaker Louis Feuillade and starring the arrestingly named Musidora as the only marginally less arrestingly named Irma Vep (an anagram, in case it has escaped you), one of the ringleaders of a band of anarchistic thugs and thieves who don black torso-hugging body stockings and slink from rooftop to rooftop across a sinister, lovingly documented, pre-First World War Paris.[1] And the point is that, no more than a decade ago, the only way of catching up with such a cumbersome classic *(Les Vampires* runs between six and seven hours) was to study the programming schedules of various cinémathèques and National Film Theatres – which would in any event screen the full version extremely rarely – and be prepared to spend an entire day, from early afternoon until late evening, hunkered down in a darkened auditorium with nothing but a tinny piano accompaniment to cut the edge off the silence. Now, as I say, one can watch the film in the privileged intimacy of one's own home, when, how and as often as one pleases. It is not unlike having an authentic Lascaux cave drawing in the cellar.

Another example. As a youthful aficionado of rare classical music, I recall trembling with irrepressible, oh-God-I-just-don't-believe-it! excitement when, rummaging through shelvesful and shelvesful of second-hand LPs in a dingy Los Angeles junk shop, I chanced upon a long-deleted recording of piano music by a composer whose work I had theretofore only ever dreamt of being able to hear, the so-called 'Spanish Satie', Federico Mompou. The music itself proved to be mildly haunting, but what I have never forgotten is the sheer euphoria of that instant of discovery. A discovery that can no longer be made: these days, virtually the complete oeuvre of the admittedly not very prolific Mompou is widely available on CD, in a generous variety of interpretations.

Still another example. Watching, as an infant, the 1953 Coronation on the near-oval eight-inch screen of my family's spanking new TV set, I remember how, at my very first glimpse of the black-and-white image flickering in a corner of the living-room without so much as a by-your-leave, my already wobbly lower lip turned to outright jelly. I remember, too, how I had to bite into it, hard, to prevent myself from bursting into tears. And I also remember, after I had had time to conquer my technophobic anxieties (the Coronation was as lengthy as *Les Vampires*), that I attempted, during what struck me as a tedious stretch of the procession, *to peek beyond the edge of the screen to see what was coming next.* Now infants far littler than I was in 1953 plonk themselves down in front of the most sophisticated of computers and instantly, but *instantly*, master them.

Life is easy, I repeat. Mortgages are easy, cable television is easy, credit cards are easy, faxes, cordless phones, microwaves, airline shuttles, take-out pizzas, PEPs, you name it, they are all easy. If you can afford them (and of course there are many who cannot), then they are yours for the asking. Progress without tears – it is, is it not, an unequivocally good thing?

I wonder.

In the first place, such facility of access and opportunity may be a little like energy. There may be a consistently stable quantity of it in the world, so that what is gained in one area is forfeited in another. Thus, if a complex network of additional telephone lines pulsating through London's infrastructure can only be beneficial to the city's social and economic welfare, it also means that its main arteries risk being permanently clogged up with construction work. Thus, more frivolously, if canned laughter on the soundtrack of a TV sitcom makes it easier for viewers to recognise when something funny has been said, it also makes it that much harder for them to feel like laughing at the joke themselves.

Of greater importance is the possibility that a surfeit of technological marvels has created a world which is rapidly losing its own capacity to marvel (just as a surfeit of amusing lines of dialogue in a play, in Tom Stoppard's *On the Razzle*, say, all too soon engenders an attitude of slumped indifference in the spectator). What is missing, surely, is the excitement, the euphoria, that I describe above. With such a range of television channels at one's disposal, it scarcely matters which of them one watches; with so many films currently released on video, it scarcely matters which of them one rents. I once queued for hours in the rain outside Covent Garden in the hope of obtaining a ticket for *Elektra* with Birgit Nilsson; now that recordings of Strauss's opera abound on CD, laser disc and videotape, I sometimes cannot help feeling I must have been mad. I wasn't, though. Almost as though, by standing for so long in line, I was, as they say, *working up an appetite*, I found the experience of the opera itself incomparably more intense than I have ever done when watching or listening to it at home.

It is not, understand, a question of the mystique of the live performance. I have already voiced my suspicion that 'liveness' has long since ceased to be enhaloed by any especial cultural prestige, and my remarks on *Elektra* are no less relevant to the experience of watching the very un-'live' *Les Vampires* inside a cinema compared to that of watching it, at ease, without anaesthetising one's backside, at home. Or, rather, it *is* a question of 'liveness', but liveness relative to the spectator's presence, not the performer's. It is the fact that the spectator is *live*, so to speak, that *he* is present, actively present, that he has had to make an effort to get there, to be there, to stay there, which engenders the consequent intensity. If one has to expend the kind of effort I expended, so long ago, just to *see Elektra*, then it becomes unthinkable not to expend a comparable effort on actually *watching* it. Whereas if the only effort required to see an opera consists of inserting a tape into a video recorder and switching on, it is likely that that very effortlessness, that inherent ease, will make it all the harder to expend the requisite effort on the work itself.

With fewer and fewer obstacles barring our paths, we are all tourists now, not travellers, and certainly not explorers, in the wide open spaces of the contemporary cultural scene. Culture, in fact, has now become essentially something we receive and has ceased to be something which we feel we have to give ourselves up to. Yet, in culture as in morality, it *is* always better to give than to receive.

Notes

1 There is undoubtedly a thesis to be written on the mythopoeic significance of the rooftops of Paris in the history of the French cinema.

On naked children

Have you ever heard of the Kuleshov experiment?

Lev (or Leo) Kuleshov (1899–1970) was a Soviet film director and theorist who, in the late teens of the century, sought to demonstrate the power and efficacy of what he termed 'dialectical montage', the now rather obsolete notion that the meaning of a cinematic image derives less from its own discrete content than from its contextual relationship with the images which directly precede and follow it. To do so, he took a neutral close-up shot of the actor Ivan Mozhukhin and juxtaposed it in turn with shots of (if memory serve, but I should point out that descriptions of the experiment, the footage of which I myself have never seen, vary considerably) a steak, a tiger and a naked woman. Subliminally influenced by each of these very different reverse-angle shots, the spectator finds himself interpreting Mozhukhin's unchanging expression as one, successively, of hunger, fear and lust.

Let us now perform a similar experiment with the printed word. Let us substitute for Mozhukhin's face the simple and in itself surely unexceptionable statement that 'A child's body is a beautiful thing' and contextualise it with three different qualifying phrases. So:

(1) *In the eyes of a parent a child's body is a beautiful thing.*
(2) *In the eyes of an artist a child's body is a beautiful thing.*
(3) *In the eyes of a paedophile a child's body is a beautiful thing.*

All of these statements are, I submit, unarguably true. The problem is that, because the third expresses an unpalatable truth, the first two have been, in Britain at least, irredeemably corrupted. Every parent *knows* that children's naked bodies are beautiful, that the contemplation of their miniature splendour is one of the authentic pleasures of parenthood. I would not even be afraid to say that there is something seriously amiss with any parent prepared to deny the assertion, sincerely or not. Yet because statement (3) is just as undeniable (and, of course, also because of our current heightened sensitivity to child abuse), adults now find it awkward to acknowledge such a source of parental gratification. They certainly have to think twice before asking a chemist to develop a set of snapshots of their children scampering naked in a garden or on a beach, since, as has been occurring more and more frequently of late, the chemist in question may well take it upon himself to forward the allegedly offending prints to the Obscene Publications Squad.

Naturally, one hopes that any chemist entrusted with unambiguously, or even ambiguously, pornographic material involving children will know where his duty lies.[1] Yet, by virtue of our extreme anxiety in these matters, we have reached a point where, as an object of visual, and more specifically photographic, representation, a child's naked body is totally out of bounds. And it is that which appears to me grotesque.

Humankind has always had an incorrigible 'representational' propensity, a need to surround itself with icons and images of its environment. And, these days, you can, in paint, photography, television and film, 'represent' virtually anything you please. You can paint, stark naked, young women or old men, old women or young men. You can photograph a woman splaying her bare thighs 'like a weird book', as Harold Brodkey once unforgettably expressed it. You can advertise knitwear with the image of an Aids victim in his death agony. You can have a television camera zoom into the face of a mother who has just learned that her daughter has perished in a plane crash. You can even film the Holocaust and transform it into a feel-good movie. But you cannot paint, photograph or film the naked body of a child.

No, I tell a lie, you can – if the child is a baby (the classic bearskin rug pose), presumably on the grounds that babies are all so identical they do not count as individuals. (Yet, as parents again know, every baby is as distinct from every other baby as every snowflake is from every other snowflake.) If, however, the age of the child is somewhere between six and sixteen, his or her body is inaccessible to representation of any kind. If, moreover, it happens to be a professional, not merely a personal, matter, the taboo is even more powerful. The

English photographer Ron Oliver, for example, often but by no means exclusively commissioned by parents to photograph their off-spring in the nude, had to resettle in Holland after the Obscene Publications Squad raided his London studio and confiscated twenty thousand negatives, transparencies and prints.

Ironically, the only instances of Oliver's work that most of us will have seen are the cluster of photographs used to illustrate journalis-tic articles about his case. These were straightforward, elegant por-traits of naked, adolescent girls, none of whom, patently, had been demeaned by the experience. And even if one imagines the sleaziest of scenarios – that someone with paedophiliac tendencies chanced to spot Oliver's photographs in some newspaper or another and decided to exploit them as a masturbatory aid – precisely what harm was done? It may not be a savoury sight to have to conjure up, but just who was hurt? The subjects of the photographs remained unaware of how they were used (which is true of any woman men-tally undressed by a male passer-by or, for that matter, vice versa), and the paedophile satisfied his desires in injurious solitude. Those desires were, after all, already *there*; they were confirmed, not cre-ated, by the existence of the photographs.

If, when divorced from all possible qualifying contexts, the seven words with which this essay opened, 'A child's body is a beautiful thing', constitute, as I suggested, an objectively true statement, then it is surely intolerable that childish nudity should be placed off-lim-its. If, on the other hand, it is argued that beauty and objectivity are ultimately incompatible categories, then it is worth making the point that obscenity, too, may be in the eye of the beholder.

Notes

1 Equally, though, it strikes me as so improbable that a child pornographer would entrust photographic material to his local Boots that willingness to do so should already constitute a presumption of innocence.

On domestic art

One could, of course, establish any number of mutually exclusive sets and subsets of paintings. For the purpose and duration of this essay, though, let me propose just two: the paintings we admire in museums and galleries and the paintings we ourselves own.

I myself am not notably flush in what might be called domestic art works. All I have hanging on the walls of my flat are one of Cocteau's spidery Orpheus profiles, scribbled by the poet on the letterheaded writing-paper of Mme Francine Weisweiller (whose sumptuous Cap Ferrat residence, Santo-Sospir, became his 'villa away from home' in the latter years of his life) and picked up by me for next to nothing in the sixties; a gaudy Lautrec print entitled *Confetti*; a large and rather insipid Chinese watercolour of a monkey-puzzle tree; a half-dozen of my own framed sketches; and a small collection of illustrations, bought directly from the artists, to books I have written over the years. Whenever I go visiting, however, I head straight for those owned by my (middle-class) acquaintances.

They tend as a rule to belong to one or other of the following genres: the wan and watery English landscape, *circa* 1930; the practically indecipherable daub by some French *petit-maître* of the eighteenth century, a *très petit-maître* of whom one has nearly heard; the styleless if perfectly competent pencil likeness of a family member, past or present; the demure, almost invariably feminine portrait whose subject one instinctively knows is unconnected with anyone living in the house (it probably 'caught the eye' at an idly browsed auction); the once fashionable silk-screen print of the Pop or post-Pop school (Hockney, Patrick Procktor, Adrian George and the like); the contemporary cultural advertisement (National Theatre, Royal Opera House, Royal Academy, etc.); the buffish, nostalgic film poster (*Casablanca*, *Pulp Fiction*); the picturesque street scene of nineteenth-century Islington, say (in an Islington flat), nineteenth-century Chelsea (in a Chelsea flat), and so on; the map of sixteenth-century

Norfolk or Suffolk; and, finally, the anonymous abstract, about which one knows neither why it was painted nor why it was purchased.

Not, you will say, a very distinguished joblot; and it is true that I do not frequent the sort of houses in which I might stand a reasonable chance of finding a Braque still life, not to mention a quattrocento altarpiece. Still, it has often struck me as strange that these acquaintances of mine, whose literary culture, as evidenced by their bookshelves, is fairly unimpeachable, who listen on record to exactly the same music they would pay to hear in an opera house or concert hall and who watch on video exactly the same films they would queue up to see in the cinema, are content to surround themselves with paintings at which, in a gallery, they would not give a second glance.

It is, to be sure, primarily a matter of economic realities. Most of us buy the paintings we can rather than the paintings we want. And the problem has been compounded by the current preponderance of installations, art works for which the only conceivable setting is a gallery. That paddy-field concoction that was shortlisted for one of the Turner Prizes – even assuming one could afford it, just where and how could it be privately 'installed'? But it cannot be a question of money alone. Think, after all, of the people one has heard claiming that they would refuse, if it were offered them gratis, a nude by Lucian Freud or one of Bacon's *Screaming Popes*. Too oppressive, they protest. Or too depressing. Or too overwhelming. Or just too big. It has reached the point where assuring a contemporary artist that, yes, one *would* rather like to own one of his works risks sounding like an insult – at the very least, like damning with faint praise.

Yes, not everyone would feel at ease with Géricault's *The Raft of the Medusa* or Münch's *The Scream* glowering from above the mantelpiece. Yet what the eye brings to domestic art is a kind of patina. Acting as a tenderising agent, regular exposure tames, it desensitizes – in a word, it *domesticates* – the most harrowing of paintings. Lived with for long enough, *The Scream* would fade away into a mere squeak, *The Raft of the Medusa* come to seem no worse than a choppy Sealink crossing. And this patina has just as tenderising an effect on the paintings we *do* own, paintings we appreciate not because they are necessarily good but because they *are* our own. It comes as a profound relief to be able to look at a painting on which we are not required to offer any considered opinion; a painting which asks only that our eyes brush against it, not bore into it; a painting which permits us for once to concentrate on content rather than form. For it is only when we have arrived at the stage of not giving a whit who painted it that we can properly enjoy a nineteenth-century townscape quaintly abuzz with costermongers and barrow boys or the portrait of some pallid young woman in a flower-print frock and Vera Lynnish hairdo or else some muddy little forest scene *à la* Corot (a classic example of the sort of artist to whose tiny and superficially uningratiating landscapes one gives short shrift in a museum when in quest of more immediately eye-fetching imagery).

These paintings, obviously, have precious little to do with 'art'. They add virtually nothing to the sum of human accomplishment. They break no new ground, stylistically, formally or technically. A critic or historian would regard them with either condescending affection or outright contempt. If ever they were to be removed from their domestic environment, they would instantly be exposed for the near-worthless botches that they are. That, though, is precisely what is most interesting about them. In this instance, uniquely, the defining context is not that of the artist but that, solely, of the purchaser. It is the purchaser alone who invests his collection of paintings with meaning, who may even be said to give them an identifiable 'style'. Uninfluenced, as no grander collector can ever be, by the prestige of a signature or the fluctuations of the art market, he effects a choice *exclusively* in accordance with his or her personal taste. And if, in an art-historical context, taste is now, more or less, a deservedly discredited concept, it is still worthy of our attention. For it is to the non-artist exactly what style is to the artist – the external expression of a sensibility. Taste is, in short, the style of the public.

On opera

Where differences of artistic appreciation are at issue, there is no chasm wider than that which divides those who like opera from those who do not. I have never heard anyone claim to take opera or leave it. There would appear to be no half-measure, no uncommitted middle ground. If you don't like it, you can't stand it.

I was reminded of this chasm when I attended a performance of *Der Rosenkavalier* at the London Coliseum. Strauss's opera is not a difficult work. Hugo von Hofmannsthal's story of the elegant, still ravishing Marschallin (textually, if not always in theatrical practice, she is actually only thirty-three) acknowledging, for the first time in her life, that a lover might abandon her rather than vice versa would not strike anyone as outlandish in the theatre or cinema. If Strauss offers few sustained arias, he almost cloys us with tunelets, deliciously tumescent shivers, spasms and swoons of melody. And the third-act trio is one of the summits of the entire repertoire, a passage so exquisite a word should be coined for it that is, proportionally, to 'sublime' what 'sublime' is to 'quite nice'. Yet, just in front of me, a middle-aged male spectator had to be jabbed out of sleep several times by his mortified wife.

If I was exasperated, it was not only by his snoring but by the fact that he was snoring through the very first opera I ever saw which prompted in me that famous suspension of disbelief that we tend to take for granted in the other performing arts. In spite of an improbable tendency to sing their way out of life's little hardships, I believed in the people on stage. I wanted to know what was going to happen to them. I even secretly identified (at twenty-five!) with the Marschallin. The operas I had previously seen (even Puccini's, even Mozart's, even Verdi's) had remained purely *cultural* events, concerts with plots, full of characters with beautiful but sometimes alienatingly 'singerish' voices (as we refer to actorish voices). I had not been bored; equally, I had never been emotionally engaged. Not,

I repeat, until *Der Rosenkavalier*: which is why I found it so hard to accept, particularly as it was sung in an English-language version, that someone could be so unresponsive to its formal beauties and psychological insights.

Perhaps, it occurred to me, the real obstacle for operaphobes is not the music at all but what they doubtless regard as the torturously stilted artifice of the whole experience. Even now, opera tends to be perceived as 'apart'. Detectable still is a pungent whiff of nineteenth-century élitism (justified to a degree, one has to say, by exorbitant seat prices) and twentieth-century philistinism (as in the popular cliché of the opera house as a place of either dutiful or fashionable attendance). There is, too, the impregnable prejudice of the opera singer as fat by definition, a prejudice reinforced by the extracurricular triumphs of a Pavarotti but statistically untenable. To be contended with, finally, is the received idea that every opera of note has been saddled with a preposterous plot. That such plots exist is undeniable. Yet the most enduring works in the repertoire were scripted by librettists of genius, da Ponte for Mozart, Boito for Verdi, Wagner for Wagner, Hoffmannstahl for Strauss, and in the contemporary era, which has seen the virtual disappearance of the professional hack librettist, by writers as various as Auden, Brecht, Cocteau, Gertrude Stein, Forster, Claudel, d'Annunzio and Colette.

The most curious thing about the abiding resistance to opera, however, is that it is exactly equivalent to that which militates against a wider following for, paradoxically, silent film. Indeed, I would argue that the generic sensibilities of these two ostensibly incompatible, not to say antithetical, forms are remarkably close to one another. For the silent cinema had at least this in common with grand opera, that only through a heightened and stylised system of physical gesticulation could any but the most elementary human emotions find expression. What makes silent film acting seem so embarrassingly bad to anyone unfamiliar with its near-semaphoric code is the absence not of speech but of *song*. Certain silent films even resembled opera productions. Look at a typical still from Erich von Stroheim's Ruritanian melodrama *Queen Kelly* – the frequently reproduced image, for example, in which a deranged Seena Owen, eyes aglitter like the twin headlamps of an automobile, brandishes a whip over a cowering Gloria Swanson – and you might easily mistake it for a faded snapshot of some turn-of-the-century staging of Strauss's *Salomé* or Massenet's *Hérodiade*. It is surely no accident that silent movie queens were known as divas.

Such stagings have become more or less obsolete. With the introduction of surtitles, moreover, no one is any longer entitled to complain that operas are hard to follow – are, in a word, 'silent'. Once haughtily indifferent to the utility of instant comprehension, opera now, like Garbo, talks. It has, like theatre and film, the capacity to lure us into its drama, to incite us to laugh or cry at will, to make us *believe*. There has ceased to be any serious excuse for its cultural ostracism.

And yet . . . every gain entails a corresponding loss. At the risk of undermining my own propaganda for the democratisation of opera, it is, I confess, one of the regrets of my life that I never did see any of those fabled sopranos who demently carried all before them. And I think, precisely, of Gloria Swanson and her lament for the passing of the silent cinema (from her own glorious swan song, *Sunset Boulevard*), and how that lament could, if inverted, serve as a valedictory epitaph for one of the gorgeous, ludicrous divas of the old, overweight school: 'We didn't need faces – we had voices!'

On controversy

From a 1994 opinion poll, conducted simultaneously in Britain, Germany, Japan and the United States, and published in the *Guardian*, *Der Spiegel*, the Japanese daily *Asahi Shimbun* and the *New York Times*, it emerged that the British were, in the poll's own word, the 'glummest' of the four nations, the most suspicious of the world at large, the most disgruntled with their present condition, the most pessimistic about their future.

What has happened to us? A number of ingenious theories have been advanced, but my own personal feeling is that this country's malaise can be directly traced to what has traditionally been regarded as its finest hour: the Battle of Britain. Viewed from the longer term, what we would have most benefited from in 1940 is defeat, not survival and eventual victory. What we needed, for the sake of our own future welfare, was to have been invaded, occupied and bombed into the Stone Age. If London had been devastated by the Luftwaffe, it would not now be the pot-holed, cone-littered dump it has become. If, like the populations of continental Europe, the British had suffered the rigours of Nazi occupation, if they had been starved and tortured (and a little starvation and torture has never done anyone much lasting harm), their moral fibre would now be considerably the better for it. If, in short, we had lost the war, we would no longer be exploiting it, a half-century on, as our sole, pathetic jibe against the Germans.

Only kidding. What I have just written is of course utter tripe, morally offensive and intellectually null. Yet I cannot help wondering how many readers, even those outraged by its premise, suspected for a moment that it might have been a hoax. Opinions not a thousand miles distant from those which I have just pretended to espouse are expressed every day in newspapers and magazines. Yet, beyond the statutory slew of furious letters which they deliberately elicit and duly receive, there would seem to be no concomitant apprehension that what might be called the *ceiling* of our culture is being ever so insidiously lowered on to our heads, like those hydraulically movable ceilings one recalls from the torture chambers of horror films. What would once have shocked, or never been published, has been reduced to yet another juicy polemical exchange. There are no scandals any longer, only debates.

Although it is hard to remember what conditions were like in the past (just as, whenever a familiar building is demolished or a friend suddenly shaves off a beard he has worn for years, it at once becomes impossible to visualise the *status quo ante*), it appears to me nevertheless that such eternal and often ephemeral controversies – controversies on sexual politics, arts funding, the influence of video nasties on patterns of criminal behaviour, the shifting goalposts of high and low culture, whatever you please – represent a relatively recent phenomenon in the media. Nor is it, in principle, a bad thing. The problem is that debating every single issue at the same decibel level – be it the murder of Jamie Bulger or Diana's fitness as an ambassadress-without-portfolio, the crisis of British fiction or the fashion for anorexia-inducing androgyny on the catwalk – means that one issue tends to have just as much impact as, but no more than, another. It might even be alleged, paradoxically, that a vocal public controversy is now the most effective means of *burying* an issue, of occluding the possibility of its ever prompting a genuinely constructive debate. Instead of by a conspiracy of silence, we are victims of a conspiracy of noise.

What specifically concerns me, however, despite the trivialising tenor of my own little spoof of sensational journalism, are not the so-called 'mischievous' articles, those articles that attack sacred cows not with real bombs, capable of doing real damage, but, Just William-style, with stink bombs, those articles whose *raison d'être* is primarily to get the reader's goat and whose ultimate destiny is to wrap up the next day's fish and chips. It is the fact, rather, that ostensibly more serious journalists are now just as much in thrall to the demon of instant controversy. In the *Guardian* again, for example, the newspaper's former literary editor, Richard Gott, once wrote a piece on what he perceived as Britain's cultural and spiritual insolvency and, in particular, its abject capitulation to an idealised,

173

mythologised and vulgarised American model. The article was, for the most part, pertinent and forthrightly argued. Except that, by some not easily discernible detour, the meanders of what started out as a sensible enough thesis eventually led Gott into making the more contentious statement that contemporary England (England, note, not Britain) was a desert, a cultural wilderness, boasting 'no English fiction to speak of, no English theatre, art, music, or English film'.

Is this true? That the English cinema is in a permanent state of crisis, indisputable. That the English theatre is less generously endowed with talent than its current reputation would suggest, agreed. That new English fiction is systematically overpraised, fair comment. That English art and music (but precisely what music? Gott did not specify) are not what they once were, more a matter of opinion, surely, than fact. Yet, even if it were a matter of fact, would it justify Gott's leap into such total, blanket pessimism? Did he himself believe what he wrote? Or else, resolved to communicate a strongly held conviction as pugnaciously as he was able, was he seduced by the sirens of instant controversy?

If it was a case of the latter, then its consequences bear out my theory of the increasingly counterproductive effect that such polemics have on public opinion. For there *were* no consequences. Gott's article did not provoke the avalanche of approving or reproving correspondence one might reasonably have expected from its intemperate tone. Unless I missed something, this was one controversy which did not 'take', and it is possible that, at least in a cultural context, we have already arrived at a point of saturation.

No one will need to be reminded of Goering's (apocryphal?) remark on the subject, his only recorded witticism: 'Whenever I hear the word culture, I reach for my revolver', an attitude which, praise be, has never been terribly relevant to the situation of the arts in Britain. Playing a rapacious film producer in Godard's *Le Mépris*, Jack Palance offered this updated paraphrase: 'Whenever I hear the word culture, I reach for my cheque book.' That, too, perhaps unfortunately, bears scant relation to typical levels of sponsorship in the private sector. No, by far the most apposite to our own overheated state of affairs is yet another paraphrase, this time from Jacques Roubaud: 'Whenever I hear the word culture, I reach for my earplugs.'

On soup

It took me a while to work out what it was that had affected me. I had been idly looking at a photograph, published in the *Guardian*, of three Siberian children, so swaddled in woollen clothes as to be of indeterminate gender, enjoying a meal (as the caption writer put it) in a Moscow soup kitchen. It was a competent but in no sense exceptional news photograph; yet I found myself unaccountably touched by it. And it finally occurred to me that what had rendered it so poignant in my eyes, beyond the pathos inherent in every image of poverty, particularly one in which children are prominent, was the fact that the 'meal' they were enjoying was, precisely, a bowl of soup.

There is surely no question but that, as one of the most basic forms of human nourishment, soup is possessed of a *mythology*. Just as, in mythological terms, milk is the food of Childhood, bread and water the food of Punishment, caviar the food of Privilege and grapes the food of Sex (no self-respecting Roman orgy, according to Hollywood, was complete without an array of silver platters heaped high with moistly gleaming grapes), so soup is still, as it has ever been, the food of Charity. Certainly, whatever may be the case in the West, it would appear that in Russia the phrase 'soup kitchen' is more literal than generic.

In consequence, even for those of us who have never had to depend on charity, soup is also invested with a *morality*. It is, in short, a food which one makes light of at one's peril. I remember, as a schoolboy (during a now unimaginable period of the British educational system when decent, three-course refectory lunches were the expected, taken-for-granted norm), passing a huge tureen of soup, without first serving myself, down the oblong trestle table at which my fellow pupils and I were seated. Suddenly, one of the supervising staff, our Latin master, an ex-army man, roared from the top table to ask me why I was not having any. 'Frankly, sir,' I replied in a supercilious voice, the memory of which, to this very day, grates on me as much as the voice itself must once have grated on everyone who knew me, 'I find soup rather a bore.' Whereupon, to my horror, he leapt to his feet, marched the length of the refectory hall and, now unnervingly puce of feature, stood over me. 'A bore?' he barked. 'You find it a bore, do you? Well, let me tell you, Adair, you putrid little twerp, had you been in a Jap prisoner-of-war camp during the last war, as I was, you would have been delighted to be bored with some soup! Oh yes, you would have got down on your knees and begged to be bored out of your gruesome little mind!' Needless to say, I ate the soup – and, from that formative moment on, I got, as it were, the hang of the thing.

We are all, of course, more 'sophisticated' now, so much so that the moral dimension which I attribute to soup tends increasingly to be diminished, even altogether obscured, by its present culinary versatility, including, as it does, recipes (transparently thin soups, summery fruit soups) at which even my former Latin master might have turned up his nose. Yet whatever kind of soup we of the middle class eat, however we eat it (cradling and sheltering the bowl as the French peasantry used to do or else deploying the spoon as though it were a miniature mill-wheel, as is the custom of the Chinese and Japanese), and even wherever we eat it (on a long rustic kitchen table in the country or in a fashionable restaurant in town), the partaking of soup permits us, for once in our lives, to experience eating not as a ritual but as a *function*.

No matter that we may strain to distance ourselves from soup's peasant or proletarian connotations – by serving it cold instead of hot, by spooning it demurely forward away from us instead of blokeishly back towards us – it is impossible entirely to sever its intimate, immemorial links with deprivation. The fact that, delicious as it may be, its flavour remains unchanged from one spoonful to the next alerts us to the more global (and easily forgotten) fact that, for many people even now – indeed, for most people in the world – the taste of what they eat is a very secondary consideration to that of its nutritious value (if any). Nor does the gesture of spooning soup up ever change, which invites allegorical analogy with other, similarly mechanical and repetitive gestures, almost all of them signifiers of poverty – the gestures accomplished, day in and day out, year in and year out, in the world's mills and factories and sweatshops. There is, finally, the weather. Even if we are fortunate enough to belong to an ethnic group or socio-economic class for which unpleasant extremes of temperature are just nuisances, not matters of potential life and death, we are still likely to 'fancy' a bowl of soup only when it is cold. For many of us, it is exclusively with soup that the linkage of climate and diet – a significant linkage among the truly deprived strata of society – has retained anything of its original force and meaning.

In my opening paragraph I mentioned how touched I was by the *Guardian*'s photograph. As I have sought to demonstrate, it was not simply that it was an image of children, and desperately hungry children at that. Beyond its immediate import and impact, it made me realise that I am always touched, in representation as in life, by the sight of someone eating soup – just as I am always touched, and to my mind a direct connection exists between the two, by the sight of a baby breastfeeding. To some slight degree still, eating soup is an activity which has the effect of desocialising and denationalising the person who performs it. It serves to remind us all of our common (eating, drinking, defecating, sleeping, dying) humanity. It is, if you like, one of the elementary symbols of life on earth.

On Ellis Island

New York is a curious place. Although one has become increasingly conscious of it as an *old* metropolis,[1] it does not of course begin to compare, in terms of real antiquity, with any of the major cities of Europe. It is in New York, nevertheless, rather than in London or Paris or Rome, that I become most alert to what I can only call 'living history'. Recently strolling through its Lower East Side, for example, along Second Avenue and into Alphabet City, from the leafy, tranquil churchyard in which Peter Stuyvesant is buried to what used to be the Yiddish theatres of Maurice Schwartz and Molly Picon, I found myself aware of the district's multilayered, multicultural past to a degree that would be inconceivable in London's East End.

Actually, I was *made* aware of these landmarks by an expert, a friend of mine, a New Yorker by birth whose passion is precisely the history of the city in which he has spent his whole life. That, too, is probably inconceivable in London; I certainly know of no native Londoner who would be capable of supplying me with a running commentary on his home town's past as we tramped its streets together. Nor, for Americans, is it New York alone which prompts this kind of quotidian fascination with their urban environment. The last time I was in Los Angeles I was chauffeured about town by one of Hollywood's young studio gofers, who kept slowing down to show me the city's very first Catholic mission or the still extant stairway up which Laurel and Hardy indefatigably toted a piano in *The Music Box*.

It may be the relative recency of American history which renders it so appealing. 'Recent history' (that, basically, which is computed in decades and of which we possess cinematic and photographic documentation) belongs to an entirely separate mytho-iconographic category from 'history proper' (which is computed in centuries and of which we possess no cinematic or photographic documentation).

And recent history, it seems, is *in*, whereas history proper is *out*. The former we have few problems 'relating to' in novels, in films like *The Age of Innocence* and *The Remains of the Day*, in TV documentaries and even commercials, whereas the latter requires on our part a massive leap of the imagination and is, in addition, tainted by mustily archivist associations. The history of New York resembles that gained from a good period movie. The history of London, to its own cultural misfortune, is more redolent of the schoolroom.

Yet there is one New York landmark which, inexplicably, has never much interested the cinema: Ellis Island. The gateway to successive waves of immigration from the middle of the nineteenth century to the middle of our own, Ellis Island has now been completely, and surprisingly tastefully, restored, as a living history lesson on one of the few unambiguously positive mass phenomena of modern times. I say 'positive' because, whatever might be one's opinion of the current society and civilisation of the United States, its immigration policy was, for once, a light that did not fail. Only a minute proportion of the huddled masses who passed through Ellis Island, and whose passage is commemorated in a permanent exhibition of photographs, artefacts and recorded testimonies, was refused entry. Even fewer thereafter ever elected to return to the old country.

It was a moving experience walking through the former central assembly hall, as well as the adjacent refectories and dormitories; and, as I did so, I could not help thinking it strange that so few Hollywood filmmakers had chosen to explore so potentially rich a repository of cinematic narrative. The only films on the subject I can name offhand are Alfred Werker's *Gateway* (an obscure little melodrama actually set on Ellis Island), King Vidor's *An American Romance*, Elia Kazan's wonderful *America, America* and, if more obliquely, Coppola's *The Godfather II*. What makes such a lack of concern even stranger is that, as I studied the snapshots of uncomprehending faces, of middle-European immigrants herded into anonymous mobs, of bewildered infants with improvised name-tags stitched to their coat lapels, of medical inspections held in cold, dark, stark rooms, of hastily piled-up luggage, neat middle-class suitcases jostling battered, string-entwined cardboard boxes, I was nagged by the sensation that I had not long before been exposed to this selfsame imagery in a totally different context. After a few moments, I realised where: in *Schindler's List*. Ellis Island was a benign Auschwitz, a Holocaust in reverse, a positive Final Solution.

For various, mostly principled reasons – in brief, because I do not believe that the Holocaust should ever be filmically 'reconstructed' – I was unable to admire *Schindler's List*. It was far from the shameless travesty I half-expected it to be, but one does not revise one's principles simply because a single film turns out to be less crass than it might have been and my fear remains that, in view of the unprecedented critical and commercial favour enjoyed by Spielberg's film, the subject will no longer be regarded as off-limits to Hollywood. Not that I expect a *Schindler's List 2*, exactly, or a Schindlerland theme park in Florida. But the Holocaust may well become, as did the Vietnam War a decade ago, the test of a director's manhood. How long, I wonder, before we are confronted with De Palma's Auschwitz movie? Or Oliver Stone's? Or even Sylvester Stallone's?

Putting it schematically, on the level of a Hollywood 'pitch', one might say that what distinguishes the story of Ellis Island from that of Auschwitz is the absence of horror. That absence, I realise, is a serious drawback in relation to contemporary filmmaking practices, yet the secret of Spielberg's success, as also the source of what subsequent backlash arose against his film, is that he contrived to make, as the American critic J. Hoberman expressed it, 'a feel-good movie about the ultimate feel-bad experience'. The popular triumph of *Schindler's List* derived, in short, from the fact that it plucked a happy ending out of the most infertile soil imaginable. Well, the Ellis Island story boasted millions of happy endings – and it didn't need a Schindler, for America itself was Schindler.

Notes

1 Taking one's cue from Le Corbusier's nostalgic invocation of an era of European history 'when the cathedrals were white', one can now speak of a virginally halcyon Manhattan 'when the skyscrapers were white'.

On intervals

When stretched out on the river bank just before her descent into Wonderland, Alice, you remember, peeped into the book that her sister was reading, 'but it had no pictures or conversations in it, "and what is the use of a book," thought Alice, "without pictures or conversations?"'

I think it a fair assumption to make that, if most of us are able to handle reading a book without pictures, we find nothing more dispiriting, especially should the book in question be a novel, than reconnoitring a few pages ahead of where we have momentarily raised our eyes from the text only to discover that what each and every one of these pages to come holds for us is a congested tablet of prose with no imminent prospect of direct speech. Not that, within a fictional context, the notion of characters speaking to one another is irresistibly alluring. What such a reaction represents, rather, is the reader's instinctive love (in diametric contrast to the writer's instinctive fear) of the white page. For us, that cool, aboriginal whiteness, the framing whiteness of margins or the honeycombed whiteness of dialogue exchanges, *irrigates* a writer's prose. It offers a soothing counterpoint to his busy, garrulous, uninterruptible discourse and diminishes our own fickle resistance to the text. Likewise with chapter divisions. What they do is alert us to the fact that some kind of an end is in sight. It is, again, not that we simply cannot wait to reach that end; just that our mental projection of its approach acts as a shaping, measuring agency. We can, if we so desire, ascertain exactly where we are, where we are headed and how long it is likely to take us to get there. That little anxiety out of the way, we can properly focus on what there is in front of us.

Plays, too, like books, have need of chapter divisions, and these are called intervals. Intervals not only enable us to satisfy a call of nature, to stretch our legs, to wet our whistle, as they say, they equally, perhaps primarily, afford us an opportunity to compare notes, to provide our companion or companions with an interim report on our reaction to the play. This is, in my opinion, a wholly legitimate and not at all frivolous itch that we should all be given a chance to scratch. In Fellini's *Ginger and Fred* a lower-middlebrow couple, forced to live without television for a month, degenerate after only a week or so into a pair of gibbering wrecks. I could certainly live without television for the rest of my life and I feel confident that, were I permanently to be deprived of even one of the genuine art forms, I could eventually learn to grin and bear that, too. But if I were told that I could see any films I pleased, or read any books, or look at any paintings, or listen to any music, but that I would never, never be permitted to communicate my views on these works to another living soul, I do indeed think I might go mad. The fact, then, that I am often impatient for an interval in the theatre is not necessarily to be interpreted as reflecting impatience with the play itself.

My problem, however, is that the interval, like the already more or less obsolete drop curtain, would appear to be on the way out. In one of New York's recent theatrical seasons both Arthur Miller's play *Broken Glass* and Stephen Sondheim's musical *Passion* were interval-free, as was, inexplicably, a revival of William Inge's three-act warhorse *Picnic*, nothing in whose creakily conventional dramaturgy invited such earnest purity of structure and performance. In London, during the same season, Stephen Daldry's production of Priestley's *An Inspector Calls*, Peter Brook's *The Man Who* and Caryl Churchill's *The Skriker* were all performed without interruption.

What has caused so apparently inexorable a progression from the five-act, four-interval stagings of the nineteenth century to the three-act, two-interval stagings of much of the twentieth century to the two-act, one-interval stagings of the last three decades and, finally, to these now fashionable one-act, no-interval stagings?

There is, I believe, a *terroristic* dimension to such a trend, a terror of silence, of empty space, of *temps morts*. Apart from the fact that the traditional observance of an interval does help to underscore any between-the-acts passage of time specified by the dramatist, I cannot help wondering whether those directors who have suppressed it hope thereby to generate an ersatz intensity, a bogus sense of theatrical ritualisation, which they suspect the plays themselves are incapable of contriving on their own. As with those EST self-fulfilment sessions during which doors are locked and no one has permission to leave the room under any circumstance, it is almost as though such directors were panic-stricken at the thought that their audiences, free to exchange views in midstream, might prove to be far less malleable, far more judgmental, in the second half; that, indeed, not a few of them might even be tempted to slip away into the night (an act of critical judgment rendered almost impossible by the absence of an interval).

But books, after all, are consumed in fits and starts, and no critic has ever insisted that only a single-sitting reading will do justice to Joyce or Proust. Our lives are full of empty interstitial spaces that are no less indispensable to our spiritual welfare for being frequently mindless. And one of the reasons I find television now practically unwatchable is its self-imposed obligation to plug up every vacant hole in the schedules. Thus I cannot watch the *Six O'Clock News* on BBC1 without first being advised what programme follows it at six-thirty, what other programme is simultaneously being screened on BBC2 and just what good value for money is the *Radio Times*. Yet, in what anyone under forty must regard as a dim and unknowable past, television once had intervals of its own, the fifties' equivalent – a potter's wheel, a tank of tropical fish, a four-minute railway journey from London to Brighton – of those screen-saving computer applications of flying toasters and exploding fireworks. Believe it or not, television actually used to shut down – or, rather, *shut up* – between five and seven o'clock in the evening.

So my advice to stage directors is this: Let the theatre, too, shut up from time to time. Let the public, too, have its say. And do not, with every production, seek to *overwhelm* us. Let us on occasion be merely whelmed.

On personality

A friend of mine, an amateur historian of British television, once showed me a treasured video recording of a programme I had not seen since it was originally screened in, I would guess, the early sixties, an old, quaintly monochromatic *Face to Face* in which an off-screen John Freeman interrogated Evelyn Waugh.

With his piglet's eyes, unrepentantly upper-crust voice and air of languorous condescension, Waugh made an extraordinary impact on the screen. Extraordinary not just because he was an extraordinary man and so could not help being so on television, but extraordinary also because he possessed what might be called a *pre-media* personality. I do not know whether this *Face to Face* session was the first time he had ever appeared on television, but he was visibly determined not to ingratiate himself with the medium. When, at one point, Freeman asked him why, if he had such scant regard for the whole experience, he had nevertheless agreed to appear on the show, Waugh replied with, for once, genuinely disarming candour, and as though no more elevated motive could ever have entered anyone's head, 'For the money.' The onscreen Evelyn Waugh was thus almost certainly, as one says of painted portraits, a good likeness. It was an Evelyn Waugh that his solicitor would have recognised, or a neighbour, or one of the waiters at his club.

Well, just how much the lapse of the intervening three decades has transformed television was made evident to me when *Face to Face* came to an end, the video recorder was switched off and up popped, on my friend's television screen, uninvited yet inevitable, *Good Morning with Anne and Nick*. The abyss was unbridgeable. Here were two people whose only imaginable existence was audiovisual, who had so completely immersed themselves in the medium's bland stream-of-consciousness (or semi-consciousness) that their faces were as marked by their chosen profession as an alcoholic's by a life-time's intake of gin. Like Henry Kelly, Phillip Schofield, Chris Evans,

Cilla Black, Judith Chalmers, Gloria Hunniford, Michael Aspel, Jeremy Beadle, Robert Kilroy-Silk, Bruce Forsyth, Anne Robinson and the inescapable Terry Wogan, like that ever lengthening list of what precisely? – presenters? emcees? hosts and hostesses? – who are presumably identified on their passports only as 'personalities', Anne and Nick have become square-eyed not by watching too much TV but by appearing on too much TV.

In this context, the basic difference between Evelyn Waugh and Anne Diamond (the 'Anne' of *Anne and Nick*) is that Waugh *had* a personality and Diamond *is* a personality. And the implication of that difference is, of course, that while Waugh was blessed with innumerable other personal qualities, most notably talent, Diamond, for her part, is not required by her vocation to 'do' anything, only to 'be'. Waugh, too, was free to assume the pre-media liberties of scowling, of being churlish, of contradicting himself, whereas Diamond's expressive range is fated to remain as narrow and unthreatening as that of a geisha. (Dorothy Parker once famously said, 'Let's go see Katharine Hepburn run the gamut from A to B.' Diamond's gamut does not even extend to B.) And, haphazardly juxtaposing the two of them, as my friend and I did, had the effect of telescoping thirty years of British television history.

Back in the medium's dark, black-and-white ages, television was commonly described as 'a window on the world'. Even then, that was an extravagant overstatement, but the phrase did reflect a widespread belief that what the medium ought to be aspiring to was a windowlike ideal of transparency, effacing itself in favour of what it elected to show its viewers: as I say, in spite of his own, by no means negligible prestige, John Freeman remained invisible throughout his *Face to Face* interrogations. As the world's 'window', it was the function of television to present viewers with luminaries from that world (actors, comedians, singers and dancers, naturally, but also writers, scientists, politicians and the like), who saw no reason to conceal the fact that they were outsiders, in temporary transit through the corridors of Television Centre. In those days, as a result, British television had relatively few 'personalities' of its own. Rather, it peopled the screen with notabilities from other spheres of activity, giving them the chance to talk about, sometimes interestingly, sometimes not, their own areas of competence. By far its most watchable performers were those who had not been raised in its own clammy cathode-ray incubator and who therefore brought to the studio a whiff of strong, fresh air from the big wide world beyond.

Then, like the cabin crew of an aircraft deciding *en masse* to take over the controls, the hosts started to pull rank on their guests. Instead of depending on the outside world to furnish it with a regularly replenished supply of 'stars', television set out to generate its own. More or less simultaneously, many of the medium's regular guests, those actors, singers, writers and politicians who were constantly turning up on the screen, started to grow sensitive to the advisability of not merely 'having' but 'being' a personality. They metamorphosed themselves into *post-media* creatures, ingratiating themselves with the medium, planing away all their behavioural angularities and idiosyncrasies and gradually inserting their individualities within quotation marks.[1] And the operation now runs so smoothly that when a supposedly 'telegenic' cabinet minister (a David Mellor, for example) is sacked from the government, there is no reason for him not to continue appearing on television as though nothing in his public status has changed.

Given the progressive 'dumbing' of our culture, it was all, I suppose, bound to happen. I still consider it drolly appropriate, though, that the French word for electronic 'interference' or 'static' is *parasites*. For, in the end, that is surely what all these television personalities are: parasites, smirking interference, human static.

Notes

1 Compare the early television appearances of John Betjeman, when he was still only 'the poet', with his later ones, when he had become, and with a vengeance, 'the poet and personality'.

On Wallace and Gromit

I once asked an advertising man of my acquaintance, an Argentinian animator and graphics artist based in London, who had just screened for me a brilliant 'demo' tape of his television work, to name his own favourite commercial. This was in the late eighties, when advertising was as modish a profession as junk bond manipulation, and I suppose I expected him to opt for one of the decade's more self-consciously classy ads, ads typically set in some neon-lit bistro with an ambience that hinted at both a romantically glamorised American past and an improbably cosmopolitan British future. I was therefore slightly taken aback when, after a moment of reflexion, he named one of those Brooke Bond PG Tips commercials whose casts, then as now, were made up of Cockney chimpanzees.

I was taken aback, as I say. Yet, oddly enough, if the same question were put to me today, I would not even need a moment to reflect. My answer would be the exact nineties equivalent: one of the 'Creature Comforts' ads directed by Nick Park for Aardman Films.

Park is an extraordinary case. His first short featuring the suburban inventor Wallace and his sardonic, long-suffering dog Gromit, *A Grand Day Out*, was nominated for an Oscar. The following in the canon, *Creature Comforts* (from which the above-mentioned electricity ads were developed), won him an Oscar. Another Wallace and Gromit short, *The Wrong Trousers*, not only won him a second Oscar (two Oscars and a nomination in nearly as many years!)[1] but became a bestselling videotape. So it might be worth attempting to analyse what it is that makes these little films so irresistible one cannot even think about them without grinning.

It is a matter of especial interest to me as, having had a weakness for animation since my infancy, I have now entirely lost patience with it, both the mainstream Hollywood variety (Disney, Tex Avery, Chuck Jones) and the less chirpy European confections of the Quay Brothers and Jan Svankmajer. What originally enchanted me about animation – its potentially limitless freedom of action and narrative – is just what I now find so tiresome and frustrating. When anything is possible, nothing is any longer meaningful: paradoxically, cartoons strike me as inhibited by their very licence to do absolutely anything they please. (It is as easy to draw a fire raging in a forest as one cosily flickering in the grate of a fireplace.) And it is significant that, coextensively with the ascendancy of special effects in the American cinema of the eighties, there came a corresponding decline in the popularity of the increasingly redundant cartoon, a decline which has since, spectacularly, been reversed by a belated return to the genre's traditional breeding-ground, the fairy-tale (*The Little Mermaid*, *Beauty and the Beast*, *Aladdin*). Significant, too, that this process has run parallel to the success of live-action adaptations of what were once exclusively cartoons (the film versions of *Dennis the Menace* and *The Flintstones*, the Broadway musicalisation of Disney's *Beauty and the Beast*).

Nick Park's relation to such reproductive frenzy is a somewhat ambiguous one. It has often been noted that, the more ingenious a television commercial, the less likely one is to recall the name and even the nature of the advertised product. What, by contrast, one tends to forget from Park's 'Creature Comforts' ads are the species of the animals interviewed in them – a lapse I regard, in this specific instance, as a compliment to the films. For their unique charm lies in a refusal, precisely, to take full advantage of the potential liberty at their disposal. Like those of the Brooke Bond ads, their settings belong to an identifiable lower-middle-class environment (lower-middle-class Plasticine models – the concept is close to revolutionary!), the only difference with live-action ads being that the denizens of that environment happen to be turtles, polar bears and suchlike. And the humour arises from the fact that, since these creatures, unlike the Brooke Bond chimpanzees, are dubbed not by actors but by 'real people', they make not just vividly *human* but unmistakably *British* turtles and polar bears. Their biotypology aside, they would not appear out of place in an episode of *Coronation Street* or *EastEnders*, in a film by Mike Leigh or Ken Loach.

To be sure, *The Wrong Trousers*, a comedy-thriller, takes a whole slew of liberties with narrative verisimilitude (although the fact that

I feel bound to write of 'verisimilitude' at all intimates the enormous abyss which separates Park's work from conventional puppetry). Its finest moments are nevertheless as always the vignettes of tenderly observed British ordinariness: Wallace remarking 'Cracking piece of toast, Gromit' at the breakfast table, just like Stanley Holloway in an Ealing comedy; Gromit opening his musical birthday card and immediately shutting it again with a startled expression on his face; Gromit greeting the entrance of a new lodger, an amazingly sinister penguin, with bemused apprehension[2] or else waiting disgruntledly outside the household's monopolised bathroom with a towel slung over his paw.

There is, finally, the 'Creature Comforts' smile, that gormlessly toothy smile which distinguishes Park's creations from all others. It is a quintessentially British smile, sickly with embarrassment, with unease at the idea of having to take responsibility for such a public display of satisfaction. Not crescent-shaped, as we all tend to draw a smile, but of contours so amorphous they can be compared only to those assumed by a slack rubber band. A smile which, in Britain, can be spotted every day of the week at a bus stop, in a pub, on the steps of a church after a service. What Park has invented, in short, is a completely new mode of filmmaking: *naturalistic animation*.

Notes

1 In 1996, subsequent to the original newspaper publication of this essay, Park received a *third* Oscar for *A Close Shave*.

2 The ultimate test of an actor's talent is surely his ability to communicate the elusively indefinable state of 'bemusement'. There could therefore not be a better indication of Park's peculiar gifts than that one of his animated blobs of clay manages to bring it off triumphantly.

On Generation W

It is a paradoxical fact about capital cities that, the greater they are, the more culturally local and parochial they tend to be. What preoccupies the culturati of London at any given moment is apt to leave those of Paris, Rome or New York utterly indifferent – and vice versa. Whenever I spend any time in Paris, for example, I find that only by radically shifting gears am I able to participate in the city's cultural discourse. None of my Parisian acquaintances has the slightest interest in, or even knowledge of, Jeanette Winterson's boundless self-puffery or Damien Hirst's naughty-boy prankishness or Suzanne Moore's 'fuck-me' footware. Contrariwise, I no sooner alight from the plane at Roissy than I am expected to offer an informed opinion on the narcissism of the rakishly handsome, publicity-mad 'philosopher' Bernard-Henri Lévy or the apparently unending ructions at the Bastille Opéra, neither of which items would have a hope of stimulating a lively debate at a dinner-table in London. Where the arts are concerned, we are still, most of us, nationalists, rabid patriots. More often than not, too, that patriotism is anchored to a city rather than to the country of which it is the capital. For all McLuhan's theories of the world as global village, each capital city continues to set its own cultural agenda, one which, with rare exceptions (e. g. the Salman Rushdie affair), is incapable of reverberating beyond the confines of the language in which its discourse has been couched.

But a related question arises: who dictates the agenda? One would have to be extremely naïve to regard the dissemination of cultural trends and movements as an ecumenical process, evenly distributed, horizontally and vertically, among the nation's various classes, regions and generations. With the first two of these categories – classes and regions – we all know that it does not work like that: the arts in Britain remain essentially a middle-class, metropolitan preserve (with certain forms, notably the theatre, almost exclusively so). I would go further, however, and argue that our current cultural scene is also primarily (or, rather, publicly) the preserve of a single generation – which, taking my cue from the self-styled Generation X which succeeded it, I will call Generation W.

What this Generation W (W for War?) would encompass are the novelists, poets, dramatists, painters, filmmakers and musicians who were born at the end, or else in the immediate aftermath, of the Second World War – from the decade extending from, let us say, 1944 to 1954. It is these artists who, if any works of art are likely to endure from the sixties onward, have been responsible for them. It is they, too (or some of them), who comprise the very last generation to date to have established irreversible reputations and acquired household-name status.

Biased as that overview may appear (I myself was born in 1944), it is not an eccentric one. When a campaign was launched in 1994 to promote the best young writers of the nineties, what its detractors focused on was the nominees' lack of lustre relative to the previous generation's crop of Amis, Barnes, McEwan, Ishiguro and company. For better or worse, these latter writers have *tenure*. Many of the younger contenders, by contrast, either haunt the shadows of their elders (Will Self, whose surname rather belies his conspicuous debt to Amis) or have sputtered out after a promising start (Winterson, the Shelagh Delaney of her generation, condemned eternally to strain after the success of *Oranges Are Not the Only Fruit*, as Delaney strained after that of *A Taste of Honey*). As writers, their successes are akin to those of the Liberal Democrats: they may chalk up the odd, momentarily intoxicating by-election victory but the clinching consecration of a general election ever eludes them. Similarly, the most keenly awaited new plays in London are still, as was true ten, even twenty years ago, those of Pinter, Stoppard, Ayckbourn, Shaffer, Hare and so on. Countless works by younger dramatists have meanwhile come and gone – gone so definitively as to be irretrievable. As for the cinema, and however feverishly the media have heralded the advent of a new generation of filmmakers, hip young creatures whose model is James Cameron rather than Eric Rohmer, their work has so far made no impact whatsoever, either critically or commercially.[1]

When people think of 'the British cinema', they think of Leigh, Loach and Frears; or else, transatlantically, of Parker, Scott (Ridley and Tony both) and Lyne.

Curiously, the same applies to works of non-fiction. A publisher (who herself belongs to Generation W) once told me that when she had been approaching thirty she was offered nothing but projects about specifically thirtysomething problems (the ticking of the biological clock, etc.). A decade on, the favourite topics had themselves aged ten years. And she fully expected, when she reached sixty, to be inundated with manuscripts claiming, from various angles of approach, that it is at sixty, precisely, that life begins. Her insight, moreover, can be confirmed by a rapid chronological survey of the books written by Germaine Greer, who seems to believe that whatever phase of life she herself has arrived at, be it characterised by promiscuity, chastity or menopause, is just that phase of life to which any sensible woman, of whatever age-group, ought to be aspiring.

So why has the younger generation not yet usurped the power and ubiquity of its elders (save in the performing arts, where youth remains the supreme ideal)? The answer, surely, lies in what the American literary critic Harold Bloom termed 'the anxiety of influence' – the looming, lowering pressure exerted, wilfully or not, by those who have already 'made it' on those who have not, a pressure cramping, crushing and on occasion castrating the creative energies of the rising generation. It has frequently been said that artists may be destroyed by premature success. Yet if there is one thing even more destructive than one's own premature success, it is the premature success of others.

Notes

1 I would now, as I rewrite, except the triumvirate of *Shallow Grave* and *Trainspotting*: Danny Boyle, John Hodge and Andrew Macdonald.

On newspaper cartoons

To illustrate an article about an officially commissioned portrait of John Major, the *Sunday Times* published a cartoon by its regular cartoonist, Newman. In Newman's version, the portrait in question was shown as fuzzily out-of-focus, the painter's excuse being, as he complains to a Whitehall mandarin, that the Prime Minister[1] 'kept shifting his position'. And the point which concerns me is that the painter himself was portrayed by the cartoonist as a bushy-bearded bohemian in beret and smock, a kidney-shaped easel in his hand.

Now I have never met Nick Newman and know nothing about him except his work. Yet I do not doubt for a moment that he was aware of the huge difference between the appearance of his caricature and the lifestyle of any living artist. That caricature was what Oliver Sacks once defined as a 'perfect specific', an emblematic image refined of every last trace of ambiguity, liberated from every conceivable social referent. Like all cartoonists, Newman was obliged to squeeze his joke into a space only slightly larger than a postage-stamp and therefore lacked the room to register anything as subtle as a nuance. We do not expect nuances from cartoons. We all understand their dependence on stereotypology, and the only potential risk is of a racial slur (e. g. the once trusty standby of loinclothed, nose-ringed natives boiling missionaries in outsized stewpots).

The first lesson, however, to be learned by the incorrigible interpreter of signs, the professional or amateur semiologist, is that *everything is about something else* – even a cultural manifestation as humble and ephemeral as a newspaper cartoon. From the example cited above one might suppose that such cartoons long ago severed every vestigial link with reality, just as the tiny single-palm desert island, which is to the cartoon what the sofa is to the sitcom, long ago severed every vestigial link with geography.[2] Yet, as the semiologist's second lesson teaches us, meaning and relevance can be nurtured in even the most minuscule of incubators.

So what sort of world is it that these cartoons depict? It is a world in which Frenchmen are infallibly identified by their berets, baguettes and onion-garlanded bicycles, Germans by their obesity and lederhosen, Americans by their cameras and Stetsons, and Australians, primarily, by the corks which dangle from their wide-brimmed outback hats. A world in which football supporters wear enormous rosettes and carry wooden rattles. A world in which convicts wear uniforms stencilled with little arrows and cat burglars wear face-masks and striped roll-neck jumpers and lug sacks over their shoulders with 'Swag' written on them. (Do they buy them from a burglars' outfitters?) A world in which all schoolmasters have gowns and mortar-boards, all schoolgirls have acne, buck teeth and pigtails and all book publishers have tweedy jackets and polka-dotted bow ties. A world in which newspaper editors sport green eye shields and newspaper reporters thirties-style felt hats with press cards tucked into their brims. A world in which door-to-door sales-men make their weary rounds bearing suitcases of combs and brushes, and film directors wear jodhpurs and bellow directions through megaphones (even if, in Hollywood, it has been many decades since the tyrants in jodhpurs were replaced by the tyros in diapers and the megaphones by megabucks). A world in which every factory has a suggestion box, every department store a complaints counter and every public library a menacing 'Silence' placard. A world in which no City boardroom wall is without its sales chart and no sales chart without its zigzagging graph-line, a graph-line which may even plummet right off the chart on to the wall itself. A world, finally, in which the Queen wears her crown to breakfast, a bushy-bearded God sits enthroned upon a cloud, and Death invari-ably shows up hooded in black and brandishing a scythe.

It is a world, in short, of simple, instantly legible archetypes and, as such, perhaps the last repository of operative, meaningful com-monplaces in our culture. Operative, yes – we continue to laugh at these cartoons (if they are any good) and their hopelessly outmoded mythology only adds to the general hilarity. But why meaningful?

Without wishing to labour the point, I would say that, if the iconography of such cartoons is, for the cartoonists themselves, merely a useful form of graphic shorthand, for their public it actually represents an alternative world, a world blissfully unlike that on which newspapers, precisely, are obliged to report, a world as we like to imagine our own world used to be. In this world a painter *looks like* a painter – which is to say, like Augustus John, not like Jeff Koons. A schoolmaster *looks like* a schoolmaster – like Robert Donat in *Goodbye, Mr Chips*, not like the motley crew of teachers with whom one has become familiar from television coverage of their annual conference. And a burglar *looks like* a burglar, not like . . . like what? Ah, but that is just the problem: no one these days quite knows what a burglar does look like, not even the police. Newman got it absolutely right. It is not only John Major but the whole country that is fuzzy and out-of-focus, because, like him, *it keeps shifting its position*. And what the traditional cartoon offers is a nostalgic, reassuringly reactionary vision of a stable, unchanging Britain, a microcosmic desert island of intelligibility amid a macrocosmic shark-infested ocean of confusion.

Donald McGill is dead, Andy Capp has given up smoking and the *Guardian*'s Steve Bell, unquestionably the finest cartoonist in the country, is beginning to take himself for Goya. Yet, as long as the crude, old-fashioned, one-off newspaper cartoon is alive, we can still claim to possess our very own *commedia dell'arte*.

Notes

1 As then was.
2 In a Gary Larson cartoon a shipwrecked sailor, swimming through a shark-infested ocean towards a desert island, discovers, nailed to its solitary palm tree, a sign which reads 'Beware of the Dog'.

On pedantry

Everyone, I am sure, knows at least one such pedant – a pedant, I mean, like the friend with whom I once flew to New York. The inflight movie, which both of us watched, if initially with no pronounced enthusiasm on either part, was *Mrs Doubtfire*; and it was afterwards, over a drink, that my friend, whose reaction to the film had been much more positive than mine, voiced his single serious reservation. *Mrs Doubtfire*, for those who have not seen it, featured Robin Williams as a voice-over artist in an animation studio who, dismissed simultaneously from his job and his marriage, conceives the notion of applying, in drag, for the advertised post of nanny to his wife's (and of course his own) offspring. And the sole plot point at which my travelling companion balked was Williams's sacking. However temperamental an employee he was shown to be, he argued, the studio would never have dispensed with the services of so brilliant a mimic.

My first response to his criticism went, as cocktail pianists say, something like this: So long as it gets the plot going, who cares if the premise is not altogether credible. But I also raised the basic illogicality (typical of these pedants) of his taking exception to such an insignificant infelicity yet swallowing without apparent strain the considerably greater implausibility that even so impeccable a female impersonator could ever have succeeded in passing himself off as a bosomy Scottish nanny to the wife and children with whom he had lived for many years. My friend was unfazed. To argument (a) he replied that, if you are going to have a plot at all, you might as well get it right; and to argument (b) he replied that, well, yes, I had a point (here he was, and he knew it, on shakier terrain), but female impersonation is a convention as ancient as Shakespeare and conventions exist to be swallowed.

To which I in turn retorted that lapses in verisimilitude, not to mention blatant narrative inconsistencies, are also as ancient as

Shakespeare. Whatever became of Mrs Lear, who is never alluded to in Shakespeare's text? How many children did the Macbeths have? None, says Macbeth, naturally anxious about the dynastic succession. Says Lady Macbeth meanwhile: 'I have given suck, and know how tender 'tis to love the babe that milks me.' Iago, for his part, starts spreading rumours of Desdemona's infidelity while she and Othello are still honeymooning in Cyprus. When on earth was she supposed to have had either the time or the opportunity to be unfaithful?

The answer to all of these questions would doubtless be that Shakespeare is an exception, and that exceptions cannot serve as examples. What, though, returning to the cinema, about the scores of westerns in which wagon trains are surrounded by marauding Indians? Why do the ambushed settlers always aim at the Indians themselves? Why not at their horses, a far roomier target? What about those thrillers in which, just before (as he intends) finishing the hero off, the villain obligingly spells out his plans to enslave the world? Or those 'women's pictures' in which, two-thirds of the way through, there inevitably occurs the Big Misunderstanding – that moment, regular as clockwork, when the hero chooses *not* to tell the heroine the real motive for his accepting a construction job in South America or the heroine chooses *not* to tell the hero the real motive for her abrupt change of heart (as when, in *An Affair to Remember*, Deborah Kerr prefers not to reveal her crippled condition to Cary Grant and thus the reason for her failure to keep their appointment on the observation platform of the Empire State Building)? What, to be more specific, about Howard Hawks's *The Big Sleep*, whose labyrinthine plot no one, not Hawks himself, nor his scenarist, William Faulkner, nor even Raymond Chandler, from whose novel it was adapted, was ever able to figure out. Or Jean Renoir's *La Nuit du carrefour* (based on one of Simenon's Maigret novels), of which, so legend has it, two whole reels were definitively mislaid? Or *Apocalypse Now*? It was, I think, Pauline Kael who asked why, when ordered to liquidate Marlon Brando, Martin Sheen was obliged to travel to the latter's jungle fastness by gunboat. Why did he not simply appropriate one of the countless helicopters that we see whirring continuously overhead, scoot downriver and be home in time for tea?

The fact remains that *The Big Sleep* is the American cinema's finest *film noir*, not a little of whose beauty and mystery derive from its plot's very incomprehensibility; that, had those two reels not gone missing, *La Nuit du carrefour* might not be quite the exquisite enigma that it is; and that, if Sheen had indeed decided to commandeer a helicopter, there would be no *Apocalypse Now* to carp at. Like settlers aiming at Indians rather than at their horses, like loquacious villains and the Big Misunderstanding, Sheen's gunboat is one of those devices of suspense and postponement by which a filmmaker holds his public in seductive, Scheherazadesque thrall. It embodies what Barthes termed a narrative's 'sense of preservation'.

The final argument employed by all such pedantic sticklers is that contemporary films, being more 'realistic' than used to be the case, can no longer accommodate the unplotted loose ends and general narrative slovenliness that went formerly unchecked. It seems to me, however, that believing that an art form can ever become, merely with the passage of time, more realistic (in, presumably, the sense of 'more lifelike') is as naïve as believing that the period one is living in, whichever it might be, necessarily represents some sort of ideal culmination towards which the history of human achievement has inexorably been converging. Every successive period behaves as though it has reached an unsurpassable apogee of naturalistic representation. Equally, the art of each of these periods is later exposed as having been just as corseted in convention and contrivance as any that preceded it – and so, one day, will our own, no matter how 'realistic' it appears to us now.

In the Stone Age the Lascaux cave drawings were probably regarded as the *ne plus ultra* in gritty realism – except that there would certainly have been some prehistorical pedant around to point out that the bison's limbs were far too spindly to support their torsos.

On posterity

In the summer of 1985 the French daily newspaper *Libération* published a special 150-page supplement, 'Pourquoi écrivez-vous?', in which a cross-section of writers from all over the world were asked why they wrote. Their responses were many and various, but by far the most intelligent was Faulkner's (he was not one of those questioned, needless to say, but was quoted by someone who was): 'Because it's worth the trouble.' *Because it's worth the trouble.* Besides being irrefutable, the force of that lapidary manifesto lay in its singleminded focus on the internal processes of literary creation, on what Flaubert called the writer's *adventures* with language, and its implicit rejection of such external incentives as the classic Freudian trio of money, fame and the love of beautiful women. It also usefully short-circuited any embarrassing fantasies about posterity, a factor that preoccupied a surprising number of the participants.

That was twelve years ago. And today? Politicians still, and for the most part ludicrously, fantasise about posterity, and probably more artists than one imagines secretly dream of it (but it is the dream that dare not speak its name). Yet, paradoxically, apart from Jeanette Winterson, whose belief in its importance is the one courageous, even moving aspect of her self-aggrandising delirium, the only contemporary British writers on whom it continues to exert a public fascination are the perpetrators of pulp, with Ken Follett musing poignantly of winning the Booker Prize and Jeffrey Archer the Nobel. No real writer would be caught dead, so to speak, ruminating aloud about still being read a hundred years hence, as Stendhal famously did, as well as the eponymous poetaster protagonist of Max Beerbohm's short story 'Enoch Soames'.[1]

So, naturally, what we ask ourselves is why? Why of late has posterity been, if not discredited, then debased? Or, putting it whimsically, why, if we can ask children what they want to be when they grow up, can we not ask grown-ups what they want to be when they die?

It is perhaps, in the first place, because we live in a more and more volatile, less and less God-fearing world. Our purchase on the future has been so diminished that the attraction of posterity, as a carrot dangled ever out of reach, has long since ceased to be what it once was. Posterity is what might be described as the afterlife of the creator, and most of us, creators or not, no longer believe in, or even care about, an afterlife. We would quite cheerfully exchange Shakespeare's five centuries of posterity for Andy Warhol's fifteen minutes of fame – always assuming we were permitted to enjoy that fame in our own lifetime.

There is, too, the uneasy conviction that posterity is beyond our control, that it reserves too many disagreeable surprises. To those, for example, who are on record as regarding *Schindler's List* as just about the most overwhelming experience the cinema has ever offered us, it might be worth recalling the sensation created in the early thirties by a similar bleeding chunk of red, raw subject-matter, *All Quiet on the Western Front*, both Erich Maria Remarque's original novel and Lewis Milestone's Oscar-winning film version. Sixty years on, things seem to have gone all quiet on that front, too. If neither work is negligible, nor could either now expect to make a prominent showing in any respectable history of fiction or film.

The most powerful of all deterrents to self-absorbed reflexions on posterity, though, is the homogenisation of quality in the postmodern world. Whatever else it may concurrently be up to, postmodernity represents the apotheosis of cultural relativism. The literary pages of newspapers and magazines now routinely review the sort of off-the-peg fiction which used to be purchased almost shamefacedly in airport bookshops and read almost surreptitiously on Mediterranean beaches. Whether such a radical broadening of horizons is a necessary corrective to a once stiflingly élitist approach to literature is open to debate. Undebatable, in my opinion, is the correlative proposition that it has led to a general, calamitous decline in standards and aspirations. One can hear the aspiring author say to him- or herself: Why bother trying to write like Flaubert when, by writing like Jilly Cooper, I can make myself lots more money and *still* be reviewed in the posh papers, often enthusiastically, just as though I *were* Flaubert? (Why bother? Because it's worth the trouble, Faulkner would reply. But Faulkner is dead and what do the dead know?)

And this postmodern relativism, this democratisation (for want of a ruder word) of literary culture, has totally altered our conception of what posterity is and how it works. It was once the case that you had to be at least Van Gogh if you hoped to be remembered a century after your death. Today, in every good bookshop, as the saying goes, next to some sumptuous monograph of Van Gogh, there sits a probably even more sumptuous monograph devoted to the canvases of Van Bloggs, a hitherto neglected, now rediscovered, *petit-maître* of the same period. Alongside the Monets and Manets in the Musée d'Orsay in Paris, the world's very first postmodern museum, hang the academic, once-derided daubs of Bouguereau and Meissonnier. If you are a woman, and you happen to have written a work of fiction in the last hundred years, then you are automatically eligible for republication as one of Virago's Modern Classics. So why, again, ruminates the writer, why strain after a Flaubertian purity of style when posterity is prepared to do the honours even if all you are capable of is a Jilly Cooperish clunkiness? No, indeed – posterity, like nostalgia, isn't what it used to be.

(However, just in case you *are* reading this in 2097, how's tricks?)

Notes

1 Having sold his soul, literally, in order that he might be granted advance knowledge of posterity's judgment on his poetry, the poor, doomed Soames is horrified to discover that the sole reference to him in the British Library's catalogue is, precisely, as the fictional hero of Beerbohm's tale – a superb, precocious example of postmodern recursiveness.

On genius

If, as a reader, you are respecting the order in which these essays have been printed, you will just have finished the one on posterity. Well, musing on posterity reminded me of another word, one with which it is intimately conjoined and which we also continue to use in spite of its now somewhat dated and hollow ring: the word 'genius'. And it might be useful to interrogate that word in its turn in order to uncover what message it currently emits.

First, a personal anecdote. When I was a small child, my (now late) father went blind. It was a horribly protracted process, rendered all the more agonising for him by the fact that the specialists whom he consulted over a number of months and even years remained unshakably optimistic right up to the unforgettable day on which a life sentence of sightlessness was abruptly pronounced upon him. I need hardly add that that particular day haunted my entire childhood. But, immature as I was, I remember already being bemused by a weird anomaly, as I saw it, in the situation. Throughout the tragedy – my father's tragedy, after all – it was my mother who was at the receiving end of all the sympathy. No one ever spoke to my father of his affliction: *it was as though his blindness had rendered him invisible*. Equally, no one could resist gabbing away to my mother about how dreadful it was, *for her*, to have a husband struck down in his prime. My father's blindness, a condition regarded as practically biblical in its pestilentiality, was *beyond* sympathy. One would not have known where to start.

Genius, true genius, is a little like that – beyond comprehension, beyond admiration and, if ever sympathy should strike one as the appropriate response (Stephen Hawking?), beyond sympathy. It goes without saying, for example, that Einstein was a genius; hence there is not much point in saying it. Someone who is not Einstein, however, but who *understands* Einstein's theory of relativity – *that*, we can cope with. *There*, we are prepared to employ the word unstintingly. ('The man's a bloody genius!') And it is probably the only level on which most of us can engage with genius at all.

Or, rather, it used to be. But genius, like posterity (and like how many other, once exalted concepts?), has been publicly demoted, its complexity reduced to the sum of its most conspicuous signifiers. 'Bad temper,' rhapsodises Joan Crawford, a grotesque patroness of the arts in the Clifford Odets-scripted film *Humoresque*, 'the infallible sign of genius!' Well, yes and no (although it is amusing to note that Odets himself was a famously temperamental man). But there can be no question that, nowadays, at least as popularly perceived, genius has become essentially a cluster of external signs.

Take the death of Dennis Potter. Potter, one obituary notice after another assured us, had been a genius. For once, no journalist felt reticent about employing the word. Yet why so, when one considers that Potter had not had a good review from these same journalists in many years; when one considers, too, how parsimoniously it has been applied to other comparable, often superior artists? Easy: (a) he worked in a medium, television, in which we do not usually expect to find the stamp of an individual sensibility; (b) his plays were sexy; (c) he himself was opinionated to the point of rudeness; (d) he had psoriasis; (e) he drank liquid morphine while being interviewed by Melvyn Bragg; and (f) he was dead. It would seem that genius, which ought by rights to be an ineffable virtue, can be disassembled without difficulty into a set of constituent cogs.

Potter was only one of the most prominent of a long line of pet British 'geniuses'. Two other contemporary artists who have had the mantle of genius thrust upon them at one time or another, more than a trifle rashly, are Ken Russell (the British cinema's perennial 'bad boy') and Julien Temple (for about five minutes that same cinema's resident *wunderkind*: then *Absolute Beginners* was released). Peter Sellers, unquestionably a less subtle actor than, say, Gary Cooper or James Stewart, was invariably described, as they never were, as 'a genius of the cinema'. Why? Because he could do funny voices and they could not; because even a fool could see that he was talented, whereas the gifts of a Cooper or a Stewart remained mysteriously indefinable. As for another recent 'genius' type, Derek Jarman, a minor figure if ever there was, but possessed of personal flamboyance, an artistic temperament that was more or less permanently on display and an undoubted courage in the face of death, it helped in his case (as in Fassbinder's and Warhol's) that he had his own entourage of hangers-on. No one is readier to proclaim genius in his idol than the kind of groupie who lives in his shadow and has therefore never had close contact with any other artist. When Brian Jones drowned, one of the surviving Rolling Stones paid this tribute to him: 'Brian *was* music.' Move over, Mozart.

Mozart, precisely. I recall, when I saw Peter Shaffer's *Amadeus*, observing to my companion that the key to its success was that it served up a platitude as triumphantly as though it were a paradox. Poor Salieri (the composer who is truly libelled by the play) cannot understand why, having sweated to become the greatest musician of his day, he should be so indecently upstaged by Mozart, an obscene tot brimming with unearned genius. Yet there *is* no paradox. The play's lewd, cavorting Mozart behaves *exactly* as orthodox opinion expects a genius to behave, and it would have been a far more intriguing exercise (probably, too, far closer to the truth) to have portrayed genius in the hard-working guise of a Salieri – genius, in short, as an infinite capacity for taking pains. Shaffer's Mozart is a cliché of genius, which Mozart himself could not have been.

Since genius has, in other words, become a mere formula, it is not surprising that the genius of geniuses in modern times is still dear old Einstein. Einstein looked like a genius, he acted like a genius and he dressed like a genius. Best of all, it was in the most beautiful, ethereally pristine formula imaginable that his genius found external expression. If, for cosmologists, $e=mc^2$ is an equation relating to arcane affinities of mass and energy, it will always be, for the rest of us, the ultimate formula for genius.

On Hollywood

In a single three-word manifesto of a sentence the film scenarist William Goldman once skewered the ignorance at the core of what everyone had always assumed was deductive reasoning of near-Byzantine complication. 'Nobody,' he declared of Hollywood's decision-making processes, 'knows anything.' It is a sentence (from his published memoir, *Adventures in the Screen Trade*) which has since been accepted as gospel by both the industry and those whose job it is to comment upon it, accepted almost as uncritically as one of those complacent but in reality all too fallible truisms which it was Goldman's purpose, precisely, to demystify. If it is really the case, though, that nobody knows *anything* – as to why certain films work and others which appear to have just as much going for them don't; as to why certain films are already commercial failures by the very first day of their release, before either reviews have appeared or word-of-mouth begun to circulate; as to why Mel Gibson's *Maverick* was a commercial success and Kevin Costner's *Wyatt Earp* a commercial flop – logic dictates that nobody knows whether Goldman's truism, too, will prove to be fallible. If nobody knows anything, then Goldman, after all, does not know anything either. And, *pace* the man himself, it is possible to argue that this at least is known about the contemporary American cinema: that the only way a new film can become a monstrous and unexpected hit (what in professional parlance is called a 'sleeper') is for its appeal to be so broad as to attract people who don't normally like films.

Note that I use the qualifiers 'monstrous' and 'unexpected'. On the question of achieving routine success in the cinema Goldman is right: nobody, patently, knows anything. Nowadays, however, the major studios are no longer content with mere routine successes – what they have set their sights on are *phenomena*. While more and more new films are released only, so to speak, on parole (these are the ones you will not even have heard of), and countless blockbusters go, more swiftly than expected, the way of all flesh (and all flash), the phenomenon is the film which breaks box-office records, which prompts a nationwide debate in the media and which, above all, attracts the sort of person who does not ordinarily go to the cinema but is curious to know, on this occasion, just what everyone else is talking about. And the strangest aspect of all about what might be termed the phenomenon of the phenomenon is that it has come to apply less to a Schwarzenegger vehicle than to a film like Robert Zemeckis's *Forrest Gump*, an airy comedy-drama in which thirty years of modern American history (the moon landing, the Black Panthers, the Vietnam War, Watergate, the Aids epidemic) drift serenely through the mindset of a moron, the titular Forrest, played by Tom Hanks. In the United States it crossed the two hundred million dollar threshold in a mere forty-six days of distribution and is now among the ten most profitable films ever made. If ever there was a phenomenon in the cinema, *Forrest Gump* is it.[1]

Yet, even if it traded in the unbeatable Spielbergian combination of good feelings and special effects – Forrest is seen amiably chatting, *à la* Zelig, with such deceased and electronically resurrected luminaries as Richard Nixon, Lyndon Johnson and John Lennon – there seemed to many of us nothing so very out-of-the-ordinary as to turn *Forrest Gump* into a precedent-setting hit. It was, in short, a film that no more than a decade ago would have done reasonably well and been forgotten. And the fact that, today, it is not simply a success but an outright phenomenon is a function not of its own extremely moot qualities but of the present state of the medium. So terminally puerile has the American cinema become, the cinema of *The Flintstones*, *The Beverly Hillbillies*, *Getting Even With Dad*, *Baby's Day Out*, *Look Who's Talking*, and so desperate, apparently, are audiences for something, *anything*, which can boast a half-respectable IQ, it now happens that films which would once have enjoyed a decent success and no more, not just *Forrest Gump* but *Sleepless in Seattle*, *The Crying Game*, *Philadelphia* and *Four Weddings and a Funeral*, currently find themselves elevated to the status of the phenomenon. In the land of the blind . . . In the land of the dumb . . .

One further point. If *Forrest Gump* is likely to be far the most profitable of all recent such phenomena, it is not least because of those special effects. Prior to the seventies, there had been three technological points of no return in the history of the American cinema: the advent of sound in the late twenties, of colour in the mid-thirties and of a variety of widescreen processes in the mid-fifties. To these, I believe, we must henceforth add special effects. Every film made today (with only the odd, eccentrically marginal exception) is a talkie; practically every film is in colour; and the great majority of Hollywood films, certainly, are screened in some form of wide-screen process (even if the staying power of that particular innovation was almost at once compromised by the conflicting requirements of television). And I would now contend that *every* film of the future will, sooner or later, visibly or invisibly, deploy special effects in one guise or another. Already, these effects can no longer be dismissed as an optional luxury, the sole preserve of multimillion-dollar budgets, an excrescence on the medium's otherwise seamless surface. They are, instead, an indispensable component of what that medium is and how it is going to evolve. As an industry, possibly also as an art, it is henceforth indissociably linked to them.

Special effects are, of course, far from new (one need think only of Méliès), but the film which first intuited their central and abiding role in the cinema was Stanley Kubrick's *2001*. It was in that intuition, rather than in his now comically dated fantasies of interplanetary communication, that Kubrick was authentically ahead of his time, authentically a prophet. By 2001 no one, I wager, will have landed on Jupiter. Film, on the other hand, will have become, *by definition*, the art of special effects.

Notes

1 In a *New Yorker* cartoon, published at the time of the film's release, a maître d'hôtel, about to seat a couple of diners, blandly enquires, 'Pro-Gump section or anti-Gump section?'

On cultural nationalism

'If, by merely pressing a switch,' goes the old poser, 'you could make Hitler (or Stalin, or Saddam Hussein, or Margaret Thatcher, or whomever you please) disappear for ever from the face of the earth, would you press it?'

These days the question is no longer a hypothetical one. The switch exists. It is the off button on a TV set. By pressing it, you can indeed remove your favourite villain from, if not the face then the screen, of the earth. And with a remote-control unit you can distance yourself even further from the act and its moral implications.

Nor need you confine yourself to politicians or even members of the human race. One of the tiny, trivial treats that I currently reserve for myself, while watching anything on BBC television, is taking remote-control potshots at the station signals by which the Corporation's programmes are preceded and followed and, in particular, at that infuriatingly cute and versatile '2' of BBC2 that either scurries across the screen like an infant's clockwork rabbit or explodes into a gaudy firework display or billows sexily out of a satiny blue background. I acknowledge that these graphics (like Channel 4's) are clever; and, yes, I know that they have won several awards. But I also believe that the connective spaces between television programmes should be set aside as brief moments of repose, of calm, of closure, opportunities of rest and relief for the eyes. Above all, I have come to wonder whether, by throwing up a smokescreen of high-powered quality where it matters least, by creating a superficial ambience of technical mastery and flair, an ambience few actual programmes can match (how often have you sat through a brilliant display of computer graphics only to discover that the programme which immediately follows it is the same old load of rubbish?), it is these graphics as much as what is sandwiched between them which are responsible for the generally high esteem in which British television is held.

For if there is one commonplace concerning our cultural life on which public opinion is all but consensual, it is that British television is the best or (as even the sceptics are prepared to concede) 'least worst' in the world. It wins prizes, it exports well and it is frequently held up as an example to others. True, a vague undertow of irritation has slowly begun to chip away at that unanimity. There is a faint suspicion that our national TV is becoming just a wee bit smug and righteous about its own virtues, a suspicion voiced by the reviewer A. A. Gill when, praising Victoria Wood's play *Pat and Margaret*, he damningly tempered his panegyric by calling it 'all so sort of "best television in the world" – English, knowing, backslapping, Bafta-winningly good'. Yet even if we understand what he means, most of us who have travelled in that world, and indulged in one of the emblematic pastimes of the contemporary peripatetic, padding naked or half-naked around a hotel room while casually zapping its television set, tend to return home with our chauvinist prejudices basically intact.

The curious thing, though, as I discovered on a trip to France, is that *everyone else feels the same way about their own television.* 'Everyone else' is of course hyperbole and not meant to be interpreted literally. I did attend a dinner party, nevertheless, at which each of my fellow guests (apart from our two French hosts) was of a different nationality: there were, around the table, an Argentinian, a German, an American and myself. And, the topic of conversation having turned to television, each of us claimed in turn (even the French, whose national TV, as I well know, is simply putrid) that, all things considered, and heaven knows most television is pretty ghastly most of the time, but, yes, ours is probably the most tolerable, the 'least worst', there is. The French couple raved about their (in reality, Franco-German) cultural channel Arte, the Argentinian about some deliriously surreal soap opera, the American about the unrivalled coverage of the O. J. Simpson trial and the German about an amazingly candid and informative series of documentaries on the penis (!), which, he insisted, doubtless justifiably, no other country would have dared to screen. As far as British TV was concerned, or as far as what any of them had seen of it, they were as one in finding the news biased, the sitcoms unfunny and the classic adaptations a bore. If there is one thing that television is not, it is 'universal'.

This is not just a convoluted restatement of some hoary, bewhisk-ered cliché: 'There's nowt so queer as folks', maybe, or 'East, west, home's best'. What such a nationalist divergence of opinions con-firms is that television is absolutely not an art form. For if no art is automatically universal, all art is potentially so. Television, by con-trast, has never been universal and never will be, and the proposition that British television is the best in the world is a meaningless one, since the comparison is being made in a void.[1] If we think British television is the best in the world, it is because it taps into our, and only *our*, memories, experiences and aspirations. It speaks to us about ourselves. It is, in a sense, a contemporary, nationwide species of home movies. It is *family*. And it is for that reason that people will always prefer their own television to any other, just as they (even the British) will always prefer their own cuisine to any other and, as Auden once mischievously remarked, will always have a secret weakness for the smell of their own farts.

Notes

1 It rather reminds me of a conversation I once had on a train with an Australian, who declared categorically that, from an *objective* point of view, there existed no finer country in the world than his own. 'Given that you feel that way,' I replied, 'what a happy coincidence you were born there. Otherwise, you would have had to go to all the trouble of emigrating.'

On light music

It sometimes seems as though nothing in the arts, no matter how minor, no matter how trivial, ever quite disappears for good. Do you remember J. R. Hartley, of *Fly-Fishing* fame, and how he eventually succeeded, after trawling through the telephone directory's *Yellow Pages*, in tracking down a second-hand copy of his memoir? Uniquely, surely, in the history of publishing, a book titled *Fly-Fishing*, by an author whom its jacket identified only as 'J. R. Hartley', was concocted in the wake of the television commercial, was purchased, was presumably read, and has since been so completely forgotten (didn't the mere mention of it again in print generate a little nostalgic frisson?), poor J. R. would probably have just as much trouble tracking it down now as in the original ad. Even so, whether in the *Yellow Pages* or from some other source, one may be sure that he *would* eventually secure a copy for himself. Somewhere it exists.

Consider, too, on a somewhat higher plane, the case of opera. It is, at least according to received wisdom, a 'dead' art, as Latin is a dead language. The supremely great operas, the only ones guaranteed to survive, have all been written already, so it is argued, and it is these alone which will continue to constitute the standard international repertoire. As an argument, it is hard to refute. With very few exceptions, the première of a new work at any of the world's opera houses is treated as an event solely because it is an anomaly; and it is not just unlikely but downright inconceivable that the finest living composer, whoever he or she may be, will ever contrive to write a masterpiece comparable to those of Mozart or Wagner. What would such an opera sound like? Would its composition not be an achievement as miraculous as the invention of a hitherto unknown colour? Indeed, does there any longer exist a potential configuration of notes and chords which, organised even with genius, would have an effect at all similar to that produced by *Don Giovanni* or *Tristan*? Art forms are not unlike those pyramid sales schemes which one tends to

211

hear about only when they end in abrupt and ignominious failure: *the people who get the most out of them are those who got in first.*

Yet operas do continue to be composed (Harrison Birtwistle's *Gawain*), just as novels in verse continue to be written (Craig Raine's *History: the Home Movie*), figurative paintings continue to be painted (Balthus, Hockney, Freud), black-and-white films continue to be shot (Tim Burton's *Ed Wood*), and all the other forms that were alleged to have been rendered redundant by modernism endure and even thrive. Culture – or, perhaps more specifically, post-modern culture (for it was not always thus, and the notion of 'neglect', so pivotal to contemporary criticism, is a relatively recent one) – is inherently anal retentive.

I can think of one creative category, however, which appears to have died for ever: light orchestral music. By that I do not mean those tired old pop standards which we associate with Frank Sinatra or Tony Bennett. I refer, rather, to the kind of music which, from the eighteenth century onward, was written by classical or semi-classical composers for the sheer, uncomplicated fun of it, the kind of undemanding if often magisterially orchestrated score (an obvious example would be Rimsky-Korsakov's *Scheherazade*) which did not have to be listened to, as Cocteau once pithily phrased it, 'with one's head in one's hands'. To be sure, classical music is again in vogue, and recordings of Gorecki's Third Symphony have sold in their tens of thousands. It is nevertheless worth pointing out, lest anyone take such unforeseen modishness as evidence to refute the claim which I have just been making, that the subtitle of the latter work is 'The Symphony of Sorrowful Songs' and that neither of Gorecki's two leading rivals in crossover popularity, Tavener and Part, is exactly what you would call a sunshine boy.

That, in any event, a demand exists for the music I am talking about is not in doubt. I could mention the recording success of a Poulenc, for example (especially when he assumes the raffish, ultra-Parisian, I'm only Poulenc-your-leg persona of his ballets and piano concertos – and who today would be able, or willing, to write music as joyous and witty as his?). Or that of the small but adventurous record company Marco Polo, which, over the past several years, has been responsible for a cycle of bestselling CDs issued under the rubric of 'British Light Music'.[1] Or that, indeed, of the umpteen recordings of *Scheherazade*.

I am aware that deploring the extinction of 'tuneful' music is a bit like owning up to a fondness for brass bands. I certainly have no desire to align myself with Keith Burstein, the composer (of sorts) who made himself a reputation (of sorts) by heckling *Gawain* at Covent Garden, and I do not wish to imply that, in the course of this century – or earlier, if one dates musical modernism from the Wagnerian and post-Wagnerian dissolution of tonality – the history of classical composition took a monstrously wrong turning. But I also tell myself that, when one comes right down to it, the word 'music' does have a basic, irreducible connotation of gaiety, of *happiness*, and I just cannot bring myself to believe in the health of an art form whose very nature seems to prevent it from ever relaxing or occasionally cracking a joke. I wonder why, during the sixties, there never occurred a musical revolution equivalent to that triggered off by Pop Art in painting, permitting the staider classical forms to draw new energy from fruitful contamination with the more seductive textures of our cultural environment. And, most frivolously, I long for the day when the hero of a film can turn to his inamorata and murmur in her ear, without any sense of incongruity on either their part or ours, 'Darling, let's make beautiful *modern* music together!'

Notes

1 These CDs (of mostly programmatic 'suites', a genre much favoured in the foothills of musical history) are endlessly charming and melodious, causing one all the more to regret the fact that many of the composers represented, Haydn Wood, Edward German, Roger Quilter, Frederic Curzon and so forth, belonged to the Edwardian era.

On Americana

Of two wholly dissimilar films whose release chanced to be more or less concurrent, Jan De Bont's *Speed* and Ken Loach's *Ladybird, Ladybird*, there could never be any contest as to which was going to make the more money. *Speed*, about a bus primed to explode if it should be driven at less than fifty miles an hour, was a roller-coaster ride of a film (a phrase used by practically every critic who reviewed it, none of whom thought it germane to point out that one of the medium's pioneers, Auguste Lumière, predicted in 1895 that the cinema was destined to remain nothing but a mindless sideshow attraction), whereas *Ladybird, Ladybird*, one of Loach's grumpier, least convivial works, centred on an unprepossessing working-class housewife whose children are systematically removed from her custody by the local authorities. Even if, from a pedantically literal point of view, the stakes were actually higher in *Speed* than in *Ladybird, Ladybird* (several lives, after all, are supposedly at risk on that bus), the former was an artlessly upbeat, crowd-pleasing entertainment, the latter, inevitably, something of an ordeal. Yet there is one other, and crucial, distinction to be drawn between them: the mere fact that *Speed* was made in America and *Ladybird, Ladybird* was not.

Made in America. I remember how intrigued I was by a TV commercial, screened many years ago now, in which a young woman, promised a new job in Paris, purringly confides to the viewer her chagrin on discovering that Paris, *Texas* was what was meant. The commercial was, in itself, an amusing enough parody of Wim Wenders's then current film, whose two-hour-plus narrative had been pulverised, in true postmodern fashion, into a sixty-second atmospheric vignette. But the ultimate, if unwitting, joke, a joke against the advertisers themselves, was that, considering all the febrile fantasising which goes on in Europe about the tumbleweedy perspectives of the American hinterland, with no more than a picturesquely lonely filling station or neon-lit diner *à la* Edward Hopper to break the delicious monotony, the prospect of living and working in Paris, Texas would probably have struck many a youthful, movie-mad viewer as actually the more appealing of the two options.

Similarly, a prominent French film critic once raved to me about what he described as the 'magically exotic' opening sequence of Vincente Minnelli's florid fifties melodrama *Some Came Running*. In fact, that sequence – a Greyhound bus pulls into a small-town square, its hydraulically controlled doors open and Frank Sinatra descends – contained absolutely nothing that would have struck an American as exotic. For Europeans, on the other hand, it crystallised that whole sociomythic mystique, that aura both cinematic and geographic, that continues to surround the United States.

If I say 'both cinematic and geographic', it is because, by now, it has become next to impossible to ascertain which came first, the cinematic or the geographic. Are we Europeans fascinated by the American cinema because we are fascinated by America? Or are we fascinated by America because, after a century of exposure to its cinema, we cannot help thinking of the country itself as one achingly, limitlessly vast film, a film whose scope for action and drama is no longer contained by a screen, however panoramic, but by the horizon itself? Anyone, certainly, who has travelled around the United States (in particular, for the first time) will recognise the eerie sensation I mean. I recall, for example, my own maiden trip across America in the late sixties. I recall my very first glimpse of the glass-and-steel Stonehenge of the Manhattan skyline, a skyline I knew by heart from a thousand films. I recall, too, crisscrossing the continent, precisely by Greyhound bus, and consulting a map from time to time, just as, at the opera, a mélomane might follow the music with the score on his knees. I recall, further, feeling assailed on all sides, like one of the passengers on John Ford's *Stagecoach*, by the neon-tipped arrows of Yankee consumerism. I recall, finally, how entranced I was by the spaghetti jumble of Los Angeles's freeways – spaghetti whose tomato ketchup (in a disorienting reversal of filmic practice) is blood. I felt, in short, during the two months of my sojourn, just as though, like the little boy in *The Last Action Hero*, I was living in a Hollywood film.

Perhaps not everyone would have had the monomaniacally cinephilic reaction to this splurge of Americana that I did. Yet the fact remains that, if a Hollywood director wishes to invest his imagery, at least as far as European audiences are concerned, with an indelible *authenticity*, a conviction that these visuals are fundamentally what the medium is all about, he has merely to train his camera on what it is that most stimulates him in his own national environment.[1] A British director, by contrast, even if his ambition is more populist, more escapist, than that of a Ken Loach, is handicapped from the start by the sheer resistance of his country to being interestingly filmed. Britain, on screen, especially when there has been little stylistic mediation on the director's part, tends to look as though it belongs more in a television programme than in a film (and British films made in the interwar years somehow managed to look like television before anyone knew what television itself was fated to look like). So British filmmakers have to work long and hard at what their American *confrères* are free to take for granted: a coherent and attractive cinematic vision of their native land. And when they do succeed in establishing an overall visual 'tone' (e. g. the hyper-British interiors and exteriors, faces, voices and accents, hats, frocks and kilts, of *Four Weddings and a Funeral*), it is often one that British spectators, not excluding those who like the film as a whole, find gratingly overdetermined.

Given Edison's pioneering experiments, the United States has as strong a claim as any country in the world to have invented the cinema. In the intervening century, the cinema has returned the compliment by reinventing America. And the two entities are now so inseparably interlinked in our culture that no one ought to be surprised that the word 'American' turns out to be an anagram of 'Cinerama'.

Notes

1 Such authenticity should not of course be mistaken for a style.

On a cultural revolution

In 1984, to celebrate what had been designated the British Year of the Cinema, the BBC commissioned a trio of first-person essays on the subject from the filmmakers Alan Parker, Lindsay Anderson and Richard Attenborough. The most exasperating (but also, perhaps not unexpectedly, the most watchable) was Parker's. Playing to the hilt his trademark persona of Islington-clapper-boy-made-good-in-an-unjust-world, Parker used the opportunity to lash out at everything in the cinema that he regarded as 'phony' (one of the philistines' pet words of abuse) – primarily art films, Peter Greenaway's in particular, and critics. The latter, he declared, were 'as useful to the industry as a scratch on a record'.

Insults, we know, have a habit of rebounding on those who trade in them, and for many that simile uncannily sums up the value of Parker's own contribution to his chosen medium. But, probably unintentionally, he had in fact raised an important issue: to whom, precisely, do critics owe allegiance? Parker himself was in no doubt. It was the critic's function to be 'useful', to be, in other words, a glorified publicist whose job was simply to coax and wheedle audiences into cinemas, no matter what was being screened in them. (Otherwise, why would he have referred to film as an 'industry'?) Most critics, however, would indignantly reject so reductive a job description, even if their writings frequently endorse it. They would claim that, if they owe any allegiance at all, it is to their readers, who look to them for informed guidance as to what they ought to see.

That, in turn, poses another problem. Consider the theatre. I once declined an offer to become a theatre critic on a national newspaper mainly because I had no idea how to reconcile the two incompatible imperatives with which I would necessarily be faced as a reviewer. On the one hand, only by a delicate balance of praise and censure, week after week, could I hope to retain the reader's sympathy and curiosity. On the other hand, the history of the theatre teaches us, and our own personal experience confirms the fact, that the vast majority of new plays (or films, or novels) are of no lasting consequence whatsoever. So that if, from posterity's hindsightful viewpoint, the most elementary measure of a critic's stature is just how often he *got it right*, then the critic whom future generations will judge to have been the sharpest and most trustworthy is logically the one who feels obliged to dismiss virtually every new play that comes his way.

For most practising critics, of course, so intransigently purist a stance would be a disaster, tantamount to discouraging anyone from going to the theatre at all. Yet overpraising a new play – either because it represents, even if inadequately, the sort of theatre one is personally seeking to promote; or else because it is the best out of a specific week's bad bunch; or, finally, because for a professional critic there is less risk attached to calling a minor work great than to calling a great work minor, as in the first case the work, and hence the opinion, will soon be forgotten – can be just as counterproductive. The reader, promised something 'magnificent', and faced with something that he himself rates no higher than 'okay', risks being alienated from a play which, had it not been so extravagantly lauded in the first place, he might unreservedly have enjoyed. As for the critic, he will have further compromised whatever reputation he once possessed for candour, taste and a sense of proportion. Indeed, it sometimes even happens that a reviewer who has, on a regular weekly basis, bandied about the most grandiose of superlatives ('Not to be missed!', 'If you see only one play this year, let it be this!') will then, in his annual round-up article in December, gripe about its having been yet another disappointing twelve months in the theatre!

What is the solution? My own belief is that, as the critic's credibility is umbilically linked to that of the dramatists whose work he is paid to review, what is urgently needed is a cultural revolution not in criticism but in the theatre itself. The dramatist David Edgar has argued that a thirty-year period of British theatre is now drawing to a close. As, I confess, a very intermittent theatregoer, I would readily agree with him, except that what strikes me as a point even more worth making is that one specific vein of theatre (of which Edgar's plays themselves are representative, as are David Hare's, Howard Brenton's, Howard Barker's, etc.) is now utterly exhausted. I mean the theatre of what I would define as *journalistic naturalism*, that theatre, be it of the TV sitcom or TV docudrama variety, whose method is to appropriate some current social issue and focus all its energies on mimicking the *textures* of the usually working- or lower-middle-class community in which the said issue is to be debated. However well, badly or indifferently done, it seems to me that such plays are stillborn, as weary, predictable and formulaic as the 'any-one-for-tennis' confections which they supplanted all of thirty (or even forty) years ago. It is now time, surely, to throw out the kitchen sink, to sling it on to the same malodorous junk heap of obsolete cultural symbols as the French window to which it once appeared to hold out such a promising alternative.

If I am right, and the British theatre *is* due to reinvent itself, the transformation is unlikely to be effected by the younger dramatists themselves, who, hypnotised by the successes of their elders, are demonstrably unable and unwilling to take the plunge. Which is where the critics are needed. It will be up to them to indicate the true way forward, to create a climate, just as Kenneth Tynan created a climate all those years ago when he championed Brecht and Beckett and Pinter. It will be up to them to encourage the creation of new theatrical forms, instead of, as tends to occur now, complacently defending what may still be valid about the old. And it will be up to them to propel the theatre, kicking and screaming if need be, into fresh (or, rather, dormant and long-neglected) modes of discourse, modes in which wit and fantasy, colour, myth and above all dreams will once more be brought into play – and into plays. For, paradox-ically, a theatre without dreams is a theatre which has lost touch with reality.

On technology

It is often said that, in the hierarchy of traumatic convulsions to which common humanity is heir, moving house comes third, preceded only by death and divorce. I seriously doubt it. Having myself moved house twice in the last decade, and finally got the point of a droll Indian curse I once heard, 'May you have the builders in!', I am now persuaded that I could take practically anything in my stride after the ordeals I have been through.

What I discovered, too, is that the trauma is exacerbated rather than diminished by the so-called technological revolution. In the eighties, when the possibility of such a revolution originally impinged itself on our minds, the new technology of faxes, computers, cellular phones, Ceefax and the like seemed little more than a vicarious *sheen*, of greater relevance to the glitteringly idealised world of television commercials than to the doggedly humdrum textures of life as it was lived around us. It also met with widespread resistance. The cellular phone became such a symbol of Thatcherism at its most unrepentantly rapacious and acquisitive that its users were jeered at in the street. Faxes long remained an unknown quantity. The sole computer with which most of us were personally familiar was that creaky old Model-T, the biliously black-and-green-screened Amstrad.[1] And, notwithstanding that their use was already relatively commonplace, even video recorders tended to flummox their proud new owners. I recall visiting an acquaintance of mine, a journalist, whom I found valiantly endeavouring to work in his study with the television humming away in a corner of the room and a dishcloth draped over it to conceal the screen. Although he had owned the recorder for a couple of months, it had still not dawned on him that, when taping a programme, he did not have to turn the set on at all.

For once in our lives, however, *the dream has come true*. The revolution has come to pass. Most of us possess at least a couple of the devices cited above, not to mention one we never then dreamt of, a sleek touch-tone telephone ('If you wish to make an enquiry, press button 1. If you wish to register a complaint, press button 2'), complete with call-waiting facilities and digitally detailed bills. Yet, for all that, as I realised when last in transit from one flat to another, we continue to live, for the most part, in a pre-high-tech Britain; we have yet to colonise, and be colonised by, the immaculate bimbo limbo of the TV commercial.

The cellular phones, for example, on which I was obliged to contact carpenters and electricians were either inaudible or switched off altogether, in which latter case a robotically dubbed message would keep me nicely fuming at the other end of the line. ('The Vodafone number you have dialled is not available at present. Please try later.') The banks and Inland Revenue offices I hoped to alert to my change of address would inform me with amazing frequency that 'The system is down' (the cybernetic equivalent of the British caff's fabled 'Cottage pie's off, luv') and no one, naturally, knew for certain when, if ever, it might become operative again. Fax machines would be crowded or jammed. Paper supplies automatically ran out in the middle of major photocopying chores. Telephone systems regularly terminated in the heartbreaking cul-de-sac of a recorded message ('I'm sorry, all our operators are busy at present, but your call has been placed in a queue'), a message reiterated every twenty seconds or so until it had been seared into the lining of my brain;[2] nor did I ever dare hold the receiver too far from my ear lest I miss the longed-for irruption on the line of an authentic human voice. As for those friends and colleagues in recent possession of a call-waiting phone facility, not one of them appeared to know how to operate it, which meant that I found myself fobbed off, more often than not, by yet another zombified speak-your-weight communication. ('The person you are calling knows you are waiting. The person you are calling knows you are waiting. The person you are calling knows you are waiting.' *Ad*, literally, *nauseam*.)

In short, it still all added up to little more than just a superficial sheen. The pioneering Mercury phone commercials, those which featured a dapper, moustachioed Harry Enfield offering, in voice, appearance and mannerisms, a creepily vivid parody of the stilted, buttoned-up pomposity of what passed for advertising in the fifties, got it more right than the company itself would probably be prepared to acknowledge. Britain is not America and never will be. Underneath the glistening crust of technology festers the same old, apparently incorrigible native incompetence.

In Cocteau's novel *Le Grand Ecart* there is a fleeting, witty allusion to an (apocryphal?) eighteenth-century English dandy, an epigone of Brummell, who, when about to put a pistol to his temple, scribbled this foppishly languid suicide note: 'Too many buttons to do up and undo. I'm killing myself.' These days buttons are perceived as only secondarily part of one's clothing. They are, supremely, *knobs*, knobs on videos, telephones, computers, faxes and the like, knobs which one has to press and turn and twiddle rather than do up and undo. But there are still too many of the damned things. I'm killing myself.

Notes

1 In the decade's earlier half, computers were still thought of, if no longer quite in science-fictional terms, then as cumbersome room-filling monoliths which had to be individually programmed.

2 Of all the teasing messages I heard, by far the most subtly sadistic was that devised by Videotron, the television cabling company. It went: 'Please do not hang up. Your call is important to us.' 'If my call is so important,' I wanted to scream, 'why the fuck . . .' But you get the picture, so let us both raise our eyes again to the body of the text.

On the *Titanic*

There is a famous episode of Noël Coward's *Cavalcade* in which a pair of poignant young newlyweds, westward bound, lean against the deck railing of the liner which is taking them to America and dreamily envision the life awaiting them there. At the end of the scene, they stroll off together along the deck and, so they suppose, into the future. And it is only then, with the theatre lights just about to dim, that we are permitted to see the lifebuoy which their two bodies have been obscuring. On that lifebuoy is stencilled the ship's name: *SS Titanic*.

In the North Atlantic, on 14 April 1912, at 11.40 p.m., an immovable object met an irresistible force, a state-of-the-art Goliath was felled by a state-of-the-nature David, and our love affair with the *Titanic* was born.

It has lasted to this very day. If you consult the internal database of any national newspaper, you will find, under '*Titanic*', a host of references to the disaster itself, as equally to the ongoing, still controversial salvage operation in the Atlantic. But you will also be pointed in the direction of numerous figurative uses of the word, under such ostensibly unrelated rubrics as opera ('At its best, opera is an overwhelming experience – but when it goes wrong it does so on a Titanic scale'), Princess Diana ('Andrew Morton's book – the latest iceberg in the monarchy's Titanic-style odyssey'), the Channel Tunnel ('"It's worse than the Titanic," said one dealer. "At least *it* left on time"') and Cliff Richard ('We sat next to two jackets kept in a glass case[1] as though they were the crown jewels: they belonged to somebody called Cliff Richard. Mum said that Cliff Richard had performed on the Titanic. But I think she was joking . . .'). MPs short of original witticisms (and which of them are not?) will automatically refer to some overly timid government measure as 're-arranging the deck chairs on the *Titanic*', a joke which apparently goes down so well in the House of Commons it can never be made too often. And, to coincide with an exhibition, held at the National Maritime Museum in Greenwich, of artefacts salvaged from the liner, the complete version of Gavin Bryars's musical fantasy *The Sinking of the Titanic* has recently been issued on record.

Why? Why has the *Titanic* always been regarded, somehow, as sacred? ('Plumbing the depths' is how an indignant Bernard Levin described media speculation on whether the entire ship might be refloated.) Why, in a century which has been little more than a catalogue of catastrophes, many of them graver, as far as their casualty rates are concerned, than the sinking of the *Titanic*, many of them, too, lending themselves just as readily to the facile seductions of instant allegory (the British Empire as *Titanic*, the American Presidency as *Titanic*), are we still fascinated by that terrifying night in 1912?

Perhaps because it no longer strikes us as so very terrifying after all. Not that I wish to imply that thrashing about helplessly in the freezing Atlantic was anything but a horrible way to die. I mean only that the popular imagery of the disaster, although scarcely bereft of horror, is of a bizarrely clean, *unmacabre* horror, a pre-Passchendaele, pre-Auschwitz, pre-Hiroshima horror. As we imagine it, the Atlantic swallowed the *Titanic* whole, as though it were an aspirin. The tales we all remember of its last hours afloat are not of the grisly, bone-crunching deaths which must have occurred but rather of old-world, almost fairy-tale manifestations of either courage (the elderly lady who gave up the place offered her on one of the lifeboats in order to stay on board at her husband's side) or of cowardice (the male passenger who allegedly succeeded in making his escape disguised as a woman). And what, of course, we remember above all else is the gallantry of the ship's musicians, that orchestra of dying swans, continuing to play (not, as legend has always had it, 'Nearer My God, to Thee', but the Episcopal hymn 'Autumn') as the *Titanic* subsided beneath them.

There was, in short, a nobility about the *Titanic*'s comeuppance which has all but but vanished from contemporary disasters (who has time to be gallant aboard a plummeting plane?), a nobility I would not hesitate to call Shakespearean. In a sense, *The Sinking of the Titanic* is the great heroic tragedy that Shakespeare did not write. Expiring in an orgy of hymns and candles, the liner was brought down, like Hamlet, Othello and Lear, by a single fatal flaw, the flaw in this instance being the classic one of hubris. And considering how far the art and wizardry of modern stagecraft have advanced of late, I find it amazing that no one seems ever to have thought of staging the disaster, in the Brechtian epic style, as a theatrical tragedy. Or possibly as a stylish postmodern opera – by John Adams? Or even, much as I abominate the genre, as a spectacular musical – Lloyd Webber? Schönberg and Boublil?[2] The subject is as rife with narrative possibilities as with historical ironies; and if a helicopter can be made to descend from the flies of *Miss Saigon*, having an ocean liner sink through an enormous stage trapdoor ought not to pose an insuperable logistical problem.

According to a *Melody Maker* review of Bryars's composition, the climax of *The Sinking of the Titanic* projects the listener 'into an imaginary future where the ship is refloated and the music returns to its previous acoustic state as it breaks surface'. At a first (and even at a second) hearing, this textural distinction was a trifle too subtle for me. But why, in any case, should such a future be regarded as 'imaginary'. The death of the *Titanic* is precisely what has kept it alive, precisely what has kept it from sinking out of sight. For it did not go down on its unconsummated maiden voyage. It ascended. It rose straight up to heaven, as all virgins do.

Notes

1 At the Hard Rock Cafe in London.

2 Such a musical did open on Broadway in the spring of 1997.

On the Death of the Author

When, in a celebrated essay, Barthes announced the Death of the Author, it was a proclamation almost as scandalous as had been Nietzsche's, a century before, that God was dead. Surely, one thought, if there was one bedrock invariable of all literary theory, whatever its methodology, it was the cult of the Author. The Author was he (or she) who, having injected a carefully calibrated shot of meaning into his (or her) prose, the same meaning that the Reader was subsequently expected to extract from it, represented the most trustworthy source – indeed, the only authoritative (or 'author-itative') source – of enlightenment on what that meaning actually meant. It was Barthes's contention, by contrast, that language itself dictated what the Author seemingly 'made it say', manipulating him in much the same way as he himself would often endeavour to manipulate the Reader.

If, as a theory, the Death of the Author eventually succumbed, like every other theory, to the endemic excesses of doctrinal delirium and intolerance, its influence on lit-crit studies throughout the seventies and eighties was nevertheless incalculable. Surprisingly, however, Barthes turned out to have been not just provocative but prescient, albeit (as invariably happens) in a manner which he did not anticipate. Who today can doubt that, if not yet dead, the Author is dying? Consider the most egregiously flagrant of examples, the supermodel Naomi Campbell's novel *Swan*. I wrote 'Naomi Campbell's novel *Swan*' as I might equally have written 'James Kelman's novel *How Late It Was, How Late*', but they were, in fact, very dissimilar entities. Yes, Campbell's name was on the cover of her book, just as Kelman's was on the cover of his. Yes, she was interviewed about her novel's contents, as Kelman also was about his. Yes, she personally signed lots of copies, as Kelman did too. But the far more significant difference between them was of course that she did not write *Swan*, whereas, at least as far as one knows, *How Late It Was, How Late* was all Kelman's own work. And the really astounding paradox was just how little this difference mattered. There was absolutely no fiction (a curious word in the context) about Campbell's lack of involvement in the fabrication of the book which bore her name. Everyone in the business (and many an informed layman outside it) was aware that it had in reality been written by the editor, Caroline Upcher, who had originally commissioned it. Rumours actually circulated that Campbell had not even read *Swan* and had to be furnished with a 250-word synopsis in order for her to offer a credible account of its plot to journalists. Yet, whether these rumours were true or not, the book existed, the public for it apparently existed (it did very well, thank you), only the Author had ceased to exist. Or, rather, the Author had died and become a Ghost.

One could say that Campbell *modelled* Upcher's text, she *wore* it, as she might have worn some flimsy see-through confection by Vivienne Westwood. To employ a metaphor that she herself ought to be capable of understanding without first being briefed, she was merely the peg on which it was hung. What we are talking about, in other words, is fiction as (in the sense in which this word is used by fashion journalists) an *accessory*.

From the British literary establishment the operation provoked a spasm of mildly amused cynicism but was otherwise a complete success. And the next time something of the kind occurs, the next time such a novel is published, by Kate Moss or Claudia Schiffer, by Diana, Keanu or Gazza, not an eyebrow will be raised. It will then be referred to, respectfully, as belonging to a 'genre', a 'tradition', as legitimate and dignified as any other, and few will notice or care that yet another nail has been hammered into the Author's coffin.

The Author is dead and the Ghost is alive. To have recourse to a filmic metaphor, the writer, or at least the sort of 'writer' exemplified by Campbell, is increasingly perceived as the star, rather than the director, of the novel to which his or her name has been attached, and his or her rivals for public attention are no longer, as they used to be, Ackroyd, Amis, Brookner and suchlike, but Emma Thompson, Elizabeth Hurley, the Marquess of Blandford and that ilk. As for novelists, genuine novelists, aside from a handful of lucky, lustrous exceptions, they have been demoted to the lowly status of, precisely, screenwriters, toiling away unsung, unloved and, unlike the Hollywood breed, not even especially well paid.

The filmic analogy is not wholly fortuitous here, since a similar process is now perceptible in the cinema itself – what might be called the Death of the Auteur. Now that more and more actors are moonlighting as directors (Redford, Gibson, De Niro) and more and more directors are moonlighting as actors (Tarantino, Scorsese, Pollack), the once impregnable notion of a filmmaker as an artist possessed of a unique, non-transferable gift is fast becoming obsolete. Ditto, for that matter, with painting. Andy Warhol's works were more or less collectively produced in what, without irony (?), he termed the Factory, while Jeff Koons retains a permanent staff of labourers to execute his 'ideas' for him. Music, too. As yet, the classical variety would appear to be uncontaminated by so broadminded a conception of creation, but Malcolm McLaren is on record as admitting that his best-known pop protégé (whose idiotic name, on principle, I refuse to commit to print) could not play, and was never recorded playing, the guitar of which he was presumed to be a virtuoso.

And I am reminded, oddly, of the 1969 moon landing and the phrase spoken, rather maladroitly, by Neil Armstrong as he set foot on the lunar surface. 'One small step for a man, but one giant leap for mankind', or words to that effect. *Or words to that effect.* Naturally, I could check the exact quote. The whole point, though, is that the conceit had almost certainly been coined by someone else, probably by committee, and that, in anticipation of the great moment, Armstrong had patently rehearsed and re-rehearsed it long before being rocketed into space. Which is why, I believe, its canonic form tends to elude one. And why, too, it is unlikely to ring down the centuries as one individual's spontaneous response to an extraordinary experience (unlike, let us say, Caesar's '*Veni, vidi, vici*', to which no one has ever felt obliged to add 'or words to that effect').

No: whatever else happens in our culture, the first person singular must never be allowed to become *persona non grata*.

On interpretation

This is an essay about 'about'. Which is to say, it is an essay about the preposition 'about' and the frequency, even incessancy, with which it recurs in a currently prevalent style of critical discourse. And it was prompted by a Channel 4 programme, *The Turner Prize*, in which a trio of critics, Sarah Kent, Cosmo Landesman and John Walsh, were invited to stroll through those rooms of the Tate Gallery in which the works of the 1994 Prize's shortlisted artists were exhibited and air their views more or less at random.

It was a scream, so much so that I began to wonder whether it was not actually a spoof. But what made it so hilarious was less the works of art on display (which, if they possessed no immediately perceptible distinction, were not at all outrageous) than the critics. Or, rather – and here I must be, I hope, uncharacteristically un*galant* – the one genuinely qualified art critic, Sarah Kent.

Walsh, too shrewd and experienced an operator to fall into any obvious trap, was foppishly witty and cynical. Landesman, who appeared, of the three, the least concerned to project a modish self-image, came across as likeable and unaffected. (It was he, too, who made the most intelligent contribution to the programme with his proposal that there henceforth be declared a moratorium on the word 'playful', by now the arch-cliché of postmodernist approbation.[1]) For her part, however, Kent was determined to conform, lock, stock and the scrapings of the barrel, to the populist stereotype of the intellectual as village explainer (as Gertrude Stein once called Ezra Pound), for whom the word 'about' is both the Open and Close Sesame of all critical judgment and opinionation.

Thus Peter Doig's fussy, blandly glamorous snowscapes – in which, to quote from Kent's coverage of the Prize in *Time Out*, 'order and meaning are seen as fragile commodities that continually have to be wrested from the ravenous void' – were not so much 'about' their subject-matter as 'about' ways of seeing. Shirazeh

Houshiary's installation of five gigantic lead cubes was 'about' the antithesis of spirituality and materiality. As for Anthony Gormley's own exhibited cube (cubes seem to be the thing at the moment), a large concrete one inside which the trace of some living presence was still spectrally perceptible, it could be read 'as a metaphor of imprisonment and, more literally, as entombment within architectural spaces that are inhuman in proportion and design'. Everything, in short, was 'about' something, and that was apparently the first, last and sole word on the subject.

Now, in fairness to Kent, depriving a critic, any critic, of the word 'about' would be like forcing someone to define a spiral staircase with both hands tied behind his back. As I ought to know, since I am still living down an absurdity I myself perpetrated more than two decades ago. It occurred at a screening of a film, *Red Psalm*, by the once fashionable and now forgotten Hungarian director Miklós Jancsó. Roughly fifteen minutes in, a young man sat down next to me, discreetly removed his overcoat, then turned to ask, in a polite, apologetic whisper, what had happened so far. Unforgivably, I hissed back at him that 'it isn't that sort of film!' (Jancsó is, or was, a director with no interest in conventionally linear plotlines) and later complained to a fellow buff, 'God, it sickens me. Latecomers always want to know what a film is "about". Why don't they ever ask about the *mise-en-scène*?' Well, quite rightly, I have never been permitted to forget that pretentiously pseudy outburst, and my friends still tease me by imagining the conversation that might have ensued had such an exchange taken place. 'Pssst. Sorry to bother you, chum, but could you fill me in on the *mise-en-scène* so far?' 'The *mise-en-scène*? Why, certainly. You see, basically Jancsó is exploring the spatial parameters of the Hungarian landscape as a means of metaphorising . . .', etc., etc. 'Right. I get the picture, mate. Cheers.'

Of course people instinctively want to know what a work of art is *about*, but it is the critic's function, rather, to illuminate what it *is*. And the fundamental impotence of exclusively interpretative criticism resides in its inherent indifference to the issue of *efficacy*. Even if Houshiary's hollowed-out cubes had always been intended by the artist herself to be 'about' spirituality and materiality, and even if, in some Platonic heaven of aesthetic values and truths, they were indeed 'about' spirituality and materiality, we would still be no better informed as to the effect, if any, that they were likely to have upon us – as to whether they had, to any persuasive extent, 'risen to' their own subject-matter. I could, after all, have an outsized fish tank installed in a gallery, fill it up with, not fish, but scores of rusty metal syringes, then blithely inform the world that this so-called artwork of mine was 'about' the depradations visited on nature by the abuses of contemporary society. Who could say I was wrong? Yet having endowed my conceptual tomfoolery with subject-matter would not automatically mean that I had also endowed it with either meaning or beauty. What critical analysis proposes is causes *after* effects, and the problem with the mode of criticism exemplified by Kent (but she is by no means alone) is that, by focusing solely on the cause, it denies all relevance to the effect.

And I am now going to offer what I would be the first to admit is an amateurish rule-of-thumb procedure, to be applied whenever you find yourself torn between an obstinately uncommunicating work of art (which might equally well be a film, play, novel or poem) and a glib critical commentary outlining what it is 'about'. (Note: the procedure tests only the validity of an *interpretation* and requires a degree of informed imagination on the spectator's part.) When confronted with a piece of sculpture, let us say, that a critic has approvingly described as being 'about the deconstruction of paternalistic images of gender', or some such cant, quickly ask yourself this question (it may be no more than gauging a subliminal gut reaction): If such an effect had *really* been intended, could it have been better, more eloquently, more powerfully, achieved? If, in your guts, you just *know* that it could have been, then either the critic (guilty of a misguided interpretation) or the artist (guilty of an inadequate execution) must be at fault.

Notes
1 Point taken.

On updating

Phyllida Lloyd's 1994 revival of *The Threepenny Opera* was set in the London of 2001, on the eve of the Coronation of King William V. It boasted the now obligatory onstage gallery of television monitors and had a new translation by Jeremy Sams which made reference to such emblematic phenomena of the nineties as drugs, the homeless, laptop computers and Torvill and Dean. Peter Sellars's more or less concurrent staging of *The Merchant of Venice* at the National Theatre also had its statutory bank of TV sets, covering Shylock's trial as though it were O. J.'s; Sellars, moreover, transformed Salanio and Salarino, Shakespeare's pair of inseparable Venetian gossips, into a chattering Siskel and Ebert offering thumbs-up and thumbs-down on the freshest dirt from the Rialto. And, again concurrently, Nick Broadhurst and Tony Britten of Music Theatre London presented a three-part televised adaptation, running ninety minutes in all, of *The Marriage of Figaro*, which featured actors who could sing (sort of) instead of singers who could act, canned laughter even during the arias (but why not canned screams for horror films, canned sobs for weepies, canned retching for *Pulp Fiction*?) and a Count Almaviva who had been reincarnated for the occasion as Sir Cecil, a 'fruity Euro fat-cat,' as one reviewer elegantly put it, 'whose randy assaults on Essex girl Susanna earn him an ice-pack on the groin'.

Thus, each of these classic texts – by Brecht and Weill, Shakespeare, and Mozart and Da Ponte – had been updated or, as it might perhaps be more accurate to say, *postdated*, like a dubious cheque. And even if gradations could be detected in their badness – the Brecht was just about tolerable thanks to Weill's indelible score, the Shakespeare excruciatingly contrived and atrociously performed, the Mozart beneath contempt and beyond criticism – their creators would presumably all have endorsed the defence of such directorial tampering put forward by Broadhurst. 'The object has never been to turn every great opera into a Crazy Gang farce,' he said, 'just to bring the real drama and contemporary relevance back to the fore-front.'

Forget the infelicity of a phrase like 'back to the forefront', the key word here is 'relevance'. Brecht, Shakespeare and Mozart must be made relevant. Unless at least one of their characters is shown using a Filofax or a cordless phone, a modern audience simply cannot connect with them.

Yet it did not strike Phyllida Lloyd, for example, that, when Brecht himself elected to update Gay's *The Beggar's Opera*, it was not to his own period, the Weimar Republic, which was patently the object of his invective, but to turn-of-the-century Soho. Nor did she appreciate that his insistence on retaining a sense of 'previousness' when modernising a pre-existent work might just have been worth mulling over by any subsequent re-adapter. More generally, it seems never to occur to any of these 'creative' directors that, to take only the most obvious cases (but then, the obvious is all they understand), people continue to read Tolstoy and Flaubert and Austen and Proust despite the fact that no ingenious publisher has ever seen fit to have their novels rewritten in an idiom likely to be more congenial to contemporary sensibilities. No one has ever reorchestrated a Bruckner symphony in the hope of appealing to fans of Sondheim or Take That. No one has ever repainted a Rembrandt self-portrait on the grounds that the sight of a wrinkled old codger in a seventeenth-century smock would prove alienating to a spectator of the nineties. Why is it only in the theatre and the opera house that updating has become the norm?

There are, I think, two principal reasons. One, because what is seen on a stage is controlled not by a writer or a composer but by a director, an interpretative artist by whom the text is increasingly perceived as a mere pretext. When the text in question is as moribund as Priestley's preposterous old warhorse, *An Inspector Calls*, fair enough. The snag is that most such directors cannot wait to get their itchy, interpretative little paws on plays which nevertheless contrived to hold the boards for several years, even centuries, without them. And, two, because those critics who systematically champion the cause of radical reinterpretation tend to forget that, although they themselves may have had to sit through a dozen *Macbeths* in as many years, each of these *Macbeths* was the very first (and, frequently, only) for a number of spectators who, if they had been asked, would probably have expressed a desire for Shakespeare's stage directions to be as faithfully respected as his text. There must be countless playgoers out there who have seen *Macbeth* set in Little Italy, *Macbeth* set in Auschwitz, *Macbeth* set in the India of the Raj, and who are still wistfully waiting for a *Macbeth* set in Scotland.

Am I turning my back on all theatrical adventurism? Precisely the contrary. Apart from the textual dislocations which inevitably ensue from the updating of a classic, that updating almost always turns out to be as schematic and reductive as the most staidly conservative reading, since it, too, has the effect of closing off every imaginative option but one – the option, indeed, that is staring us all in the face. Watching *The Threepenny Opera*, I felt insulted by the fact that Lloyd, judging me too obtuse to draw my own analogies between the polemical thrust of the original and what I see around me every day in the Britain of the nineties, felt it incumbent upon herself to make those analogies conspicuously, sometimes glaringly, visible on the stage. Like her colleagues, she no doubt believed that she was 'metaphorising' her material. What, however, I detected in such an approach was instead a crude literalism, a complacent negation of the past and the lessons it might still have to teach us.

If a play or an opera is not about today, so runs the argument, then it is about nothing. What I would reply is that only the dated need be updated. Only the irrelevant need be made relevant. And a work of art that was once new will always be new.

On 'quotation marks'

When I lived in Paris many years ago I used to buy my copy of *Le Monde* every day from the same local newspaper kiosk. Once a week, at that kiosk, I would run into a neighbour of mine, a chic, fortyish *bourgeoise*, who would also buy *Le Monde*, along with *Le Nouvel Observateur*, the (only just) left-of-centre political journal. Whereupon, having apparently taken her leave, she would make an unfailing U-turn, so unfailing I used to exchange a complicitous smile with the newsagent, she would casually throw a handful of coins (always the exact change) on to the counter and she would then murmur under her fragrant breath: 'Oh, and give me a copy of *France-Dimanche*, why don't you. It's completely brainless, but it's something to read in the bath. And my maid enjoys it.'

To understand that anecdote you have to know that *France-Dimanche* (which still exists) was a precursor of *Voici!*, the French *Hello!*. Its tawdrily illustrated pages, consecrated to what was then known as *le café-society*, would salivate over the lifestyles of the international jet set, from the late Princess Grace of Monaco to the Comte de Paris (the eternally forlorn pretender to the French throne), from the ageing playboys José-Luis de Villalonga and Gunther Sachs to a slew of gruesome French pop stars, Claude François, Johnny Hallyday, Sylvie Vartan and Michel Polnareff. And since it was universally derided as a rag that only concierges would be seen dead reading, it occurs to me now that my poor shamefaced neighbour was a precursor herself.

In view of the *mise-en-scène* (the last-minute change of mind, the unvarying allusions to her bathtub and her maid) without which she simply would not have been capable of purchasing the magazine, she was arguably a pioneer of the quintessentially postmodern mechanism of inscribing one's taste for the basest forms of popular culture within ironic – or what one likes to think of as ironic – quotation marks. By systematically delaying her request for it, the message that my neighbour was hoping to send out was that *France-Dimanche* had been the very last thing on her mind when she approached the kiosk; that even if, in truth, she had not missed an issue in years, each purchase was still a 'one-off', so to speak, a once-in-a-lifetime indulgence by the gratification of which she herself was the first to be taken by surprise. Compared to one of *France-Dimanche*'s targeted readers, she saw herself as resembling an athlete closing in on a rival whom he has in fact already lapped: although they appear to be running shoulder to shoulder, a crucial, invisible distance separates them.

We still believe in the power of those ironic quotation marks. We still believe that an invisible distance does actually separate the unembarrassed purchaser of *Hello!*, who takes a naïve pleasure in gawping at the palatial homes of the stars, from the sort of person who, caught red-handed with a copy, will react just as defensively as did my former neighbour. To be sure, no 'sophisticated' reader of *Hello!* would any longer dare pretend that it had been bought for the maid; no one today would expect to get away with that old chestnut. But implicit in the self-satirising, *faux-naïf* tone of what such a reader *does* say ('It's a scream! I adore it! I read it from cover to cover, I really do!') is the same basic message: the difference between me and an ordinary reader is that *I know Hello!* is brainless. We may appear to be running shoulder to shoulder, but I am always that crucial lap ahead.

In response, however, let me propose this axiomatic truth: *If you imitate something for long enough, you will finally turn into it.* You may start watching *Blind Date* as a consciously assumed exercise in postmodern cultural slumming, confining your comments to its inexhaustible vulgarity ('Only in Britain!') or else paying good-humoured if still *de-haut-en-bas* tribute to the dexterity with which its presenter has dealt with a potentially awkward participant ('You've got to give Cilla Black her due!') – eventually, fatally, you will find yourself caught up in heated conjecture as to which of the couples on the show will be paired off and whether the coupling is going to prove as ill-matched as it seems. Similarly (and here I am prepared to switch to the first person singular), I bought a ticket in the first week of the National Lottery because I felt it would be churlish of me not to participate in a new nationwide ritual and without any real interest in whether I would win or not. (Given the ridiculous odds, I knew I wouldn't, and sure enough I didn't.) Now, even if I have long since ceased to be able to exploit the sociological defence, I continue to buy a ticket every week; and, when asked why by incredulous acquaintances, I hear myself using *exactly* the same arguments as any other punter. 'Heavens, it's just a bit of inexpensive fun,' I say airily. 'What's wrong with adding a little excitement to your life?' And although I am just as opposed as I always was to the whole idea of a lottery, a lottery at least as a privately run operation, and try to persuade myself that the quotation marks of my ironic detachment are still there, hovering just above my head, I cannot deny that they have been irrevocably tarnished, eroded to the point of virtual invisibility, by overuse.

What has happened to me? Just the same as happens to someone who reads schlocky novels 'only on the beach' and, before he knows it, ends up reading nothing else; who, pleading fatigue, decides to give a miss to the Chinese film he originally intended to see, goes to *Speed* instead and never sees another Chinese film in his life. I am yet another willing victim of the mass culture which demands from us, and all too often receives, not the suspension of our disbelief, as we say of traditional, illusionistic fiction, but the suspension of our *distaste*.

On the Queen

Although rationality is, as we know, an exclusively human attribute, it is possible to wonder on occasion just how rational we human beings are in our day-to-day existence.

Consider (and I refuse to believe that this happens only to me): I am browsing in a shop, I see something I wish to buy (a record, a book, an *objet d'art*, whatever), but ultimately decide against buying it because it turns out to cost more than I am prepared to pay. On the way home, however, I decide after all that I have to have the thing. I return to the shop the following morning, now with a queasy foreboding as to what awaits me; I discover, naturally, that it has meanwhile been sold; and I curse myself for having so stupidly procrastinated. By such antics I am, I realise, already flirting with less than wholly rational behaviour. But where that behaviour topples over into downright irrationality is when I return to the shop telling myself that what I want must have been sold, discover to my amazement that it is still available and, rather than gratefully securing it once and for all, get into exactly the same lather of indecision as before – to the point where I leave the shop empty-handed a second time, the object of my desire still unpurchased.

That is nothing, though, compared to the irrationality I routinely display in my relations with other people. Let us say that I have three close friends, B, C and D; I myself am A. Now, when I am in the company of B and C, I cannot deny that we three talk about D in terms that, were he ever to be apprised of what had been said, he would find extremely hurtful. It does not mean (as we, B, C and I, keep reassuring ourselves) that we appreciate D any the less; merely that we know him well enough to be conscious of his faults and are unable to resist airing them from time to time among ourselves. Likewise, with B and D, I find myself talking about C, about *his* faults, *his* little personal squalours and meannesses, with a candour, a brutality, I would never dare express to his face. Yet, somehow, stubbornly, and aware as I am that such a belief is utterly irrational, I simply cannot credit that when my friends B, C and D get together in *my* absence, they talk about me in the same heartless fashion. They do, of course – I may *believe* they don't, but I *know* they do – and they probably rationalise their candour with arguments exactly identical to mine.

Consider, now, a case of human irrationality on a national scale: the Queen. Although I have strong and even frankly unprintable opinions about several members of the Royal Family, and regard the very fact of having a Queen at all as an extraordinarily irrational aberration for the late twentieth century, I have never known quite what to make of the woman herself. To be more precise, I have never made up my mind about the constant stream of (often indecent) jokes at her expense in the media; about the caricatures, the impersonations, the Spitting Images; about the fact that, while one would be arrested for scrawling graffiti on the walls of Buckingham Palace, stand-up comics get away scot-free with drawing rude appendages (in a figurative sense) on its most famous occupant. As a confirmed, albeit not too fussed, republican, I might be expected to enjoy these jokes, but I don't. For I cannot help asking myself if the Queen really deserves to be bullied so, to be positively tortured? If, as is becoming clear, the general British public increasingly resents her free enjoyment of the wealth and privilege she has inherited, why does it not just disinvest her of that wealth and privilege and be done with it, instead of systematically subjecting her to what can only be called cruel and unusual punishment? How, I think, would *I* like it? How, for that matter, would *you* like it?

But therein lies a strange paradox. Notwithstanding a now widespread assumption that, if the Windsors are the closest our nation has to a Holy Family, the British themselves are growing more and more atheistic, opinion polls continue to suggest that the great majority of the population is monarchist at heart. So how (apart from a universal taste for salacious gossip from any quarter, the more exalted the better) can such diametrically opposed positions be reconciled? My own theory is that there is a fundamental difference between the attitude of the writers, actors, comedians and cartoonists who regularly pillory the Queen and that of the public which, seemingly without protest, laps up their work. In the first case, I detect real hostility, or at least cynicism; in the second, it strikes me that, where she is concerned, a taste for royal ribaldry is in reality a measure of public affection.

We British, in short, are willing to take the same liberties, and see the same liberties taken, with the Queen as with our closest friends (assuming again that the double standard of behaviour I describe above is not peculiar to me alone). When we talk about her, it is with the same brutal candour with which we might speak our minds about a close friend behind his or her back. If we view her as frumpy and philistine, it does not necessarily follow, as we may infer from the intimate opinions that we hold of our closest friends, that she has completely forfeited our sympathy or that we could easily imagine our lives without her. Nor, finally, does the negative publicity she has received over the past few years, and occasionally merited (the reluctant payment of income tax, the initial proposal that the financial brunt of restoring Windsor Castle be borne by the taxpayer, the eternal antics of Diana and Fergie, the Merry ex-Wives of Windsor), mean that her disappearance would not provoke a national trauma, the kind of trauma, indeed, that would be provoked on a personal level by the disappearance of a close friend who had also led a less than blameless life.

It was Peter Ustinov who remarked that our closest friends are not those we like the best but those we have known the longest. That, I believe, is indisputable. I also believe, *pace* Bagehot and his contemporary disciples, that no mystique need be postulated to explain our affection for the current monarch; that, as with Victoria before her, it is primarily a matter of longevity. How many of us, after all, have known *any* of our friends, close or not, for as long as we have known the Queen?

On the death of a poet

No lover of musicals, I have never been what you might call a fan of Stephen Sondheim. But there was one show of his which I recall finding oddly disturbing. I refer to *Pacific Overtures*, about Commodore Matthew Perry's expedition to Japan in 1853 and the successful termination, through Yankee gunboat diplomacy, of that nation's self-imposed policy of social and economic isolation.

For practically all of *Pacific Overtures'* running time what was evoked on stage was the arch-traditional (and traditionally arch) Japan of parasols, kimonos, decorative screens and impeccable clockwork-doll manners. Nothing very disturbing in that: in fact, the exquisiteness of the spectacle verged more than once on the twee. In its final scene, however, the show simply, astoundingly, self-destructed. With an unforeseeably abrupt change of tack, Sondheim projected the action forward into the Japan of the late twentieth century and bombarded his startled audience with all that has been most detestable in the country's Americanisation. As the genteel cod-Oriental melodies and Gilbert-and-Sullivanish patter songs gave way to grating rock music, the stage was filled with teenagers in jeans, sneakers and baseball caps, with fat, middle-aged women in polyester pants, and with toothy, bespectacled junior executives.

That was a rather lengthy preamble for an essay that is about neither Japan nor Stephen Sondheim nor what Billy Wilder once described as 'Coca-colonisation'. It is, instead, about the American poet James Merrill, whose death in February 1995 from a heart attack (he was sixty-eight) did nevertheless make me think, for the first time in more than a decade, of *Pacific Overtures'* closing tableau.

Merrill led something of a charmed life. His parents owned both an elegant New York townhouse and a multi-bedroom mansion in the Hamptons; and although his father, the Merrill half of Merrill Lynch, the mighty Wall Street brokerage firm, had early hopes, as fathers will, of James being tempted into the same line of business, he eventually conceded that it was never going to be and even paid for a privately printed volume of his son's juvenilia, claiming that he 'would rather have a first-rate poet for a son than a third-rate polo player'. Nor did James's homosexuality appear to be a source of especial disquiet to anyone. In 1954 he left New York altogether and, with his companion, David Jackson, settled permanently in Stonington, a small, pretty coastal village off the Long Island Sound, filled with 'clever wrinkled semi-famous people whom by the end of our second season we couldn't live without'. In 1959 he and Jackson purchased their second residence, in Athens, and thereafter spent six months of every year in Europe. Even the one shadow which had fallen over his adolescence, his parents' separation and acrimonious divorce trial, he managed to assimilate with no excessive emotional strain, exorcising the trauma as ever in a poem: 'Always that same old story – /Father Time and Mother Earth,/A marriage on the rocks.' (For all details of Merrill's life and most of the quoted verse I am indebted to a beautifully written memoir by J. D. McClatchy, Merrill's friend and fellow-poet, published in the *New Yorker*. Various peregrinations over the years have left me without a single handily accessible collection of the poetry.)

Merrill was brilliant, good-looking and of course wealthy. He was both lucky in love and lucky at words. (He was probably lucky at cards, too.) His poetry – of an 'aloof, lapidary glamour', in McClatchy's unimprovable description – has little in common with the rowdy, free-verse and what we Brits tend to regard as *echt*-American tradition stretching from Whitman to Ginsburg. Think rather of the sculpted stanzas of Wallace Stevens or those, closer to home, of Richard Wilbur. His words speckle the page with the restless glitter of besequinned insects. Here he is, for example, on the gorgeous asperities of the Greek language (a language which, naturally, he took no time at all to master): 'kaló-kakó, cockatoo-raucous/Coastline of white printless coves/Already strewn with offbeat echolalia'. And, as the life grew ever more domestic and downhomey, so the work, repudiating the faintly chi-chi mysticism which had been its only real blemish, became more directly, transparently, autobiographical. The later poems were, in Merrill's own phrase, elliptical 'chronicles of love and loss'.

Is this interesting? Is this fit material for the closing essay in a book titled *Surfing the Zeitgeist*? Not really, I suppose. Merrill, after all, deliberately exiled himself from the zeitgeist I have been surfing. He didn't promote his poetry on talk shows. He didn't pose for Gap. He didn't date Elizabeth Hurley – or Hugh Grant. And he didn't die of Aids. He won the National Book Award in 1967, but who cares about that? Or the Bollingen Prize, which he won in 1973? The Pulitzer Prize, awarded him in 1976, is a bit more newsworthy, but even so. It's not like it's an Oscar.

Basically, he worked. He wrote. And he wrote. And he wrote. He knew, as McClatchy puts it, that he had always been 'meant to end up as books on a shelf'. As far as the 'literary life' was concerned, he remained admirably impervious to its coarsening attentions. Like every true artist, he *cultivated his deafness*: like Satie, who died leaving scores of personal letters not just unread but unopened; like Proust, who, for want of being deaf himself, corklined his room and made *it* deaf.

Deafness to what, exactly? To the Coca-colonisation of culture. To grating rock music and teenagers in jeans and women in polyester pants and I'm mad as hell and I'm not going to take it any more and hasta la vista baby and go on punk make my day and lunch is for wimps and greed is good and gotcha and freddie starr ate my hamster and loadsamoney and read my lips and where's the beef and we are a grandmother and come on down and get a life and life is like a box of chocolates you never know what you're going to get and cor what a scorcher and famous for being famous and turkeys voting for christmas and we had an exceptionally rich crop of titles to choose from this year and ere we go and you know what they call a quarter-pounder with cheese in paris and pushing the envelope and you just don't get it do you and everything else of which the rich and glorious pageant of our contemporary culture is composed.

James Merrill, 1927–1995. Rest in Peace.

Index

A la recherche du temps perdu, 6, 34, 93, 135
A l'ombre des jeunes filles en fleur, 93
Abba, 50
Abbott and Costello, 108
Abish, Walter, 127
Abraham's Valley, 78
Absolute Beginners (film), 203
Ackroyd, Peter, 12, 227
Adams, John, 225
Adventures of Robin Hood, The, 61
Adventures in the Screen Trade, 205
Aeneid, The, 74
Affair to Remember, An, 197
Age of Innocence, The, 141, 156–7, 179
Aids and its Metaphors, 86
Akerman, Chantal, 143
Aladdin, 188
Aldrich, Robert, 66
Ali, 90
Alice in Wonderland books, 3, 127, 181
All My Sons, 31
All Quiet on the Western Front, 200
Allen, Woody, 2, 45, 71, 110
Alma Cogan, 88
Alma-Tadema, Laurence, 100
Alphabetical Africa, 127
Altman, Robert, 141, 143
Amadeus, 204
Amants du Pont-Neuf, Les, 101
America, America, 179
American Romance, An, 179
Amerika, 35
Amis, Martin, 33, 38, 127, 191, 227
Ammer, Christine, 132–4
Amphitryon 38, 73
Amphitryon 39, 73
And Life Continues, 103
Andersen, Hans Christian, 23

Anderson, Lindsay, 217
Andre, Carl, 53, 56
Andrews, Dana, 65, 66
Annaud, Jean-Jacques, 7, 9
Annie Hall, 45
Annunzio, Gabriele d', 170
Anouilh, Jean, 74
Antonio das Mortes, 101
Antonioni, Michelangelo, 4–5, 56, 101
'Anything Goes', 17
Apocalypse Now, 197, 198
Apprentis sorciers, Les, 124n.1
Après-midi de Monsieur Andesmas, L', 1
Arcadia, 90
Archer, Jeffrey, 95, 199
Arlen, Michael, 95
Armstrong, Neil, 228
Arnold, Malcolm, 145
Arrivée d'un train en gare de La Ciotat, L', 40
Artaud, Antonin, 122
Asahi Shimbun, 172
Aspel, Michael, 185
Assassins, 31
Asya, 88
At Play in the Fields of the Lord, 9
Attenborough, Richard, 37, 217
Auden, W. H., 49, 170, 210
Austen, Jane, 233
'Autumn', 224
Avery, Tex, 187
Avventura, L', 56
Ayckbourn, Alan, 191

Baby of Mâcon, The, 101
Baby's Day Out, 206
Bacon, Francis, 167
Bagehot, Walter, 240
Balthus, 78, 139, 212

Balzac, Honoré de, 35, 140
Barb Wire, ix
Barker, Howard, 219
Barnes, Julian, 38, 191
Barth, John, 74
Barthes, Roland, xiv, 4, 198, 226
Bartók, Béla, xii, 18
Basic Instinct, 118
Bateman, H. M., 157
Battleship Potemkin, 5
Baudelaire, Charles, 117
Baudrillard, Jean, 10
Beadle, Jeremy, 185
Beauty and the Beast, 188
Beaverbrook, Max, 3
Beckett, Samuel, 35, 56, 57, 219
Beerbohm, Max, 199
Beethoven, Ludwig van, 5
Beggar's Opera, The, 233
Bell, Steve, 195
Belle Noiseuse, La, 101, 102, 141, 142
Ben-Hur, 143
Benjamin, Walter, 10, 36
Bennett, Tony, 212
Benson, E. F., 73
Bentsen, Lloyd, 31-2
Berg, Alban, 92, 108
Bergman, Ingmar, 19, 56, 66, 101
Bergman, Ingrid, 112
Bergson, Henri, 29
Berio, Luciano, 18
Berkeley, Busby, 26, 136-7
Berlin, Irving, 108
Bernard, Kate, 99
Bernstein, Leonard, 17
Bertolucci, Bernardo, 4-5, 101
Betjeman, John, 186n.1
Betrayal, 32-3
Beverly Hillbillies, The, 206
Big Sleep, The, 64, 197, 198
Billington, Michael, 37, 43-4, 45
Birth of a Nation, The, 142
Birtwistle, Harrison, 18, 212
Bitter Moon, 8-9
Black, Cilla, 185, 236
Blandford, Marquess of, 227
Bleak House, 38-9
Blind Date, 236
Bloom, Harold, 192

Blue, 102, 158
Blue Bird, The, 17
Blues Brothers, The, 143
Boeuf sur le Toit, Le, 19
Boito, Arrigo, 170
Boléro, 17
Bonfire of the Vanities, The, 34-5
Booth, John Wilkes, 132
Borges, Jorge Luis, 11-12, 54, 74
Boty, Pauline, 49-50
Boublil, Alain, 225
Bouguereau, Adolphe-William, 201
Boulez, Pierre, 92
Bourges, Elemir, 60
Boyd, William, 38
Boyle, Danny, 192n.1
Bragg, Melvyn, 203
Brando, Marlon, 197, 198
Breath, 56
Brecht, Bertolt, xii, 19, 74, 170, 219, 232, 233
Brenton, Howard, 219
Bresson, Robert, 4-5, 101
Bringing Up Baby, 135-6
Britten, Benjamin, 3
Britten, Tony, 232
Broadhurst, Nick, 232-3
Broch, Hermann, 74
Brodkey, Harold, 58, 59, 164
Broken Glass, 182
Brook, Peter, 182
Brookner, Anita, 2, 227
Brooks, Louise, 62
Browning, Tod, 19
Browning Version, The, 157-8
Bruckner, Anton, 233
Brummell, Beau, 59, 222
Bryars, Gavin, 224-5
Brynner, Yul, 101
Bulger, Jamie, 47-8, 173
Buñuel, Luis, 43, 101, 123
Burchill, Julie, 3
Burke, Edmund, 3
Burn, Gordon, 88
Burstein, Keith, 213
Burton, Tim, 212
Bush, George, 31, 32, 154
Butch Cassidy and the Sundance Kid, 5

Cabaret, 5, 63
Caesar, Julius, 228
Cage, John: 4'33", 56
Cahiers du Cinéma, 36
Calvino, Italo, 35, 74, 127, 128n.1
Cameron, James, 191
Campbell, Naomi, 226–7
Campion, Jane, 101, 102, 158
Capra, Frank, 24, 38–9
Caractères, Les, 92
Carax, Leos, 101
Caro, Anthony, 49
Caron, Leslie, 156
Carousel, 37
Carrie (musical), 64
Carroll, Lewis, 127
Carter, Jimmy, 32
Carver, Raymond, 143
Casablanca, 65, 166
Castle of Crossed Destinies, The, 127
Cat on a Hot Tin Roof, 31
Cats, 60
Cavalcade, 223
Céline, Louis Ferdinand, 35, 120
Cerha, Friedrich, 92
Cervantes, Miguel de, 11–12
Cézanne, Paul, 43
Chabrol, Claude, 117
Chagall, Marc, 19
Chalmers, Judith, 185
Chandler, Raymond, 64, 197
Chaplin, 37
Chaplin, Charlie, xii, 5, 19, 37, 38–9
Charme discret de la bourgeoisie, Le, 123–4
Chayefsky, Paddy, 32
Cheers, 83
Chen Kaige, 141
Chereau, Patrice, 92
Chevalier, Maurice, 156
Chocolate Kiddies, 61
Christmas Carol, A, 24
Churchill, Caryl, 182
Circus, The, 19
Citizen Kane, 5
City of Angels, 64, 66
Claudel, Paul, 126, 170
Clinton, Bill, 2, 32–3
Clooney, Rosemary, 22

Close Encounters of the Third Kind, 41
Close Shave, A, 189n.1
Cocteau, Jean, 19, 74, 75, 93, 131, 166, 170, 222
Colette, 170
Collard, Cyril, 86
Collins, Jackie, 3
Come and Go, 56
Conformist, The, 50
Cooper, Gary, 203
Cooper, Jilly, 200–1
Cope, Wendy, 148
Coppola, Francis Ford, 40, 179
Corot, Jean-Baptiste-Camille, 168
Costner, Kevin, 205
Coward, Noël, 223
Cox, John, 13
Coyote, Peter, 8
Cozarinsky, Edgardo, 124n.1
Crawford, Joan, 203
Creature Comforts, 187
Critics' Forum, 82
Cronin, A. J., 50
Crosby, Bing, 22
Crying Game, The, 206–7
Curtiz, Michael, 38, 65
Curzon, Frederic, 213

Daldry, Stephen, 182
Damage, 44
Dances with Wolves, 9
da Ponte, Lorenzo, 170, 232
Dark is Light Enough, The, 91n.1
Darlington, W. A., x
David Copperfield, 88
Davies, Terence, 14
Davis, Carl, 92
Day-Lewis, Daniel, 43, 156
Death of a Salesman, 32
Death in Venice (film), 50
Death in Venice (novella), 35
Death of Virgil, The, 74
de Bont, Jan, ix, 214, 237
Debussy, Claude, xii, 18
Defoe, Daniel, 34
Degas, Edgar, 19, 100
Delacroix, Eugène, 3
Delaney, Shelagh, 191
De Mille, Cecil B., 19

Deneuve, Catherine, 124n.1
De Niro, Robert, 228
Dennis the Menace, 188
De Palma, Brian, 117, 180
Depardieu, Gérard, 85
de Souza, Edward, 122
Detour, 66
Diamond, Anne, 184–5
Diana, Princess of Wales, 93, 114,
    140, 173, 223, 227, 240
Diary of Anne Frank, The (film), 141
Dick Deterred, 32
Dickens, Charles, 2, 22–3, 35, 38–9,
    133
Dictionary of the Khazars, The, 35,
    127
Diderot, Denis, 122
Dietrich, Marlene, 62
*Discreet Charm of the Bourgeoisie,
    The*, 123–4
Disney, 187, 188
Disparition, La, 125–7
Divertimento, 142
Dr Faustus, 74
Doctor Finlay, 50
Doig, Peter, 229
Don Giovanni, 211
Don Quixote, 11–12
Donat, Robert, 195
Don't Dress for Dinner, 90
Dostoevsky, Fyodor, 35
Double Indemnity, 66
Double Life of Véronique, The, 101
Dovzhenko, Alexander, 4
Dracula, 40, 41
Drag, 111
Dreyer, Carl Theodor, xii
Duffy, Carol Ann, 148
Dufy, Raoul, 19
Duras, Marguerite, 1–2, 9
Dylan, Bob, 147–8

Eastwood, Clint, 158
Eco, Umberto, 2, 35
Ecoute voir . . . , 124n.1
Ed Wood, 212
Edgar, David, 218–19
Edison, Thomas, 216
Editions de Minuit, 1
Eh Joe, 56

8½, 19
Einstein, Albert, 72, 202–3, 204
Eisenstein, Sergei, 5, 26, 60
Eisler, Hans, 62
Elektra, 161
Elgar, Edward, 17–18
Eliot, T. S., 74
Elizabeth II, Queen, 160, 239–40
Ellington, Duke, 61
*End of History and the Last Man,
    The*, 154
Eneide travestita, L', 74
Enfield, Harry, 221–2
'Enoch Soames', 199
Entartete Musik, 61–3
Esquire, x
Europa, 101
Evans, Chris, 184–5
Everage, Dame Edna, 124n.2
Eyre, Richard, 44

Face to Face, 184, 185
Family Plot, 117
Farewell, My Concubine, 141
Farquhar, George, 45
Fassbinder, Rainer Werner, 204
Fatal Attraction, 118
Faulkner, William, 197, 199, 201
Fellini, Federico, 19, 101, 182
Fermat, Pierre de, 93
Ferreri, Marco, 85
Feuillade, Louis, 4, 159
Film, 56
Finlandia, 17
Fitzgerald, F. Scott, 40
Flaubert, Gustave, 95, 97, 199,
    200–1, 233
Fleming, Ian, 95
Flintstones, The (film), 188, 206
Fly-Fishing, 211
Follett, Ken, 199
For Services Rendered, 157–8
Forains, Les, 19
Ford, Gerald, 32
Ford, Harrison, 118
Ford, John, 215
Forrest Gump, 206–7
Fors, 98
Forster, E. M., 50, 170
Forsyth, Bruce, 185

Foucault, Michel, 70, 76
4'33", 56
Four Weddings and a Funeral,
   206–7, 216
1492, 9
Fowles, John, 127
France-Dimanche, 235–6
François, Claude, 235
Franju, Georges, 26
Frau ohne Schatten, Die, 13
Freaks, 19
Frears, Stephen, 115n.3, 192
Freeman, John, 184, 185
French Lieutenant's Woman, The,
   127
Freud, Lucian, 167, 212
Freud, Sigmund, 70–2, 139
Front Page, The, 157–8
Fry, Christopher, 89, 91n.1
Fugitive, The, 118
Fukayama, Francis, 154
Fuller, Samuel, 5
Fumaroli, Marc, 55

Gainsborough, Thomas, 2, 140
Gallimard, 1
Garland, Judy, 136
Gascoigne, Paul, 29, 227
Gateway, 179
Gawain, 212, 213
Gay, John, 233
Genet, Jean, xii, 35
Genette, Gérard, 73
Genevieve, 5
George, Adrian, 166
Géricault, Théodore, 167
German, Edward, 213
Gershwin, George, 16, 17, 108
Gertie the Dinosaur, 118
Getting Even With Dad, 206
Giant, 143
Gibson, Mel, 205, 228
Gide, André, 74
Gift of the Gorgon, The, 90
Gigi, 156
Gilda, 65
Gill, A. A., 209
Ginger and Fred, 182
Gingold, Hermione, 156
Ginsberg, Allen, 242

Giraudoux, Jean, 74
Glengarry Glen Ross, 32
Godard, Jean-Luc, 42, 43, 46,
   103n.1, 174
Gödel, Kurt, 72
Godfather Part II, 179
Goering, Hermann, 174
Gold Diggers of 1935, 136–7
Gold Rush, The, 5
Golding, William, 12
Goldman, William, 205
Good Morning with Anne and Nick,
   184–5
Goodbye, Mr Chips, 195
Gore, Al, 33
Gorecki, Henryk, 212
Gormley, Anthony, 230
Gott, Richard, 173–4
Götterdämerung, 60
GQ, x
Grace, Princess, 235
Graf, Steffi, 2
Gramsci, Antonio, 70
Grand Day Out, A, 187
Grand Ecart, Le, 222
Grant, Cary, 36, 135–6, 197
Grant, Hugh, 243
Great Dictator, The, 39
Great Gatsby, The, 50
Greatest Show on Earth, The, 19
Greenaway, Peter, 57, 101, 102, 217
Greene, Graham, 131
Greer, Germaine, 192
Gregory's Girl, 5
Grieg, Edvard, 17
Griffiths, D. W., 142
Grosz, Georg, 51, 62
Groundhog Day, 79–81
Guardian, 37, 43, 172, 173–4, 175,
   177, 195
Gutenberg, Johann, xiii

Hair, 50
Hall, Peter, 44
Hallyday, Johnny, 235
Hampton, Christopher, 44
Hancock's Half-Hour, 84
Hanks, Tom, 206
Hardy, Thomas, 73
Hare, David, 44, 147, 191, 219

Harlequinade, 157–8
Hartley, J. R., 211
Hartley, L. P., 102, 155
Hawking, Stephen, 202
Hawks, Howard, 64, 65, 135, 197, 198
Haydn, Franz Joseph, 145
Hays, Will, 112
He Who Gets Slapped, 19
Heaven's Gate, 143
Hecht, Ben, and Charles McArthur, 157
Heidegger, Martin, 108
Heimat, 142
Heisenberg, Werner Carl, 72
Hellman, Lilian, 157
Hello!, 236
Hemingway, Ernest, 35, 40
Henry VIII, 133
Hepburn, Katharine, 135, 185
Hergé, 129–31
Hérodiade, 171
Heston, Charlton, 36
Heywood, John, 133
Hi Fi Review, 145
High Noon, 5
Hill, Susan, 73
Hindemith, Paul, 62
Hirst, Damien, 190
Hislop, Ian, 86–7
Histoire(s) du cinéma, 46
History: the Home Movie, 212
Hitchcock, Alfred, 5, 36, 65, 116–18
Hitler, Adolf, 25–6
Hoberman, J., 180
Hobson, Harold, 104
Hockney, David, 49, 166, 212
Hodge, John, 192n.1
Hodgkin, Howard, 49
Hofmannsthal, Hugo von, 74, 169, 170
Hogan, David, ix
Holloway, Stanley, 189
Hollywood vs America, 46
Holm, Ian, 122–3
Holt, Tom, 73
Homer, 74, 131
Homère travesti, 74
Hopkins, Anthony, 43
Houshiary, Shirazeh, 229–31

How Late It Was, How Late, 226–7
Howard, Leslie (pianist), 145–6
Hugo, Victor, 34, 73
Human Condition, The, 142
Humoresque, 203
Humphries, Barry, 124n.2
100 Best Films of the Century, 4–6
Hunniford, Gloria, 185
Hurley, Elizabeth, 2, 227, 243
Hypothetically Murdered, 19
Hytner, Nicholas, 37

'I Got Rhythm', 17
If on a Winter's Night a Traveller, 127
Ignatieff, Michael: Asya, 88
Iliad, The, 74
Illness as Metaphor, 85–6
Importance of Being Earnest, The, 89
In the Line of Fire, 118
Independent on Sunday, 10
Indigo, 73
Inge, William: Picnic, 182
Innocent, The, 97
Insdorf, Annette, 25
Inspector Calls, An, 182, 233
Invisible Cities, 35
Iosseliani, Otar, 103n.1
Isherwood, Christopher, 62
Ishiguro, Kazuo, 35, 191
It Runs in the Family, 90
It'll Be Alright on the Night, 28–30
It's a Mad, Mad, Mad, Mad World, 143
It's a Wonderful Life, 24, 39
Ivan the Terrible, 60

Jackson, David, 242
Jackson, Michael, 93, 110
Jacquot, Guillaume, 1
Jagger, Dean, 22
James, Henry, 96
Jancsó, Miklos, 101, 230
Janssen, David, 136
Jarman, Derek, 203–4
Jeanne Dielman, 23 Quai du Commerce, 1080, Bruxelles, 143
Jesus Christ, 3
Jew Suss, 120

JFK, 50, 143
John, Augustus, 195
Johnson, Lyndon, 32
Johnson, Samuel, 59
Jones, Brian, 204
Jones, Chuck, 187
Jonny spielt auf, 61, 62, 63
Joplin, Scott, 50
Joseph and his Brothers, 74
Jourdan, Louis, 156
Joyce, James, xii, 2, 6, 35, 74, 183
Jurassic Park, 60, 94

Kael, Pauline, 80, 197
Kafka, Franz, xii, 35, 43, 131
Kandinsky, Wassily, xii
Kant, Immanuel, 72
Kaufman, George S., and Moss Hart, 32–3
Kaye, Danny, 22
Kazan, Elia, 179
Keaton, Buster, 37, 56, 93
Keats, John, 147–8
Keeler, Ruby, 27n.1
Kelly, Henry, 184–5
Kelman, James, 226–7
Kennedy, John F., 31, 32, 154
Kennedy, Robert, 32
Kent, Sarah, 229–31
Kern, Jerome, 108
Kerr, Deborah, 197
Kiarostami, Abbas, 42, 103, 103n.2
Kieślowski, Krzysztof, 101, 102, 158
Kilroy-Silk, Robert, 185
King, Stephen, 97n.1
King and I, The, 101
King Kong, 36, 136
King's Row, 61
Kiss Me Deadly, 66
Kiss of the Spider Woman (musical), 64
Kissinger, Henry, 3
Klossowski, Pierre, 78
Knight of the Burning Pestle, The, 90
Kobayashi, Masaki, 142
Kollwitz, Käthe, 51
Koons, Jeff, 100, 195, 228
Korngold, Erich Wolfgang, 61, 62
Krenek, Ernst, 61, 62, 63

Kubrick, Stanley, 41, 42n.2, 207
Kuleshov, Lev (Leo), 163

La Bruyère, Jean de, 92
Lacan, Jacques, 70
Ladybird, Ladybird, 214
Lady's Not for Burning, The, 89
Laforgue, Jules, 74
Lambert, Verity, 67
Lamorisse, Albert, 97
'Land of Hope and Glory', 17–18
Landesman, Cosmo, 229
Landscape Painted With Tea, 127
Lane, Anthony, ix
Lang, Fritz, 66
Lanzmann, Claude, 142
Larson, Gary, 195n.1
Last Action Hero, 110, 215
Last of the Mohicans, The, 9
Last Woman, The, 85
Last Yankee, The, 90
Late Show, The, 83
Laura, 65, 66
Laurel and Hardy, 178
Lavers, Annette, xvn.4
Lear, King, 197
Le Corbusier, 180n.1
Lee, Spike, 141
Lee Anderson, Pamela, ix
Léger, Fernand, 19
Leigh, Mike, 192
Leighton, Frederic Lord, 100
Lejeune, C. A., x
Lessing, Doris, 1
Lessness, 56
Levin, Bernard, 224
Lévy, Bernard-Henri, 190
Lezard, Nicholas, xivn.1
Liberace, 147–8
Libération, 199
Lichtenstein, Roy, 11, 139
Lincoln, Abraham, 132
Lineker, Gary, 2
Liszt, Franz, 145–6
Literary Review, 60, 148–9
Little Mermaid, The, 188
Lloyd, Phyllida, 232, 233, 234
Lloyd Webber, Andrew, 225
Loach, Ken, 192, 214
Loaded, x

Lola Montès, 19
Long Day Closes, The, 14
Long Day's Journey Into Night, 31
Longest Day, The, 143
Look Who's Talking, 206
Lotte in Weimar, 74
Lover, The (L'Amant), 7, 9
Love's Labour's Lost, 90
Loyd, Sam, 136
Lukacs, Georg, 70
Lulu, 92
Lumière brothers, 40, 214
Lynch, David, 101
Lyne, Adrian, 192
Lyotard, Jean-François, 10

Macbeth, 197, 233–4
MacBird, 32
MacCarthy, Desmond, x
McCay, Winsor, 118
McClatchy, J. D., 242, 243
McCowen, Alec, 156
Macdonald, Andrew, 192n.1
MacDowell, Andie, 79–81
McEwan, Ian, 38, 97, 191
McGill, Donald, 195
MacKinnon, Catherine, 150–2
McLaren, Malcolm, 228
McLuhan, Marshall, 190
Madonna, 93, 110–12
Maeterlinck, Maurice, 17
Magnificent Ambersons, The, 5
Magritte, René, 100
Major, John, 51, 140, 193, 195
Malade imaginaire, Le, 129
Malcolm X, 50, 141
Malevich, Kurt, 56
Mallarmé, Stéphane, x, 100, 117
Malle, Louis, 44
Mamet, David, 32, 119–20
Man Who . . . , The, 182
Manet, Edouard, 201
Manhattan Murder Mystery, 110
Mann, Thomas, xii, 35, 62, 74
Mapp and Lucia, 73
March, Jane, 7
Margolyes, Miriam, 156
Margot et l'Important, 1
Marivaux, Pierre, 74
Marker, Chris, 26

Márquez, Gabriel García, 35
Marriage of Figaro, The, 232–3
Marty, 32
Marx, Groucho, 45
Marx, Karl, 50, 70, 72
Massenet, Jules, 171
Massey, Anna, 122–3
Masson, Jeffrey, 151
Mathews, Harry, 128n.1
Matisse, Henri, xii
Maugham, W. Somerset, 157
Maverick, 205
Medved, Michael, 46
Meet Me in St Louis, 136
Meissonnier, Juste-Aurèle, 201
Méliès, Georges, 42n.1, 207
Mellor, David, 186
Melody Maker, 225
Mendelssohn, Felix, 18
Mépris, Le, 174
Merchant Ivory, 50
Merchant of Venice, The, 232
Meredith, Burgess, 31–2
Merrill, James, 241–3
Merrily We Roll Along, 32–3
Methuen Dictionary of Clichés, 132–4
Michelangelo Buonarroti, 55
Miférables, Les, 73
Milestone, Lewis, 200
Milhaud, Darius, 19
Miller, Arthur, 31, 32, 182
Miller, Glenn, 50
Milton, John, 133
Minnelli, Vincente; *Gigi*, 136, 156, 215
Misérables, Les, 34, 73
Miss Saigon, 225
Mizoguchi, Kenji, 4
Modern Review, 10, 38
Molière, 129
Mompou, Federico, 159–60
Monde, Le, 235
Mondrian, Piet, xii, 56
Monet, Claude, 99, 201
Monroe, Marilyn, 36n.1, 110, 111
Monsieur Verdoux, 5
Moon is Blue, The, 8
Moonlight, 122–3
Moore, Demi, 80
Moore, Suzanne, 190

Morand, Paul, 115n.1
Morrell, Ottoline, 3
Morton, Andrew, 223
Moss, Kate, 227
Mother Courage and Her Children, 19
Mourning Becomes Electra, 89–90
Mozart, Wolfgang Amadeus, 169, 170, 204, 211, 232–3
Mozhukhin, Ivan, 163
Mrs Doubtfire, 196
Mudd, Samuel, 132
Muir, Frank, 132
Münch, Edvard, 167
Murdoch, Rupert, 3
Murray, Bill, 79–81
Music Box, The, 178
Musidora, 159
Mythologies, xiv
Myths & Memories, xii

Nabokov, Vladimir, 124, 127
Name of the Rose, The, 3, 35
Naming Names, 150
Nation, 150–2
National Geographic Magazine, 8
Navasky, Victor, 150, 151
Navigator, The, 93
'Nearer My God, to Thee', 224
New York Times, 113, 172
New Yorker, ix, 143, 207n.1
Newman, Nick, 193, 195
Newsnight, 83
Nietzsche, Friedrich, 12, 70, 226
Night Porter, The, 50
Nilsson, Birgit, 161
Nineteen Eighty-Four, 153
1941, 143
Nixon, Richard, 31, 32
No Man's Land, 55
Nocturne in Black and Gold, 98, 99
Norden, Denis, 28–30
Norman, Barry, 4–6
Norman, Philip, 26–7
North by Northwest, 117, 118
Notorious, 118
Nouvel Observateur, 235
Nuit de carrefour, La, 197, 198
Nuit de Putney, La, 115n.1
Nuits sauvages, Les, 86

Nunn, Trevor, 16
Nymphéas, 99

October, 26
Odets, Clifford, 203
Odyssey, The, 74, 131
Of Mice and Men, 32
Old Curiosity Shop, The, 39
Oldman, Gary, 43
Oleanna, 119–21
Oliveira, Mañoel de, 4–5, 78, 103n.1
Oliver, Ron, 164–5
Oliver Twist, 34, 88
Olympiad, 25, 26
On the Piste, 90
On the Razzle, 161
One Hundred Years of Solitude, 35
O'Neill, Eugene, 31, 74, 89–90, 91n.2
Only Words, 150–2
Ophüls, Max, 4, 19, 38
Oppenheim, E. Phillips, 95
Oranges Are Not the Only Fruit, 191
Orlando, 101
Orwell, George, 51, 153
Othello, 197
Ouida, 95
OuLiPo (Ouvroir de Littérature Potentielle), 128n.1
Owen, Nick, 184–5
Owen, Seena, 170–1
Ozu, Yasujiro, xii, 4

Pabst, G. W., 62
Pacific Overtures, 241
Palance, Jack, 174
Pale Fire, 127
Palestrina, Giovanni Pierluigi da, 145
Palimpsestes, 73
Pandora's Box, 19
Parade, 19
Paradzhanov, Sergei, 4
Paris, Comte de, 235
Paris By Night, 44
Paris, Texas, 214
Park, Nick, 187–9
Parker, Alan, 192, 217

Parker, Dorothy, 185
Parsifal, 60
Pärt, Arvo, 212
Passion, 182
Pastiches et Mélanges, 74
Pat and Margaret, 209
Pavarotti, Luciano, 170
Pavic, Milorad, 35, 127
Peer Gynt (Grieg), 17
Perec, Georges, 125–6
Perfect World, A, 158
Perfume, 35
Perry, Commodore Matthew, 241
Philadelphia, 206
Phoenix Too Frequent, A, 91n.1
Pialat, Maurice, 4
Piano, The, 101, 102, 158
Picasso, Pablo, xii, 19, 43, 100, 139
Picnic, 182
Picon, Molly, 178
'Pierre Menard, Author of Don
  Quixote', 11–12
Pile, Stephen, 29
Pinter, Harold, 32, 55, 57, 122–3,
  191, 219
Pirandello, Luigi, xii, 89
Pisier, Marie-France, 124n.1
Play, 56
Playboy of the Western World, The,
  89
Plunder, 157–8
Poe, Edgar Allan, 54, 117
P. O. L., 1
Polanski, Roman, 8–9
Pollack, Sydney, 228
Polnareff, Michel, 235
Porgy and Bess, 16
Porter, Cole, 17, 108
Potter, Dennis, 84, 203
Potter, Sally, 101, 102
Poulenc, Francis, 212
Pound, Ezra, 74, 229
Praz, Mario, 112n.1
Preminger, Otto, 8, 65, 66
Priestley, J. B., 182, 233
Private Eye, 148
Procktor, Patrick, 166
Prospero's Books, 101
Proust, Marcel, xii, 3, 6, 35, 43, 53,
  74, 93, 96, 97, 135, 183, 233, 243

Psycho, 5, 65, 117, 118
Puccini, Giacomo, 169
Pulp Fiction, 166
Pursued, 65

Quay Brothers, 187
Quayle, Dan, 31–2
Queen Kelly, 170–1
Queensberry, 8th Marquis of, 112
Queneau, Raymond, 128n.1
Quignard, Pascal, 54n.1
Quilter, Roger, 213

Racine, Jean, 74
Racing Demon, 44
'Raft of the Medusa, The', 167
Raine, Craig, 212
Rattigan, Terence, 157
Ravel, Maurice, 17
Reagan, Ronald, 31, 32
Rebecca, 73
Red Balloon, The, 97
Red Psalm, 101, 230
Redford, Robert, 50, 228
Redgrave, Vanessa, 2
Reeves, Keanu, 227
Reitz, Edgar, 142
Remains of the Day, The, 35, 179
Remarque, Erich Maria, 200
Rembrandt van Rijn, 233
Renoir, Jean, 197, 198
Resnais, Alain, 4–5
Rhinoceros (musical), 64
Rhys, Jean, 74
Richard, Cliff, 223
Riefenstahl, Leni, 25–7
Riley, Bridget, 49
Rilke, Rainer Maria, xii
Rimsky-Korsakov, Nikolay, 212
*Rise and Fall of the City of
  Mahagonny, The*, 62
Rivette, Jacques, 4–5, 101, 102, 141,
  142
Robinson, Anne, 185
Robinson Crusoe, 34
Rocha, Glauber, 101
Rodgers, Richard, 108
Rodin, Auguste, 140
Rohmer, Eric, 4–5, 42, 103n.1, 117,
  191

Rolling Stones, 204
Romantic Agony, The, 112n.1
Romero, Carlin, 150–2
Ronde, La, 19
Roosevelt, Franklin D., 33n.1
Rosencrantz and Guildenstern Are Dead, 57
Rosenkavalier, Der, 53, 169–70
Rossellini, Roberto, 4
Rothko, Mark, 98–9
Rouault, Georges, 19
Roubaud, Jacques, 128n.1, 174
Runaway Soul, The, 58, 59–60
Rushdie, Salman, xii, 2, 190
Ruskin, John, 98, 99
Russell, Ken, 203
Ryder, Winona, 156

Sacks, Oliver, 193
Safire, William, 113
Saint Laurent, Yves, 2, 56
Salieri, Antonio, 204
Salomé (Strauss), 171
Salomé (Wilde), 74
Salon de Würtemburg, Le, 54n.1
Sams, Jeremy, 232
Santiago, Hugo, 124n.1
Sargent, John Singer, 140
Sarris, Andrew, 56
Sartre, Jean-Paul, 74
Satie, Erik, 19, 243
Sauguet, Henri, 19
Sawdust and Tinsel, 19
Scarface, 65
Scheherazade, 212, 213
Schiffer, Claudia, 227
Schindler's List, 180, 200
Schlagobers, 54n.2
Schoenberg, Arnold, xii, 62, 63
Schofield, Phillip, 184–5
Schönberg, Claude-Michel, 225
Schopenhauer, Arthur, 72
Schreker, Franz, 62
Schubert, Franz, 145
Schwartz, Maurice, 178
Schwarzenegger, Arnold, 36, 58, 110, 206
Scorsese, Martin, 2, 141, 156, 228
Scott, Ridley, 192; *1492,* 9
Scott, Captain Robert, 23

Scott, Tony, 192
Scream, The, 167
Scully, Sean, 99
Sea Hawk, The, 61
Sea of Love, 118
Self, Will, 191
Sellars, Peter, 232
Sellers, Peter, 29, 114, 203
Serres, Michel, 130
Seth, Vikram, 59, 75
Seurat, Georges, 19
Seven Year Itch, The, 36n.1
Sex (Madonna), 110, 112
Seyrig, Delphine, 143
Shaffer, Peter, 191, 204
Shakespeare, William, 2, 67, 72, 74, 133, 197, 200, 232–4
Shallow Grave, 192n.1
Shape of Things to Come, The, 153
Shaw, George Bernard, 133
She Stoops to Conquer, 90
Sheen, Martin, 197, 198
Sheltering Sky, The, 101
Shining, The, 42n.2
Shoah, 142
Short, Nigel, 29
Short Cuts, 141, 143
Shostakovich, Dmitry, 19
Sibelius, Jean, 17
Silence, The, 56
Simenon, Georges, 197
Simpson, O. J., 209
Simpson, Robert, 145
Sinatra, Frank, 212, 215
Sinking of the Titanic, The, 224–5
Sirk, Douglas, 38
Six Characters in Search of an Author, 89
Six O'Clock News, 183
Sixties Art Scene in London, The, 49
Sjöström, Victor, 19
Skriker, The, 182
Sleeper, 5
Sleepless in Seattle, 206–7
Sliver, 118
Smith, Maggie, 3
Smith, Stevie, 93–4
Snow, Peter, 83
Some Came Running, 215
Someone to Watch Over Me, 118

Sondheim, Stephen, 31, 32–3, 182, 241
Songs Without Words, 18
Sontag, Susan, 26, 85–6
Speed, ix, 214, 237
Spellbound, 117
Spender, Stephen, 3
Spiegel, Der, 172
Spielberg, Steven, 40, 180
Spy, 113
Stagecoach, 215
Stallone, Sylvester, 180
Stanislavski, Konstantin, 122
Steel, Danielle, 95
Stein, Gertrude, 86, 170, 229
Steinbeck, John, 32, 51
Steiner, George, 25, 26
Stendhal, 106, 199
Stevens, George, 141
Stevens, Wallace, 242
Stevenson, Robert Louis, 35
Stewart, James, 39, 203
Stone, Oliver, 50, 143, 180
Stoppard, Tom, 44, 57, 161, 191
Strangers on a Train, 117
Strapless, 44
Stratas, Teresa, 92
Straub, Jean-Marie, 103n.1
Strauss, Richard, 13, 53, 54n.2, 161, 169–70, 171
Stravinsky, Igor, xii, 18
Streetcar Named Desire, A, 89
Stroheim, Erich von, 170–1
Stuyvesant, Peter, 178
Suchet, David, 119
Suitable Boy, A, 59–60, 75, 94
'Summertime', 16
Sunday Times, xiv, 86, 99, 193
Sunset Boulevard, 171
Suspicion, 36, 118
Süsskind, Patrick, 35
Svankmajer, Jan, 187
Swan, 226–7
Swanson, Gloria, 171
Syberberg, Hans-Jürgen, 25, 26
Sykes, Eric, 132
Synge, J. M., 89

Tarantino, Quentin, 228
Tarkovsky, Andrei, 4

Taste of Honey, A, 191
Tati, Jacques, 4
Tavener, John, 212
Taverner, John, 145
Tchaikovsky, Pyotr, 17
Tempest, The, 73
Temple, Julien, 203
Temple, Shirley, 108
Tennant, Emma, 73
Terminator 2, 41, 42
Tess, 73
That Was the Week That Was!, 84
Thatcher, Margaret, 51
Theophrastus, 94n.1
Thirty-Nine Steps, The, 5
Thompson, Emma, 227
Thorpe, Adam, 54n.1
Threepenny Opera, The, 232, 233, 234
Time, 113
Time Out, 229
Time's Arrow, 33, 127
Tinker, Jack, 104
'Tis Pity She's a Whore, 90
Titanic, SS, 223–5
Titian, 138–40
Toch, Ernst, 62
Tolstoy, Leo, 233
'Tonight', 17
Touch of Evil, 5
Toulouse-Lautrec, Henri de, 19, 166
'Towards the Millennium', 49
Trainspotting, 192n.1
Travers, Ben, 157
Trial, The, 34
Tristram Shandy, 127
Triumph of the Will, The, 25–7
Trojan War Will Not Take Place, The, 89
'Trolley Song, The', 136
Trollope, Joanna, 60
Truffaut, François, 114, 117
Turner, J. M. W., 98
TV Hell, 29
Twister, ix
2001, 41, 136, 207
Tynan, Kenneth, 219

Ulmer, Edgar G., 66
Ultima donna, L', 85

Ulverton, 54n.1
Ulysses, 6, 74, 127
Until the End of the World, 101, 102
Upcher, Caroline, 227
Usage des plaisirs, L', 76
Ustinov, Peter, 240

Valéry, Paul, 56, 117
Vampires, Les, 159, 161
Van Gogh, Vincent, 201
Vanity Fair, x, 80
Vartan, Sylvie, 235
Velázquez, Diego, 140
Vera-Ellen, 22
Verdi, Giuseppe, 169
Victoria, Queen, 240
Vidor, Charles, 65
Vidor, King, 179
Vigo, Jean, xii, 4
Villalonga, José-Luis de, 235
Virago Modern Classics, 201
Virgil, 74
Virgile travesti, 74
Visconti, Luchino, 50, 101, 156
Voici!, 235
Void, A, 125–7
Voix humaine, La, 75
von Trier, Lars, 101
Voyage in a Balloon, 97

Wagner, Richard, 60, 141, 170, 211, 213
Waiting for Godot, 57
Walsh, John, 229
Walsh, Raoul, 65
Wardle, Irving, 104
Warhol, Andy, 47, 200, 204, 228
Warner, Marina, 73
Warning Shot, 136
Watch on the Rhine, The, 157–8
Waterworld, 41
Waugh, Auberon, 60, 149
Waugh, Evelyn, 59, 184, 185
Waxman, Franz, 62
Wedekind, Frank, 19
Weill, Kurt, 62, 232
Weisweiller, Francine, 166
Welles, Orson, 5
Wells, H. G., 153

Wenders, Wim, 4–5, 101, 102, 214
Werker, Alfred, 179
West, Mae, 110–12
West Side Story, 17
Westwood, Vivienne, 227
Wetherby, 44
Where Is the Friend's Home?, 103n.2
Whistler, James Abbott McNeill, 98, 99
White Christmas, 22
Whitman, Walt, 242
Wide Sargasso Sea, 74
Wilbur, Richard, 242
Wild at Heart, 101, 102
Wilde, Oscar, 39, 45, 74, 89, 106n.2, 112
Wilder, Billy, 36n.1, 66, 241
Williams, Lia, 119
Williams, Robin, 196
Williams, Tennessee, 31, 89
Winters, Shelley, 141
Winterson, Jeanette, 190, 191, 199
Wiseman, Frederick, 26
Wogan, Terry, 185
Wolfe, Tom, 35
Wolfes, Peter, 50
Woman in Black, The, 90
Woman in the Window, The, 66
Wood, Haydn, 213
Wood, Victoria, 209
'Words Are in My Heart, The', 136–7
Wrong Trousers, The, 187, 188–9
Wunder der Heliane, Das, 61, 62
Wuthering Heights, 34
Wyatt Earp, 205
Wycherly, William, 45

Xenakis, Iannis, 18

Yeats, W. B., xii
York, Sarah Duchess of, 93, 114, 240
'You'll Never Walk Alone', 37
Young, Toby, 10
Young and Innocent, 116–17

Zelig, 206
Zemeckis, Robert, 206